THE GALLOWS IN THE GROVE

Civil Society in American Law

GEORGE W. LIEBMANN

PRAEGER

Westport, Connecticut
London

Library of Congress Cataloging-in-Publication Data

Liebmann, George W.
The gallows in the grove : civil society in American law / George W. Liebmann.
p. cm.
Includes bibliographical references and index.
ISBN 0–275–95886–8 (alk. paper)
1. Law—United States. 2. Civil society—United States.
3. United States—Social policy. I. Title.
KF384.L49 1997
301′.0973—DC21 97–11083

British Library Cataloguing in Publication Data is available.

Library of Congress Catalog Card Number: 97–11083
ISBN: 0–275–95886–8

First published in 1997

Praeger Publishers, 88 Post Road West, Westport, CT 06881
An imprint of Greenwood Publishing Group, Inc.

Printed in the United States of America

The paper used in this book complies with the Permanent Paper Standard issued by the National Information Standards Organization (Z39.48–1984).

10 9 8 7 6 5 4 3 2

Copyright Acknowledgment

The author and publisher gratefully acknowledge permission to quote from the following article:

George W. Liebmann, *Delegation to Private Parties in American Constitutional Law*, 50 Indiana L.J. 650 (1965). Permission granted by the Indiana Law Journal and Fred Rothman & Co.

All the pleasing illusions, which made power gentle, and obedience liberal, which harmonized the different shades of life, and which, by a bland assimilation, incorporated into politics the sentiments which beautify and soften private society, are to be dissolved by this new conquering empire of light and reason. All the decent drapery of life is to be rudely torn off. All the super-added ideas, furnished from the wardrobe of a moral imagination, which the heart owns, and the understanding ratifies, as necessary to cover the defects of our naked shivering nature, and to raise it to dignity in our own estimation, are to be exploded as a ridiculous, absurd, and antiquated fashion.

On this scheme of things, a king is but a man; a woman is but an animal; and an animal not of the highest order. All homage paid to the sex in general as such, and without distinct views, is to be regarded as romance and folly . . .

On the scheme of this barbarous philosophy, which is the offspring of cold hearts and muddy understandings, and which is as void of solid wisdom, as it is destitute of all taste and elegance, laws are to be supported only by their own terrors, and by the concern, which each individual may find in them, from his own private speculations, or can spare to them from his own private interests. In the groves of their academy, at the end of every vista, you see nothing but the gallows. Nothing is left which engages the affections on the part of the commonwealth. . . . These public affections, combined with manners, are required sometimes as supplements, sometimes as correctives, always as aids to law. . . .

But power, of some kind or other, will survive the shock in which manners and opinions perish; and it will find other and worse means for its support . . . plots and assassinations will be anticipated by preventive murder and preventive confiscation, and that long roll of grim and bloody maxims, which form the political code of all power, not standing on its own honour, and the honour of those who are to obey it. Kings will be tyrants from policy when subjects are rebels from principle.

—Edmund Burke

Contents

Introduction

This book is about the mediating structures of American civil society, their depreciation by the courts, and the means for their revival. The title chapter is a survey of American institutions and the effect of post-World War II constitutional decisions on them. The second chapter is an exploration of the original intention concerning the functioning of American courts and political institutions. The third chapter discusses the power of governments to delegate functions to private institutions.

The second part of the book describes some of the changes necessary if the courts are to be returned to a more appropriate and restricted role as guardians of the political process and of freedom from fear of political actors. The first chapter considers the appropriate scope of the First Amendment by an assessment of the writings of the late Professor Harry Kalven, its most influential modern commentator, and calls for abrogation of the "commercial speech" doctrine; the second attempts to define the appropriate scope of government-provided legal assistance. The last two chapters discuss the dangers presented by federalization of the enforcement of criminal law and of social issues such as abortion.

The concluding part of the book is not about judicial doctrine, but about some positive measures that might be considered to restore damaged social institutions. The essays provide examples of the sort of political discussion that would become commonplace if our elections and political process were no longer dominated by "rights talk." The chapters successively consider policies toward law enforcement, welfare, land use, the schools, social services, the aging, and urban renewal. This part complements the discussion of neighborhood institutions in the author's *The Little Platoons: Sub-Local Governments in Modern History* (Praeger, 1995).

Because the tenor of this work is generally "conservative," two criticisms of its design may be anticipated. The first is that excessive blame for the predicament of our social institutions is placed on the courts, as opposed to market institutions. However, some of the worst depredations upon American civil and political institutions wrought by the market would not have been possible but for misguided judicial activism: One may instance the commercial speech decisions; the recasting, without benefit of congressional action, of the labor and antitrust laws; the extravagant immunities conferred on the mass media; and judicial mischief-making with attempts at regulation of campaign finance.

The second inevitable criticism is that the work does not devote much time to addressing distributive issues and that, to the extent it does address them, it is concerned with the wider distribution of social capital rather than economic capital. Concern about economic distribution obviously provided the emotional fuel or subtext for many of the judicial decisions most severely criticized, which had as their object coercing more equal economic distribution. To this the author would tender two rejoinders. The first is that, over time, the expansion of welfare state institutions does little for economic redistribution, since benefits are in disproportionate measure designed by and claimed by the more fortunate classes in the community.[1] This does not mean that there is not a case on other grounds for welfare-state institutions: This work favors expansion of them in such areas as maternity homes and the provision of primary health care. The second rejoinder is that those interested in redistribution would do better to address themselves to the erosion of threshholds in the income tax system and the increased resort to payroll taxes that have no thresholds at all. The British experience is similar to the American and the consequence of it has been succinctly described:

> in 1949 a married man with two children had to earn three-quarters of average earnings to pay any income tax, by the late 1960s such a family was paying tax at just under half average earnings. For manual workers the picture was even bleaker. In the late 1940s an unskilled man with two children had to earn more than average pay in order to pay any direct tax at all. By the late 1960s the taxman was taking his share at little more than half the average manual wage.[2]

The appropriate agenda for those concerned with economic redistribution should be found not in "welfare rights" litigation, destructive of social capital, but in seeking restoration of the value of personal exemptions and standard deductions in the income tax systems (including those of the states) and in adding minimum thresholds to social security and unemployment taxes, as in most European countries. They would do well to recall John Stuart Mill's emphasis on:

> the difference between a tax which can be saved from luxuries and one which trenches, in ever so small a degree, upon the necessaries of life . . . the smallest income which labour ought to be able to command, the government ought not to be a party to making . . . smaller . . . any tax on these either permanently degrades the habit of the labouring class or falls on profits and burthens capitalists with an indirect tax.[3]

Portions of chapters 3 and 10 were previously published in the *Indiana Law Journal* and the *Real Property, Probate and Trust Law Journal*, and are included with permission. The author is also indebted to Patricia Garside, Christopher Miller, and Denise Rennie of the University of Salford (U.K.) for a visiting fellowship in early 1996, during which period this book was edited for publication, and to my colleague, Orbie R. Shively, and my secretary, Jeanette I. Scott, for assistance in preparing the manuscript.

NOTES

1. See, e.g., J. Le Grand, *The Strategy of Equality* (1982).

2. N. Timmins, *The Five Giants: A Biography of the Welfare State* (London: Harper Collins, 1995), 265.

3. J. Mill, *Principles of Political Economy* 829.

Part I

THE COURTS AND CIVIL SOCIETY

1

The Gallows in the Grove: Civil Society in American Law

The Judiciary Committee of the American Senate has recently given its considered response to the nation's current ills: amendments to the criminal code that include more than fifty new capital offenses. Sir Henry Maine would have understood: "In their eagerness to escape . . . a superstition of the priests, [they] flung themselves headlong into a superstition of the lawyers." The nation now has a Jacobin Club, in the form of a Civil Liberties Union, in each congressional district. Hence, as Burke said, "Laws are to be supported only by their own terrors, and by the concern, which each individual may find in them, from his own private speculations, or can spare to them from his own private interests. In the groves of *their* academy, at the end of every vista, you see nothing but the gallows. Nothing is left which engages the affections on the part of the commonwealth."

Today's America is crazed with "rights," including those relating to commercial speech, "privacy," "takings," family relations, sexual equality, and a variety of other causes, none of them having anything to do with the freedom of political discussion and freedom from fear for political actors that were at the root of the Bill of Rights and its English precursors. At the same time, little thought is given to institutions or to their legitimate powers and functions. Thus the nation's malaise, its depressing poll results, and its disconcerting fondness for Ross Perot, Oliver North, and other demagogues. Does the reader doubt this? Let us proceed to a survey.

THE CIVIL SERVICE

The federal civil service is an unlikely choice for the first institution to be considered. It is appropriate, however, because, for both celebrators and critics of present tendencies, the expanded federal bureaucracy is the anticipated endpoint. The enthusiasts of the administration implicitly rely on its adequacy. The latter-day followers of Tocqueville fear a "despotism . . . more extensive and more mild [which] would degrade men without tormenting them." On recent form, the pessimists are too optimistic. America does not have a professional civil service. Any despotism that it might impose will therefore not be mild.

There is nothing in America comparable to the system of selection examination familiar in Britain or to the French grands ecoles. None of the public administration schools have the selectivity and prestige of the leading law and business schools, nor has any effort been made to convert any of the plethora of the latter to more useful objects.

Since each federal agency has several layers of political appointees at the top chosen on a system of quotas and as their functions in turn are interfered with by an ever-expanding White House staff, there are few prizes worth having. Morale is undermined by overelaborated internal grievance procedures. In-service training of any serious nature appears lacking.

The external discipline of the civil service is dependent almost entirely on judicial review. The results the courts produce are driven by sympathies rather than institutional concerns; the process does not foster better administration. Yet, despite urgings by the late Judge Henry Friendly and by Professor Kenneth Culp Davis in their writings on administrative law and by George F. Kennan in his most recent memoirs, there is no ombudsman or any system such as the hierarchy of administrative tribunals headed by the French Conseil d'Etat.

When Mr. Churchill in the 1945 election campaign prophesied that widespread nationalization in Britain would result in a Gestapo, his claim was widely and rightly dismissed as ridiculous. When Friedrich Hayek wrote his *Road to Serfdom*, sounding a similar theme, one of the Labour government's leading defenders declared that it was intellectually and morally a grand book and gave the assurance that the quality and discipline of the civil service rendered freedom and planning not incompatible. That proved true in Britain. Can any serious observer of our contemporary doppelgängers, Rebecca West's "plastic gnomes of Washington," believe that it would be true in the United States?

THE JUDICIARY

The American judiciary has become a vast engine that feeds on its own excesses. The greater the diminution of the authority of the professions, lower levels of government, private institutions and the family, the greater the demand for more courthouses and jails.

There are now twenty- or thirty-man federal appeals courts, which once had three members; more than a thousand federal district judges; and an unending Kulturkampf against subordinate institutions waged by our civil liberties unions (and some right-wing think tanks). Juvenile curfews are invalidated; dress codes and drug searches in slum schools are under attack; single-sex education is assailed; work requirements for welfare recipients are objected to, as is the control of public beggary; drug testing of students is opposed; efforts to limit television obscenity and violence in the afternoon hours are said to contravene imperishable concepts of liberty. The right for its part asks courts to eviscerate protections for labor unions and small businesses, and to dampen the belated movement toward local land use control of sprawl development.

Increasingly, ideological abstractions govern constitutional discourse. "More than ever before," the late Justice Walter Schaefer of Illinois observed, "the lawyer's quest has become a search for quotable words which, regardless of their initial context, can be read in the abstract to bear upon the situation at hand. The pressure is thus toward a jurisprudence of words or phrases divorced from facts and capable of generating new words and phrases with independent lives."

The danger of judicial review on the American pattern, as Peter Calvocoressi has noted, is that it can readily become a vehicle for "making the law so much more inflexible as to deflect it from the service of society to the service of a class." Constitutional provisions directed at the maintenance of a political system founded on free discussion and freedom from fear by political actors have been transformed into frivolous and trivial protections of upper-Bohemian lifestyles.

There is a chasm between Justice Holmes's view of a constitution made for people of fundamentally different views, on the one hand, and the express declaration of Ronald Dworkin, on the other, that "jurisprudential issues are at their core issues of moral principle." A profession increasingly educated in a priori deduction from ideology is not receptive to Learned Hand's vision of a constitutional system that "[g]ives a bloodless measure of social forces—bloodless, have you thought of that?—a measure of continuity, a principle of stability, a relief from the paralyzing terror of revolution."

Other nations have dealt with their abortion controversies without transforming elections and judicial confirmations into religious wars.
Even in the realm of race relations the most important judicial contribution was the proper protection of the First Amendment rights of civil rights demonstrators; nor were judicial decisions, once made, effective until supported with the congressional power of the purse. Judge Hand's words, "Men do not gather figs of thistles, nor supply institutions from judges whose outlook is limited by parish or class," have not been recently honored by either party.

Neither in private nor public law does Hayek's ideal of "uniform rules laid down in advance" bulk large. Instead, the characteristic mode of judicial decision involves the use of elaborate multifactor tests, whose use is frequently destructive of predictability, trust, contract, voluntary association, private ordering, and social capital.

Notwithstanding the Progressive objections to "government by injunction," the courts have been exuberant in their use of restraining orders against both private groups and new state statutes. The first practice raises the danger that large-scale military enforcement will be needed and that violent clashes will ensue; the second practice effectively accords the lower federal courts a suspensory veto over legislation. Most movements of social amelioration in America have had to move to curtail the federal injunction. The American courts also increasingly fail in the maintenance of fair trials and freedom from fear, particularly for political actors. The Bill of Rights is nothing so much as a recital of grievances arising from abuses in British state trials. Behind many of its provisions was a determination to secure to political offenders the ordinary course of law, including clear charges, a jury derived from the defendant's vicinage (a guarantee twice repeated in the Constitution), rights of confrontation, and the privilege against self-incrimination. The last has now been vitiated by use immunity. Provisions for trial in the defendant's vicinage have been undermined by latitudinarian mail-fraud statutes and venue rules. Almost all important prosecutions now lie in the District of Columbia, where (over the dissent of its four most distinguished recent justices) the Supreme Court has permitted government employees to serve on juries. Political offenders are now pursued not by congressional investigations or by the constitutionally contemplated impeachment mechanism, but by specially appointed special prosecutors, worthy adjuncts to a revived Star Chamber. All federal judges begin their judicial careers by supplying dossiers to the law enforcement agency whose abuses they are supposed to curb. A Judicial Conference committee is now exploring whether the televising of trials should now be extended to the federal system,with all the coercion that will ensue when trials are turned into national referenda. The right to clear charges has been impaired by the vagueness of the conspiracy and racketeering statutes nd by multicount indictments; even the confrontation clause no longer means what it says, at least where the accusing witness is female or of tender years. Heart-balm actions, abolished in the 1930s because of their use as tools of blackmail, have been revived as actions for sexual harassment; and the courts have even tolerated bizarre "recovered memory" uses permitting charges of child abuse to be presented decades after the event. Thus we have, with full judicial sanction, the criminalization of politics, which the framers of the constitution sought to avoid.

THE PRESIDENCY

The date the distempers of the modern presidency began can be fixed with great precision: January 20, 1961. The selection of President Kennedy, whose first term at least would have been regarded as disastrous but for his martyrdom, represented the convergence of the presidential primary and the influence of paid television.

The framers of the Constitution settled on a unified executive with reluctance. They undertook to guard against Caesarism by two features of the Constitution that have fallen into desuetude: indirect election of the president and Senate confirmation of the principal officers of state.

The electoral college, to be chosen by state legislators, now survives only in ruins. Its successor, the nominating convention, fell victim to the 1960s. Recent presidential nominees have included governors of small states, members of the Senate commanding little respect from their colleagues, and the unusual phenomenon of President Reagan, whose appeal owed most to his television personality. The exceptions, vice presidents anointed by their predecessors, were by almost any judgment worthier and more competent than the self-promoted nominees.

The recent changes derive from a misplaced desire to subordinate party organizations to a fictitious general will. Learned Hand, reminded us: "If it is hard to see any answer to this, the day has clearly gone forever of societies small enough for members to have personal acquaintance with each other, and to find their station through the appraisal of those who have any first-hand knowledge of them. Publicity is an evil substitute, and the art of publicity is a black art." Clearly the process of candidate selection at the national level should be a candidly indirect one, as it used to be in the United States and continues to be in every parliamentary system.

The corruption of the nominating process has been accompanied by the transformation of the executive from constitutional to personal government. The present administration features a mediocre cabinet, selected on quota principles, the wholesale importation of campaign staff into the White House, a bevy of part-time assistants, and a new role for the First Lady founded on former Argentine and Romanian practice. No good can come of this; nor, if Article II, Section 2, of the Constitution is taken seriously, is this arrangement consistent with the president's oath of office. Senate confirmation, Hamilton observed in the *Federalist*, no. 74,

> [w]ould be an excellent check on a spirit of favoritism in the President, and would tend greatly to prevent the appointment of unfit characters from State prejudice, from family connection, from personal attachment, or from a view to popularity. . . . He would be both ashamed and afraid to bring forward, for the most distinguished or lucrative stations, candidates who had no other merit than that of coming from the same State, to which he particularly belonged, or of being, in some way or another, personally allied to him, or of possessing the necessary insignificance and pliancy to render them the obsequious instruments of his pleasure.

Nothing in modern society or technology renders these methods necessary to effective political leadership.

The political parties, if left unmolested by the courts, have the ability to reconstruct their nominating conventions. A determined Congress can use its power of the purse to shrink the White House staff. Finally, attention needs to be given to the corrupting effects of presidential reelectability. The Mexican slogan "effective suffragio, no reelection" has given even a semiauthoritarian self-perpetuating regime impressive powers of adaptation. By contrast, as Tocqueville observed, "It is impossible to consider the ordinary course of affairs in the United States without perceiving that the desire to be re-elected is the chief aim of the President, that the whole policy of his administration, and even his most indifferent measures, tend to this object; and that, especially as the crisis approaches, his personal interest takes the place of his interest in the public good."

CONGRESS

Congress as now organized has abandoned its central function, the enactment of considered statutes which partake of the ideal of uniform rules laid down in advance. This evil flows from self-entrenchment through the multiplication of staff; misguided "reforms" of campaign finance; the perpetual political campaign; the balkanization of the committee system; reapportionment with its destruction of organic constituencies; and the failure to publicize the substance of important pending legislation.

Congress also fails in its responsibility to oversee the administration. Because of the jealousy of its members, no ombudsman system that would allow grievances to be centrally processed and oversights in administration to be systematically corrected has been devised. Similarly Congress has abdicated to the judiciary and to special prosecutors the responsibility for correcting serious official misbehavior.

The consequence is a climate in which other social actors have no clear idea of the parameters of their authority. Since the constitutional controversies of the early New Deal, Congress's favorite legislative device has been the conditional grant-in-aid. This practice destroys the initiative of lower levels of government, while being singularly cumbersome as a method of administration. The suggestion by former Senator Eugene McCarthy that the quality of the Senate be improved by repealing the Seventeenth Amendment is also not an entirely facetious one. Partial repeal, so that one of each state's senators was selected by the governor or state legislature, might well lend greater dignity to both the direct and indirect processes of election, while restoring one of the lost "political safeguards of federalism."

The *Congressional Record* is a singularly uninformative document, and Congress has failed to require that bills of obvious major importance be published in full text. Politics in this system becomes an insider's game.

The devices suggested by Justice Brandeis to avoid destroying local autonomy have found decreasing favor. These include central government circulars of the sort discussed in the last, unfashionable, chapter of Mill's *Essay on Liberty*; federal taxes with credits for state taxes imposed for similar objects (the basis of the unemployment compensation system); enhanced use of the Full Faith and Credit Clause to prevent progressive state legislation from being undermined; tax and revenue sharing; and the use of interstate compacts.

The prevailing mythology in Washington is that modern developments make centralization inevitable. Postwar German, French, and Italian experience belies this contention. Yet the modest revenue-sharing measures of the Nixon administration were swiftly withdrawn at the earliest opportunity.

STATE GOVERNMENTS

State governments continue to suffer from the constraints of the grant-in-aid system, together with some self-inflicted wounds of their own. They have failed to recruit competent civil servants and have been reluctant to devolve revenues to municipal and voluntary institutions. There is little effort to systematize what was once known as "the Wisconsin idea."

The decline of inner cities, in important ways a consequence of federal policies relating to highway and sewer construction and school desegregation, has been aggravated by reapportionment, which has discouraged revenue and tax sharing with declining areas. The affected large cities thus are driven to seek relief through state takeover of local services.

In many states, failure to reform property taxation has caused it to be limited by constitutional amendment (as in California) or replaced with state taxes and grants-in-aid (as in Michigan).

The states are frequently faced with a Hobson's choice between state monopolization of services and an unwarranted discrimination against religious institutions if voluntary agencies are used. Inner city churches thus are no part of most states' social strategies.

State systems of higher education, once one of the glories of American government, are now beset with federal mandates relating to student and faculty composition, student records, sexual harassment, crime control, and even women's gymnasia, now statutorily preferred to physics laboratories as an object of state expenditure. They also are the first victims of the new demands on state revenue that ensue when local property taxation is curtailed by litigation.

The most ominous specter hovering over the liberties of Americans is the increase in the size and jurisdiction of federal policing agencies. The courts, initially prompted by abuses in the South, have burdened the criminal law with numerous procedural restraints, which have decreased the perceived effectiveness of state criminal justice systems and fostered careless demands for federal intervention, gratified by the Senate Judiciary Committee, which has more than its fair portion of demagogues, of both right and left.

Macaulay described a somber precedent: "[w]hile the Houses were exercising their authority thus it suddenly passed out of their hands. It had been obtained by calling into existence a power which could not be controlled. . . . In the summer of 1647, about twelve months after the last fortress of the Cavaliers had submitted to the Parliament, the Parliament was compelled to submit to its own soldiers."

MUNICIPAL GOVERNMENT

A century has passed since James Bryce observed that the greatest failure of the American political system was its municipal governments. Constitutionally, municipalities have been the stepchildren of the states, possessing, under a principle known as Dillon's Rule, only the powers specifically granted them from above. Municipalities are denied the right to levy sales and income taxes or earnings taxes, and powers of annexation.

There is little tax and revenue sharing with state government, and none at all with the national government. The effect of this is a mutually destructive regime. Suburban municipalities favor infrequent tax reassessments and heavy real estate transfer taxes, to cause burdens to fall disproportionately on newcomers. Cities attempt to take their revenge with parking and hotel taxes, earnings taxes when allowed, and special taxes on business utilities. Few of these devices would be a part of a rational tax system.

While persons who reside in unincorporated areas may freely organize special taxing districts, once a municipality has been incorporated, the creation of any submunicipal body requires the assent of the state legislature. While unincorporated suburban areas witness a civic explosion of residential community associations, condominiums, and special taxing districts, large cities are denied these means of local improvement. Loss of economic capital thus is joined with prohibition of the development of social capital.

With rare and brief exceptions (mostly during the Progressive period), involvement in local government has never been part of the American liberal agenda. As Rebecca West observed, "[t]he Webbs urged their followers to . . . follow all sorts of political activities, including standing for local government; and for that reason the English left wing has been preserved from the lack of practical experience which makes the northern liberalism of the United States so sterile."

The development of submunicipal communities is further hindered by traditional zoning practices discouraging mixed uses. State law (unlike German law, for example) generally confers extravagant procedural rights on those who object to development. Any improvement is therefore much more easily carried out in a "greenfield" location.

The development of civic pride is also retarded by the uniform grid system, as well as by the legal difficulties attendant upon street closing or the consolidation of small lots. Even creation of new small-unit accessory apartments is heavily burdened. Efforts to cultivate distinction in some public schools succumbed to the leveling of the 1960s, rendering cities unattractive to migratory industries. There has been little use of volunteers or even employed civilians to relieve the burdens of police paperwork, no attempt to vindicate the validity of drug testing in public schools to discourage the development of a new generation of career criminals, and no neighborhood law enforcement publications of the type originated by Henry Fielding in England and still prevalent in Japan. Publicity is given to crimes, but never to arrests, convictions, or sentences. Nor have there been attempts to revive the nineteenth century English practice of "friendly visiting" among deprived groups or the later institution of Citizens'

Advice Bureaux. The development of so-called amenity cooperatives for the delivery of day care services such as the British Pre-School Playgroups Association and the old age clubs of Japan has not been fostered.

Most strikingly of all, most cities have failed to replicate their nineteenth-century efforts to foster immigration, though the economic strength of cities rests on their diversity and the resultant agglomerative economies. Civic pride is not fostered by the rattling of begging bowls, nor is the sympathy of higher legislatures enlisted by those who quite manifestly are failing to help themselves.

THE BAR

The bar has been transformed by judicial interference. Competition among lawyers traditionally was competition for reputation—in quality of services, range of contacts, community participation, political candidacy, and sometimes even scholarship.

Legal service is now a commodity, by reason of decisions relating to advertising applying the First Amendment to carry out a disputable economic policy. Justice Holmes' proposition that "when the ignorant are taught to doubt, they know not what they may safely believe" has been fully operative. All regulations designed to limit professional overreaching have been impaired. The more mundane areas of practice have become concentrated in the hands of advertisers, hiring bevies of young lawyers in a sort of franchise system, as sellers of indulgences rather than transmitters of values. The new atmosphere has infected the corporate as well as the personal bar. The enforced collapse of the notion that professional engagements should be initiated by the client and not the lawyer has multiplied the amount of trivial personal-injury and class-action litigation conducted for the benefit of lawyers rather than clients and has diminished the ability to say no to clients.

The judicially compelled expansion of legal and public defender programs has rendered federal and state governments the legal employers of last resort. The absence of self-determining clients and the judicial erosion of restrictions on professional malpractice and products liability actions, in which jurors could award damages without putting themselves at risk for higher taxes or insurance rates, has multiplied lawsuits.

Litigation, once the stepchild of most law offices, became their mainstay. The bar developed a massive vested interest in resisting curtailment of causes of action or simplification of the discovery process. These influences are the product in almost equal measure of doctrinaire free-market philosophy and doctrinaire egalitarianism.

Legal education in America is at once radical and reactionary. Where once legal literature was inductive, seeking to distill principles from decided cases exposing new social needs and to propose reforms in legislation, today it is theoretical and devoted to "constitutional" principles. The legal academy has divided itself into feminists and critical legal scholars on the one hand and law and economics partisans on the other.

The ideal faculty candidate is a Supreme Court clerk, with no experience of private practice, the protégé of identical faculty members. The principal contribution of academia to the profession has been to explode its numbers, rather than to raise its standards. The impulse is toward greater and greater specialization. But so far as their political role is concerned, lawyers are generalists or they are nothing. As the new developments have waxed, the participation of lawyers in government office has waned; other professions more constructively involved in community life have increased their influence in high politics.

THE MEDICAL PROFESSION

The medical advertising unleashed by the Supreme Court—promotions of cosmetic surgery and potentially dangerous eye operations—is at least as unattractive as its legal counterpart and operates to increase aggregate demand, not to allocate work to "efficient" producers.

The practice of abortion in the United States has been concentrated in large clinics, whose counseling practices frequently do not bear close scrutiny. The judicial opinions, with their dubious legitimacy, called into being a virulent antiabortion movement, further discouraging the performance of abortions by mainstream physicians, a phenomenon not duplicated in Europe. To the extent that the advice of family physicians and gynecologists acted as a restraining influence on sexual practices, that influence has been removed.

Government policy has fostered the growth of large group practices, to provide incentives to limit the overuse of specialists. But this destroys the small-group professional practice traditional in medicine, which today survives more fully in the British National Health Service than in America's supposedly private system.

The design of new proposals does not flow from an analysis of deficits in public health services. There is reason to believe that larger investments in parenting education, nutritional education, epidemiology, and neighborhood nurse-visitors would produce a more dramatic improvement in mortality statistics than would the insurance reform that is being proposed,and that first-dollar coverage of initial physician visits would do more to promote early diagnosis than "reforms" of the whole system accompanied by large deductibles. As a political issue, health care reform is driven by consumer and bureaucratic rather than professional or public health interests. The matters that bulk large are the inconvenience of filling out insurance forms and the fear, not of denial of care, for that has been guaranteed in hospital settings since 1985, but of ensuing debts, garnishments (limited by law to 25% of wages), and bankruptcy.

The one approach not considered is a change in the basis of compensation of primary care physician to one largely based on capitation grants, as in the British system. Since these doctors derive little benefit from insurance, it is hard to believe that such a scheme would meet intense resistance.

Medical research funds, once professionally allocated, are increasingly earmarked for fashionable diseases. The response to recent venereal disease epidemics has been directed by advocacy groups and civil liberties groups, not public health officers; and the contact tracing and testing used in connection with the postwar syphilis epidemic has therefore been forsworn. The appointment of surgeons general has been used as a means of appeasing constituency groups, at the cost of professional leadership.

All this impacts the recruitment, and morale of the profession, as to which Tocqueville's words remain pertinent: "It would seem as if the rulers of our time sought only to use men in order to make things great; I wish that they would try a little more to make great men; that they would set less value on the work and more upon the workman; that they would never forget that a nation cannot long remain strong when every man belonging to it is individually weak."

THE CHURCHES

The devaluation of religious institutions worked by the courts has been systematic, though marked by a few dramatic episodes. The working assumption has been that all public aid to religious institutions is suspect, a principle turned against not merely church schools benefitting from the compulsory education laws but also hospitals, colleges, institutions for the elderly, and day care centers.

It was only in the late 1930s that the Supreme Court, creditably motivated by the religious persecutions in Europe, found religious freedom to be part of "liberty" and not until 1947 was the Establishment clause so applied, Congress having previously, in the 1870's, rejected the Blaine Amendment, which would have done so because of its origins in prejudice against Catholic and Jewish immigrants.

Religious institutions now play a diminishing role in education, and even the most mild acknowledgments by public schools of religious values are proscribed, even where they result from the judgment of particular teachers rather than systemwide policy. The result of has been to induce a lassitude and passivity into the mainstream churches. The political energies of the Catholic Church, once engaged in seeking public aid for parochial schools, are devoted to a rearguard action against legal abortion. No effort has been made, even by now black-dominated municipal governments, to encourage the rendition and delivery of social services by the evangelical churches that are important in slum neighborhoods. But the social value of religious impulses cannot lightly be dismissed; as Lord Devlin observed: "There are individuals who can lead perfect lives from charity alone but for men and women as a whole, and so for society, there must be faith and hope." It is worth recalling Adam Smith's observations about some earlier casualties of industrialization:

> A man of low condition . . . as soon as he comes into a great city . . . is sunk in obscurity

> and darkness. His conduct is observed and attended to by nobody, and he is therefore likely to abandon himself to every sort of low profligacy and vice. He never emerges so effectually from his obscurity, his conduct never excites so much the attention of any respectable society, as by his becoming the member of a small religious sect. . . . In little religious sects the morals of the common people have been almost always remarkably regular and orderly; generally much more so than in the established church.

The "mainstream" churches for their part have retreated almost entirely from social involvement: one finds today none of the impulse toward friendly visiting, and the creation of youth movements, maternity homes, schools, and colleges, characteristic of the past. The liberal vision of the state as the monopolist of social services has been absorbed into the internal life, of religious institutions, to the nation's loss. It is this conviction of its own inconsequence that is the most alarming feature of American church life however full the churches on Sundays. Simone Weil would have understood this phenomenon: "The State has morally killed everything smaller than itself."

THE UNIVERSITIES

In Justice Frankfurter's stillborn concurring opinion on academic freedom in *Sweezy v. New Hampshire*, there appears the protest of the South African university chancellors against the imposition of apartheid on their universities, with its reference to "the four essential freedoms of a university—to determine for itself on academic grounds who may teach, what may be taught, how it shall be taught, and who may be admitted to study." This serves well as a concise expression of the standards that major American universities have renounced. Since the late 1960s they have behaved as thoroughly coerced institutions. Notwithstanding that most leading universities, at least in the North, had no modern histories of racial discrimination, they have been subjected to affirmative action regimes relating not merely to the recruitment of students but also to the hiring of faculty, quotas being imposed even at the department level. Vague codes of behavior have become a cloak for the suppression of unfashionable views. There has been a flight to "think tanks" of politically incorrect scholars. The degree to which the universities have abandoned any tutelary function is attested by the virtual disappearance of meaningful course requirements, and by the adoption of systems of student evaluation of faculty that treat college teaching as a branch of the entertainment business. The unfashionable portions of President Eisenhower's farewell address, cautioning against a condition in which "federal research grants become a substitute for intellectual curiosity" have gone unheeded.

Particularly outside the sciences, the current system of permitting each course to stand on its own minimizes curricular requirements, independent study, and comprehensive examinations and places a premium on the regurgitation of lecture notes. The system has functioned as well as it has by reason of its diversity and competition, factors that are rapidly diminishing. The recent phenomenon of grade inflation, unchecked by any system of external examiners, does not bode well; the deterioration of political discussion and practice in the United States is in no small measure due to the slow and quiet hollowing out of the study of the social sciences and humanities in its universities.

SOCIAL WORK

Social work was conceived as a means of helping individuals who had failed to integrate themselves with society to lead productive lives. Its premise was that the role of the social worker was to call to the aid of troubled individuals,the friends, neighbors, teachers, and ministers who would be provide opportunities that would lead to a reformation of behavior. Its effective American founder, Mary Richmond, was the author of a leading manual on "friendly visiting" and, twenty years later, of *Social Diagnosis*, the first social work text. The early social workers were vehement opponents of indiscriminate distribution of cash aid. With respect to the modest proposals for state widows' pensions put forward in 1915, Richmond declared, "If individualized care is not necessary at this point, if 'case work' has no place, then we are confronted here with the solitary exception in the whole range of social endeavor." Cash relief, for Richmond, was a mere auxiliary of social work, which was conceived as a form of moral rehabilitation.

This approach to social work was altered in the 1930s by what has been described as "the psychiatric deluge." The excesses of this line of development helped to discredit social work.

The final blow was delivered by the decision of the Supreme Court in *Goldberg v. Kelly*, requiring an individualized quasi-judicial hearing for each denial of public assistance. This decision was at once denounced by Henry J. Friendly, then the nation's most distinguished sitting federal judge, as "making government impossible." What it made impossible was any individualized conditioning of welfare assistance.

State welfare departments responded by completely separating income maintenance from other functions. The "social training" and "therapeutic" functions were not separately administered; they rapidly became nonexistent, there being no serious incentive for welfare recipients to take part in them. Any proposals for mandatory work requirements or drug testing and treatment were strenuously resisted. By 1993, the columns of *Social Work* contained lamentations by social workers who, drawn into their profession by a desire to help the underclass, found themselves in private practice catering to middle-class neuroses.

Can it really be said that Mary Richmond was wrong and that the United States has benefitted from the judicial destruction of her profession?

THE SCHOOLS

A great deal has been written about the decline of American public school teaching. As with social work, much is due to the "epidemics of ideas" against which Learned Hand warned. But a disconcerting number of the recent problems have their roots in the courts.

Mandated school busing was not a necessary result of the *Brown v. Board of Education* decision; immediately following *Brown* a distinguished lower court construed it as prohibiting segregation but not compelling integration. The "integration" required by the later *Green* decision left large-city schools even more segregated than before and in addition bereft of a large portion of their tax base. The courts also promulgated decrees solidifying the position of black teachers. While this served the purpose of protecting the only portion of the black community that had secured higher education before 1954, it also resulted in preferring the interests of a defectively educated older generation to those of the one that was to follow. In pursuit of similar aims, the Court imposed hearing requirements that rendered teachers virtually irremovable irrespective of their tenure status, mandated bilingual instruction, and spurred large-scale illegal immigration from Mexico by holding that the children of illegal immigrants could not be excluded from the public schools.

Cumbersome requirements for student discipline were imposed, and students were held to have free speech rights entitling them to conduct political demonstrations in classrooms. Efforts by schools to use drug testing to deter drug use by their students met with immediate objections, notwithstanding the successful similar programs of the military.

It is hard to understand why the daily reading of a varying text from the King James Bible (as once proposed by Mrs. Roosevelt in her famous correspondence with Cardinal Spellman) had to be invalidated, particularly when the decision to require it was that of a community rather than a state legislature. Still harder to understand is the recent decision holding that the fleeting utterances of a one-time commencement speaker deprived those who did not share his religious views of a constitutional right. Demands for tolerance are to be directed ever outward, never inward.

Public education even at its best is perceived as being uniform, uninnovative, and bureaucratic. The efforts in other English-speaking countries to enhance self-government of schools have scarcely begun in America.

Finally, the quality of the teaching force has suffered from the consequences of exaggerated feminism. The effect of glorification of "nontraditional" occupations and devaluation of "traditional" occupations such as teaching and nursing whose schedules are more readily rendered compatible with child care has been to lead women into law offices and executive suites at the cost of teaching.

THE PRESS

The phenomenon of concentration of control over the media has been little remarked upon since the deaths of Morris Ernst and Robert Hutchins. The courts and enforcement agencies have ignored the concerns expressed in Judge Learned Hand's opinion in the *Associated Press v. United States* case. In consequence, we are today left with a condition in which there are essentially three newspapers with national impact or, more accurately, one newspaper (the *New York Times*) and two half-newspapers (the *Washington Post* and the *Wall Street Journal*). Virtually every important provincial paper, with the exception of the *St. Louis Post-Dispatch*, has been absorbed into a chain. The only significant newspaper established in recent years is the right-wing *Washington Times*; the hundreds of millions in losses it has incurred are testament to the barriers to entry that exist.

The Antitrust Division of the Department of Justice has been equally incurious about events in book publishing, where both horizontal and conglomerate mergers have been endemic. It and the Supreme Court allied themselves in the 1950s to destroy the resale price maintenance system, which survives in the book trade of almost all other major Western nations. The consequences of this were dramatically illustrated at the time of the Rushdie affair when a controversial work was rendered unobtainable in the United States by a boycott by the three leading bookstore chains. It is no accident that the number of book titles published in the United States remained virtually constant for the last forty years and has recently plummeted while in England and Germany, each with a fifth of our population, the number of titles issued has more than doubled in the same period and in each country far outstrips the American figures.

The concentration of outlets has virtually eliminated freelance writing and has left even senior well-established journalists in a chronic state of vocational insecurity, with all the conformity and timidity that result therefrom. The atrophy of the provincial press assures that there are no longer any sages to be found in Emporia or Baltimore.

The press may libel with impunity or, if it so chooses, suppress facts without fear of competition. Journalists are all too ready to trade on rumors or anonymous accusations. Those who recall the systematic use of defamation, particularly sexual defamation, in the course of Hitler's rise to power will not be convinced that nearly total immunity is an aid to liberty, however acceptable it may be in quiet times.

LABOR UNIONS

Eighty years ago the Clayton Antitrust Act declared an important half-truth: "The labor of a human being is not an article of commerce." Today, without change in the law, the right to collective bargaining has effectively been sent to its graveyard, for that is the practical effect of the Supreme Court's "permanent replacement" decision respecting strikers.

The court has also displayed sudden solicitude for the right of dissenting beneficiaries of union membership to opt out of the use of their dues for political purposes, even though industry political action committees wax and no one inquires very closely into the voluntariness of the "individual" political contributions bundled by them. The inarticulate premise is that, because of international competition, the trade union movement has seen its day and that it is therefore the function of the courts to give it a decent, or indecent, burial.

But the union movement, though brain-dead (perhaps for the reasons suggested in Michael Young's *Rise of the Meritocracy*) still has important functions to perform: in asserting particularized employee grievances, reorganizing work practices, lobbying for social legislation, returning to its initial function as an agency for mutual aid, and providing an organized bulwark against the violent seizure of political power.

THE MASS MEDIA

Television has been left almost entirely to regulation (or nonregulation) by market forces. Once franchises are granted (by a process that does not bear much public scrutiny), virtually no limitations are placed on the behavior of franchisees, nor are the internal traditions and restraints that in some respects regulate newspapers present here.

The salient fact about television as a medium is its power. This, the late Fred Allen observed, is unusual in that television, more so than theater or the radio or the printed word, deprives its listeners of their imaginations and therefore induces uniform rather than varying reactions.

Recent congressional efforts to limit the broadcasting of certain types of sexually explicit material during afternoon hours resulted in decisions by the United States Court of Appeals for the District of Columbia Circuit holding two federal statutes unconstitutional in one day, as many as Learned Hand invalidated in a career spanning fifty years.

More modest suggestions that manufacturers be required to install blackout switches on television sets as a measure to allow parents to more readily regulate their children's television viewing have met with doctrinaire opposition from devotees of untrammeled markets. There has not been even rudimentary consideration of methods of divorcing the purchase of advertising from the sponsorship of particular programs. No efforts have been made to improve the quality of political advertising by limiting it to "talking head" presentations, as in England, where a five-minute minimum is applied, nor have the FCC's licensing powers been used to impose minimum quantitative standards on news programs.

Since the First Amendment "commercial speech" doctrine is currently a hypertechnical minefield, the prospects for change are not good.

THE FAMILY

The active role of the courts in family law began with the *Williams v. North Carolina* cases after the war, which interpreted the Full Faith and Credit Clause so as to undermine restrictive state divorce laws. The rather tormented reasoning employed gave rise to a memorable statement by Justice Jackson in dissent: "I believe it desirable that people should know whether they are married, and, if so, to whom."

More dramatic developments came later. The states were held not entitled to deny AFDC benefits to households where there was a man present who was not married to the benefit claimant or to deny benefits to illegitimate children, even where benefits were in fact received by a parent. Most states adopted equal rights amendments, under which laws erecting a presumption in favor of maternal custody were invalidated and men as well as women were given the right to claim alimony from spouses. Other decisions gave fathers of illegitimate children rights in adoption proceedings and hinted that adoptive children had rights to identify the natural parent who consented to adoption.

The effects of these decisions were not at all what were desired. Legislatures drastically curtailed alimony rights. Estranged husbands used the withholding of custody as a bargaining counter to reduce support obligations. The process of divorce was rendered more complex and expensive. Perverse incentives were created. The stigma attaching to illegitimacy was lessened, not only for children; also for their parents. The process of adoption was encumbered with new legal risks.

A "right of marital privacy" was established and promptly converted into a "right of non-marital privacy," the authority of the state to distinguish between relationships inside and outside of wedlock being denied. Finally, "liberty" in the Fourteenth Amendment was held to confer a right to abortion substantially on demand, even as to viable fetuses after six months of pregnancy, a rule unparalleled anywhere, declaring situation ethics to be a principle of constitutional law. The law of obscenity was recast to eliminate any meaningful assessment of the social value of the challenged work, thus upsetting the balanced approach to the law derived from the 1930 decision of the Second Circuit Court of Appeals in the *Ulysses* case.

The number of illegitimate births did not decline but rose sharply, the looser mores promoted by the Court causing more women to place themselves at risk of pregnancy, many of them, particularly the young in inner cities, then finding that they had scruples about abortion or a desire to bear a child. The new sexual explicitness did not usher in a golden age of American literature. Not only has a religious right been called into being, but an equally fanatical feminist movement has risen to resist it. Judicial confirmation hearings have been transformed into religious wars. The divorce rate continues to climb, and adoptions fail to keep pace with illegitimate births. The greatest losers from the depreciation of responsible behavior have been the most susceptible groups in the community, among whom indices of social breakdown have sharply risen, crime and disease statistics not being far behind. The interests of women with more traditional aspirations have been sacrificed to those of feminist professionals. Family allowances and increased tax exemptions are no significant part of the new agenda, and for every new lady financier there are several bank tellers and supermarket clerks who would rather be at home while their children are young. Congressman Barney Frank's appropriate reflection on the hypocrisies of the right-to-life movement can be extended. While life does not begin at conception and end at birth, neither do the distinctive obligations of motherhood begin at birth and end with the severance of the umbilical cord. Yet the feminism vindicated in American policy is one that claims for women not the ability to accommodate career and family but rather an equal right to abandon their young.

BUSINESS AND BANKING

The federal courts and legislature have not significantly compromised the vitality of businesses. Overlapping employment discrimination laws, have generated a culture of complaint and have caused some industries to avoid the problem by fleeing cities with large minority populations. In addition, business must cope with the habit of careless and frequent tinkering with the federal tax code, which gave rise to the overbuilding of commercial buildings, followed by a federally mandated collapse in their value, as well as with the failure of a series of administrations to invest political capital in eliminating the double taxation of corporate dividends.

These concerns are incidental: there are three problems of larger consequence. One is the carelessness recently displayed about business structure, which denies the legitimacy of any socially motivated limits on economic size or dominance. This has led to a judicial repeal of the Celler-Kefauver and Bank Merger acts and a growing concentration of control over the banking industry, the functioning of which has never been characterized in the United States by a high degree of professionalism. The combination of large size, rapid growth, the lack of a professional culture, and the lack of adequate regulation may ultimately produce collapses. The political consequences may pose dangers to a mixed economy.

A second is the undermining of commercial morality and prudence in lending worked by the excessive liberality of the Bankruptcy Code and the Supreme Court's undermining of state usury restrictions on credit card lending.

Most ominous are the recent proposals for expansion of the federal criminal law, some of them enacted, that are careless in their reduction of requirements of willfulness and give unscrupulous prosecutors a whip hand over the business community. The great sociologist Karl Mannheim once warned, "It is only . . . through a legal system . . . which deliberately uses the political weapon of criminal prosecution to shape the economic system according to its ideology that old traditions of strength can be comparatively quickly destroyed."

CONCLUSION

To what may one attribute the willingness of the American political classes to sweep away all institutions beneath the national state? Principally to a fixation by both right and left on the economic; in important ways, American politics has resolved itself into a competition between rival materialist philosophies that uneasily coexist in separate parts of society. But the society that makes markets possible rests in part on precapitalist foundations. Complete dominance by the national government is likewise no way to realize equality.

The enthusiasm for destruction of mediating structures has been hastened by the cause of attaining racial equality. But the consequences of forty years of action has not been the elevation of deprived blacks to meaningful full citizenship but the effective transformation of an underclass from peons to wards of the state. The weakening of the institutions that have sustained other groups in their rise in society has conferred no benefits on the dispossessed, nor has the devaluation of standards of personal behavior. The fostering of an ideology of extreme individualism in both morals and economics has been destructive of social capital. American slums are not poor. Their diet and housing stock compare favorably to those of even advanced Asian nations. They suffer from a culture of family breakdown, social isolation of households, a lack of mechanisms for civic cooperation, and a lack of mutual trust. The dominant judicial logic has been that satirized by Professor Philip Kurland in his critique of the Warren court: "equality of rules is inconsistent with a multiplicity of rule-makers."

A sensible agenda for national government would demand that it first do no harm. Although the original premise of income taxation as stated in Mill's *Principles of Political Economy* was that the tax was fairly applied only to income beyond that necessary for subsistence, exemptions have been allowed to wither. Correction of this should supply the appropriate egalitarian agenda. For the rest, government cannot provide equality: As Hume wrote two centuries before the collapse of Communism, "So much authority must soon degenerate into tyranny, and be exercised with great partialities."

The road away from our present discontents is found not in invention of new "rights" but in respect for what was once thought to be a distinctive American value, what Justice Black called "the right of each man to participate in the self government of his society." As the much-maligned Judge Bork pertinently observed, "The Constitution assures the liberties of self-government, not merely those liberties that consist of being free of government. The freedom to govern is enormously important to the individuals who make up a community, for it is freedom to control the environment—physical, aesthetic and moral—which they and their families live."

The renewal of our institutions requires a willingness not only to honor these principles but to look the facts of decline in their face. A surprising number of the needed reforms entail only repudiation of invented judicial doctrines or return to the original constitutional design. The Gorbachevs and Havels, raised under a totalitarian system, perceived the need for reconstruction of their civil societies, as did the American military when confronted with its wreckage following the Vietnam War. There are indeed dangers in a condition in which the last has reason to conceive of itself as the only American institution that has yet faced facts.

2

A Political Constitution

Recent years have seen mounting dissatisfaction with the course of American domestic policy. This has manifested itself in declining voter turnouts, public disaffection with major social institutions—the Congress, the courts, the schools, the professions—hostility toward incumbent officeholders and increased receptivity to muckraking concerning them; and a general malaise manifesting itself both in receptivity to leaders of opinion from outside the political system and poll results indicating a belief that society is moving in the wrong direction. Assessment of the reasons requires an accurate, rather than idealized, description of America's current political system. Such a description would take note of the following features.

Primary responsibility for domestic policy theoretically is reposed in state governments. The executives of these governments are chosen for short, two- to four-year terms, as are their legislatures. Legislators represent artificial, not organic, constituencies, which are sharply realigned every ten years to ensure that economically declining and depopulating areas suffer prompt reductions in their representation.

In each state, there are on average, twenty federal district judges, enjoying life tenure and increasingly appointed on quota principles to provide representation of interests. Each of these judges enjoys the equivalent of a three-year suspensory veto, similar to that retained by the British House of Lords collectively during the period 1911-49, over the acts of the state legislature. This veto may be exercised on a variety of grounds, the more common of which are that particular legislation disadvantages racial minorities; that its regulation of verbal behavior impairs free speech; that it is a regulatory taking of property; that it intrudes on rights of inter- or intrastate travel or rights of personal privacy; that it fails to provide individualized hearings or that the procedural rights at such hearings are inadequate; that portions of it are vague or under- or overinclusive; that its use or recognition of religious institutions offends the Establishment or Free Exercise clause; or that legislation is expressly or impliedly preempted by some provision of the United States Code or the Code of Federal Regulations, each of which now runs to several hundred volumes.

The funding of state programs of any consequence is increasingly partially dependent on federal grants, the receipt of which involves time-consuming reviews, waivers, and clearances; compliance with conditions relating to labor standards, affirmative action, public bid solicitation, advertising, nonuse of religious agencies, public hearings, user or recipient advisory councils, and elaborate 'impact statements.' Lest judicial zeal and bureaucratic caution prove inadequate to enforce limitations on action, federal appropriations of approximately a billion dollars a year are provided to foster tests of legislation by offices whose members have legal training, but no training in economics, social work, or public administration. Generous tax deductions are provided to private advocacy groups, whose litigation activities are treated as charitable in nature, and successful plaintiffs have their counsel fees restored from the public fisc.

The persons administering federal programs are not part of a meritocratic civil service, any impulses in this direction being constrained by the threat of "equal protection" litigation. Their effective political supervisors increasingly are not constitutional officers who have been confirmed by the Senate but the personal retainers of the president, recruited from campaign staffs, who are in turn selected on the basis of their zeal, youth, and independence of family and civic ties.

The President for his part is no longer selected by a system of indirect nomination and election, through electors chosen by state legislators or by party conventions, from among serving senior officeholders known to many of the electors. Instead, he is a person willing to abandon his public or private occupation for a period of years to devote himself to the production of short television advertisements and the raising of funds to broadcast them. These funds he is constitutionally privileged to provide himself: but if he lacks a fortune, he may not call upon others who possess them. Instead, he must curry the favor of industry groups and trade associations, who bundle contributions for him. Similar disabilities are imposed on members of Congress, since the Senate is no longer indirectly elected, even though most of its more distinguished modern members gained their seats by being appointed to fill vacancies. Members of the House no longer represent organic constituencies by reason of decennial reapportionment.

This exquisitely constructed political system can no longer rely on the aid of strong nongovernmental institutions. The traditional professions are no longer either self-confident or self-governing, their traditional codes of ethics having been shredded by the Supreme Court's commercial speech decisions and displaced by market values, distorted by the perverse incentives that professional knowledge bestows. By grace of the Establishment Clause, discovered in 1946, the churches have been marginalized in their educational and social service roles. The family as a social institution has been diminished by judicial exaltation of the individual rights of its members.

Reapportionment has diminished the political weight of great cities, in favor of that of their prospering suburbs, and affirmative action litigation has similarly destroyed any centers of excellence in their education systems and public services. Labor unions have similarly been diminished by judicial celebration of the individual rights of their members. The ability of either state or national societies to constrain or organize individual behavior has further been precluded by judicial restriction of state residence requirements and expansion of the rights of illegal immigrants.

The result is a society characterized by extreme individualism, qualified by a popular culture seeking meaning in fads and cults rather than in the traditional agencies of civic participation. The constraints on behavior that do exist are highly complex and rule based, hence the proliferation of the legal profession. In Edmund Burke's words about the Jacobins: "Laws are to be suppported only by their own terrors, and by the concern, which each individual may find in them from his own private speculations, or can spare to them from his own private interests. In the groves of their academy, at the end of every vista, you see nothing but the gallows. Nothing is left which engages the affections on the part of the commonwealth."[1]

The thesis of this chapter is that this regime is not the regime contemplated by the framers or ratifiers of the Constitution, or the proposers of the Bill of Rights. For them, the Constitution was to be a self-regulating system for the resolution of conflicting values: the constitution of a polity, not of a utopian social or economic order,[2] and one in which the role of the courts was highly limited. Even for the Radical Republicans in the group once delicately referred to as "the perhaps somewhat less gifted framers of the Fourteenth Amendment,"[3] judicially enforced constraints were literally an afterthought, reliance initially being placed on congressional enforcement under sections 2 and 5 of the amendment and on the enfranchisement of blacks, for which a two-thirds majority in Congress could not be mustered until 1869, three years after the Fourteenth Amendment was proposed. In Gordon Wood's words, the Constitution was "a charter of power granted by liberty rather than, as in Europe, a charter of liberty granted by power," it was "a political device designed to control the social forces the Revolution had released,"[4], and "intrinsically an aristocratic document designed to check the democratic tendancies of the period."[5] As for the Bill of Rights, "the Antifederalists in their demand for amendments and a bill of rights had actually been more concerned with weakening the federal government in its relation to the states in matters such as taxation than with protecting 'personal liberty alone.'"[6]

THE FRAMERS

A number of the premises shared by the most influential of the framers have been forgotten. Madison, though favoring popular election of the House of

Representatives, declared himself "an advocate for the policy of refining the popular appointments by successive filtrations . . . in the appointment of the second branch of the legislature, and in the Executive and judiciary branches of the government."[7] Even the popular election of the House had its critics, Elbridge Gerry expressing the fear that the people "were too little informed of personal characters in large districts, and liable to deceptions."[8]

A proposal, favored by Madison, to vest veto power in the president acting together with Supreme Court justices as a Council of Revision was rejected on three separate occasions. Of this scheme Gerry, noted "It was quite foreign from the nature of office to make them judges of the policy of public measures[9], while Rufus King observed that "the judges ought to be able to expound[10] the law, free from the bias of having participated in its formation,"[11] and Nathaniel Gorham noted that judges were "not to be presumed to possess any peculiar knowledge of the mere policy of public measures."[12] After John Rutledge declared that "judges ought never to give their opinion on a law until it comes before them, Luther Martin summed up by saying that: "Knowledge of mankind cannot be presumed to belong in a higher degree to the Judges than to the legislature. . . . It is necessary that the Supreme Judiciary should have the confidence of the people. This will soon be lost, if they are employed in the task [of coercing the states]. The use of force against a state would look more like a declaration of war than an infliction of punishment."[13]

The fear of self-aggrandizement by the executive was also a real one, and was initially sought to be checked, as Tocqueville would have preferred,[14] by a single seven-year term, favored by George Mason as "the best expedient both for preventing the effect of a false complaisance toward unfit characters and a temptation on the side of the Executive to intrigue with the legislature for a re-appointment."[15] The proposal also won the support of Benjamin Franklin, who, after noting that the people were the masters in a democratic state, said of presidents, "It would be imposing an unreasonable burden on them, to keep them always in a state of servitude and not allow them to become again one of the masters."[16] When this course was forsworn, largely because of fear of changing leadership during a war, provisions requiring Senate confirmation of principal officers were provided, Roger Sherman declaring, "Many officers in the Executive Department should be so appointed [without Senate confirmation]—but many ought not, as general officers in the army in time of peace. Herein lay the corruption in Great Britain. If the Executive can model the army, he may set up an absolute government."[17] Senate confirmation, Hamilton wrote in the Federalist No.74, in terms that have contemporary resonance,

> would be an excellent check on a spirit of favoritism in the President, and would tend greatly to prevent the appointment of unfit characters from State prejudice, from familv connection, from personal attachment, or from a view to popularity. . . . He would be both ashamed and afraid to bring forward, for the most distiguished or lucrative stations, candidates who had no other merit than that of coming from the same State, to which he particularly belonged, or of being, in some way or another, personally allied to him, or

of possessing the necessary insignificance and pliancy to render them the obsequious instruments of his pleasure.

The political abuse of the power of criminal prosecution, which had inspired the English Petition of Right and the bills of rights in some state constitutions, were sought to be dealt with by a restrictive definition of treason. The requirement of two witnesses to an overt act was provided on Benjamin Franklin's premise that "prosecutions for treason were generally virulent, and perjury too easily made use of against innocence."[18] The effect of the limitation was largely vitiated by Rufus King's unfortunate remark, echoed in the prevailing opinion in the Rosenberg case, that "the legislature might punish capitally under other names than treason."[19]

Even the problem of slavery, it was hoped by some delegates, would vanish once importations were prohibited in 1808. Oliver Ellsworth expressed the view that "poor laborers will be so plenty as to render slaves useless. Slavery in time will not be a speck on our country."[20] Madison, however, thought otherwise: "Twenty years will produce all the mischief that can be apprehended from the liberty to import slaves."[21]The suggestions at the end of the convention that a bill of rights was needed were met with reliance on the proposition that the federal government was a government of limited powers. Thus, as pointed out by Roger Sherman, "The power of Congress does not extend to the press."[22] Further, "the State Declarations of Rights are not repealed by this Constitution, and being in force are sufficient."[23]

The premise of the framers was that the horizontal and vertical division of powers, not judicially enforced individual rights, supplied the basis of liberty, which, in Franklin's words, "can only end in Despotism when the people shall have become so corrupted as to need despotic government, being incapable of any other."[24]

THE RATIFIERS

The debates of the ratifying conventions, like those of the constitutional convention, make plain a design to avoid the direct coercion of state governments. At the Massachusetts convention, Thomas Dawes observed, "A whole state can be compelled only by an army, but taxes upon an individual imply only the use of a collector of taxes."[25] In Connecticut, Oliver Ellsworth similarly observed, "I am for coercion by law—that coercion which acts only upon delinquent individuals. This constitution does not attempt to coerce sovereign bodies, states, in their political capacity. No coercion is applicable to such bodies, but that of an armed force. If we should attempt to execute the laws of the Union by sending an armed force against a delinquent state, it would involve the good and the bad, the innocent and guilty, in the same calamity. [26]At the New York convention, similar sentiments prevailed. Robert Livingston stated that the Articles of Confederation "operated upon states in their political capacity, and not upon individuals [and] carried with it the seeds of domestic violence and tended ultimately to its dissolution."[27] Alexander Hamilton proclaimed "to coerce the states is one of the maddest projects that was ever devised. A failure of compliance will never be confined to a single state. This being the case, can we suppose it wise to hazard a civil war."[28] At the North Carolina convention, Samuel Spencer similarly observed, "Laws could not be put in execution against states without the agency of the sword; which instead of answering the ends of government, would destroy it."[29]

The ratifiers were also assured that the states would be unimpaired in their normal functions. At the New York convention Hamilton declared, "Were the laws of the union to newmodel the internal police of any state; were they to alter or abrogate at a blow the whole of its civil and criminal institutions; were they to penetrate the recesses of domestic life and control in all respects the private conduct of individuals there might be more force in the objection."[30] Further: "Can the state governments become insignificant while they have the power of raising money independently and without control . . . the states have certain independent powers in which their laws are supreme; for example in making and executing laws concerning the punishment of certain crimes, such as murder, theft etc, the states cannot be controlled."[31] At the North Carolina convention, William R. Davie, who had been a member of the federal convention, after emphasizing the limited powers of the national government, observed: "There is not one instance of a power given to the United States, whereby the internal policy or administration of the states is affected. There is no instance that can be pointed out wherein the internal policy of the state can be affected by the judiciary of the United States."[32] James Iredell, also a member of the Federal Convention, assured the convention that except for treason, piracies, felonies on the high seas, and offenses against the law of nations, the Congress "have no power to define any other crime whatever."[33,34] As in the federal convention, the restrictive definition of treason was pointed to to demonstrate the lack of need for a bill of rights to protect controversial criminal defendants.[35] James Wilson declared to the Pennsylvania convention in his magisterial opening statement, "This punishment, and the description of this crime, are the great sources of danger and persecution, on the part of government against the citizen. Crimes against the state! and against the officers of the state! History informs us that more wrong may be done on this subject than on any other whatsoever. But under this Constitution, there can be no treason against the United States, except such as is defined in this Constitution . . . a very great part of . . . tyranny over the people has arisen from the extension of the definition of treason."[36] At the North Carolina convention, Richard Irspaight, a member of the federal convention, observed, citing the restrictive definition of treason, "Complaining, therefore, or writing, cannot be treason."[37]

The indirect election of the Senate and the president was extolled as a mechanism for assuring the competence of government and the protection of state interests. Governor Huntingdon of Connecticut declared to his state's convention,

"It is not only inconvenient but dangerous to liberty for the people of a large community to attempt to exercise in person the supreme authority." John Jay told the New York convention that legislatures "will certainly choose those who are most distinguished for their general knowledge; they will also instruct them." Fisher Ames in the Massachusetts convention referred to senators as "the ambassadors of the states" and to the states as "a shelter against the abuse of power the natural avengers of violated rights," while Theophilus Parsons declared, "The legislatures are the constituents of the senate."

The majorities of the legislatures constituted by this checking process were themselves regarded as the appropriate guardians of private rights. John Hancock, concluding the Massachusetts convention, declared that the people "until they themselves become corrupt . . . will always have upright and able rulers. . . . They will never forsake the first principle of society—that of being governed by the voice of the majority."[38] Oliver Ellsworth opening the Connecticut convention similarly stated, "In republics, it is a fundamental principle that the majority govern, and that the minority comply with the general voice . . . a minority, a very small minority, has governed us."[39] Edmund Pendleton., the president of the Virginia convention stated "The idea of the poor becoming rich by assiduity is not mere fancy. This could not have been the case without a government to protect their industry . . . the greatest security of liberty is regular government."[40] Madison told the Virginia convention, "If the bonds of the government be relaxed, confusion will ensue. Anarchy ever has produced, and I fear ever will produce, despotism . . . the rapid growth of population in every state is an additional reason to check dissipation and licentiousness."[41] Hamilton, in the New York convention declared himself for "strength and stability in the organization of our government, and vigor in its operations."[42] The general prevailing sentiment was that expressed by James Wilson in Pennsylvania: "Liberty has a formidable enemy on each hand: on one there is tyranny, on the other licentiousness. In order to guard against the latter, proper powers ought to be given to government; in order to guard against the former, those powers ought to be properly distributed."[43]

For protection of property, reliance was placed not on any specific constitutional guarantee but on the independence of judges, without which, Thomas Thacher told the Massachusetts convention, "all property is precarious and personal security is at an end; a man may be stripped of all his possessions and murdered, without the forms of law."[44,45] Edmund Pendleton similarly assured the Virginia convention, "Whenever, in any country in the world, the judges are independent, property is secure."[46,47] Beyond that, significance was attached to the provisions sweeping aside state duties and obstructions of commerce, precluding the states from issuing currency, and precluding impairments of contract, James Wilson citing these provisions and further observing, "If we mean to restore either public or private credit, . . . foreigners, as well as ourselves[must] have a just and impartial tribunal to which they may resort."[48]

As in the Philadelphia convention, proponents of ratification justified the absence of press guarantees on the basis that the national government had limited powers. Thus Wilson Nicholas told the Virginia convention, "Is the disputed right enumerated? If not, Congress cannot meddle with it. [England has] no express security for the liberty of the press. They have a reliance on Parliament for its protection and security."[49]The constitutional provisions barring ex post facto laws and bills of attainder and providing habeas corpus and jury trials in criminal cases were likewise pointed to with favor.

The diverse nature of the nation's population (influenced by Congress's power over naturalization laws), the provision of the Constitution prohibiting religious tests for office, and the limited powers of the national government were relied upon to secure religious freedom. Thus Madison told the Virginia convention, "If there were a majority of one sect, a bill of rights would be a poor protection for liberty . . . that multiplicity of sects which pervades America is the best and only security for religious liberty in any society; for where there is such a variety of sects, there cannot be a majority of any one sect to oppress and persecute the rest."[50] Oliver Wolcott told the Connecticut convention, "Knowledge and liberty are so prevalent in this country, that I do not believe that the United States would ever be disposed to establish one religious sect, and lay all others under legal disabilities. But as . . . any test would be exceedingly injurious to the rights of free citizens, I cannot think it altogether superfluous to have added a clause, which secures us from the possibility of such oppression."[51] Edmund Randolph told the Virginia convention , "I am a friend to a variety of sects, because they will keep one another in order and will forever oppose all attempts to infringe religious liberty."[52] In North Carolina, James Iredell referred to the provision prohibiting religious tests as "calculated to secure religious liberty by putting all sects on a level." He further pointed to the limited powers of the national government: "Can they pass a single act to impair our religious liberties?"[53] Madison had similarly argued, "I have no reason to conclude that uniformity of government will produce that of religion. The government has no jurisdiction over it."[54]

As in the federal convention, there were ratifiers who thought that the terms of the unamended constitution would mean the ultimate end of slavery. Thomas Dawes told the Massachusetts convention "every particular state is left to its own option totally to prohibit the introduction of slaves into its own territories . . . we may say that, although slavery is not smitten by an apoplexy, yet it has received a mortal wound, and will die of a consumption."[55] James Neal, noting the prohibition on importation after 1808, stated, "The step taken toward abolition of slavery was one of the beauties of the constitution."[56] Judge Francis Dana and Samuel Adams "rejoiced that a door was now to be opened for the annihilation of this odious abhorrent practice in a certain time."[57] It was also pointed out by William Heath that "the migration or importation is confined to the states now existing only; new states cannot claim it,"[58] though he doubted that slaves in the South would be emancipated after 1808. James Wilson lauded the Constitution as "laying the foundation for banishing slavery out of this country . . . the new states to be formed will be under the control of Congress in this particular, and slavery will never be introduced among them."[59] The flaws in this optimism were summarized by Charles Pinckney at the South Carolina convention: "We have a security that the general government can never emancipate them, for no such authority is granted. We have obtained a right to recover our slaves in whatever part of America they might take refuge, which is a right we had not before."[60]

Throughout the deliberations of the conventions, there was emphasis on institutional rather than parchment guarantees and recognition that the whole apparatus was dependent on the civic virtue of the populace. "If there is no virtue among them, what will Congress do? . . . If they set heaven at defiance, no arm of flesh can save them."[61] (Phillips of Massachusetts). "If ignorance and depravity prevail, they will inevitably lead to slavery and ruin."[62] (Huntingdon of Connecticut). "Without the prevalence of Christian piety and morals, the best Republican constitution can never save us from slavery and ruin."[63] (Turner of Massachusetts). "There is a remedy to every distemper in government if the people are not wanting to themselves; if they are wanting to themselves, there is no remedy."[64] (Wilson of Pennsylvania). "No free government can be preserved to any people but by a firm adherence to justice, moderation, temperance, frugality, and virtue."[65] (Nicholas of Virginia, quoting the Virginia Declaration of Rights).

THE BILL OF RIGHTS

With the exceptions of North Carolina, which refused to ratify the Constitution until after it had taken effect and amendments had been proposed, and Rhode Island, which did not ratify until 1790, the other states of the original thirteen ratified the Constitution. Beginning with Massachusetts, the sixth state to ratify, the ratifying conventions appended to their resolutions requested amendments to the Constitution. The initial set of amendments, those of Massachusetts, related to reserved powers of the states, monopolies, grand juries, civil juries, and titles of nobility. New Hampshire then requested amendments relating to the right to arms and quartering of troops, as well as laws "touching" religion. Virginia added freedom of the press, a general due process clause, limitations on penalties, search and seizure, speech, and assembly. New York added double jeopardy to the list, as well as a proposal resembling the Eleventh Amendment. The later resolutions tended to cumulate the earlier. Almost all of the resolutions also requested other amendments relating to taxation, representation, and other matters; none requested a restriction on takings.[66]

The resolutions relating to religion,[67] with the exception of the New Hampshire language ("touching religion, or to infringe the rights of conscience") all ran to a type. Virginia's version referred to "free exercise of religion" and went on "and that no particular religious sect or society ought to be favored or established by Law in preference to others." The New York language was "freely and peaceably to Exercise their religion" and "no Religious Sect or Society ought to be favored or established by Law in preference of others." North Carolina referred to "free exercise of religion" and "that no particular religious sect or society ought to be favored or established by law in preference to others; the Rhode Island language was identical in both respects. This language seems calculated to dispel any notion that nondiscriminatory congressional aid to religion was proscribed. The version of the Bill of Rights presented by Madison to the House of Representatives used the language, "no religion shall be established by law, nor shall the equal rights of conscience be infringed." He explained it as meaning that "Congress should not establish a religion, and enforce the legal observation of it by law, nor compel men to worship God in any manner contrary to their conscience," which he said would prevent the danger that "one sect might obtain a preeminence, or two combine together and establish a religion to which they would compel others to conform."[68] The Senate adopted a condensed version reading, "Congress shall make no law establishing articles of faith, or a mode of worship, or prohibiting the free exercise of religion." The final version, substituting the words "an establishment of religion" was the work of a conference committee whose members were Madison, Roger Sherman, and John Vining for the House and Oliver Ellsworth, Charles Carroll, and William Paterson for the Senate.[69]

Madison's version of the amendments would have prevented states as well as the national government from infringing the rights of free speech,press, and conscience and that of trial by jury[70]; and he indicated that he thought this provision binding the states "the most valuable on the whole."[71] Nonetheless, it was rejected by the Senate.

The Bill of Rights was in its essence a concession by the federalists to the antifederalists, designed to head off what were seen as more damaging amendments relating to direct taxation and the treaty power. For Jefferson, they would "produce probably further guards to liberty without touching the energy of the government and this will bring over the bulk of the opposition to the side of the new government."[72] Madison, acquiescing in this view, feared that rights would be too narrowly defined, and was under no illusions as to the value of parchment barriers, in view of "the inefficacy of a bill of rights on those occasions when its control is most needed . . . [dangers] chiefly to be apprehended from acts in which the Government is the mere instrument of the major number of the constituents."[73] For Madison, the value of a bill of rights was found in its educative effect, and in curbing occasional instances of arbitrary government not reflecting majority opinion.[74]

CASE LAW PRIOR TO THE FOURTEENTH AMENDMENT

"In the first century," David P. Currie, perhaps the most disinterested historian of the Supreme Court has written, "it is not common to find an important decision that clearly distorted the Constitution."[75] The failures he lists are nonetheless significant ones, which gravely distorted the original design: "The capstone again is Dred Scott,[76] where five Justices outdid one another in concocting ever more ludicrous excuses for the preconceived and untenable conclusion that Congress lacked authority to ban slavery in the territories. I have trouble believing that Article III authorized suits against states[77], that the eleventh amendment did not preclude injunctions against state officers, that the Constitution somewhere forbade state taxation of federal instrumentalities . . . that due process limited substantive legislative powers . . ."[78]

Dred Scott doomed the hopes of those who looked for the ultimate abolition of slavery through the withering and isolation of its political base as more states were admitted. Although the court in *Barron v. Baltimore* was explicit in holding that the Bill of Rights did not apply to the states, the progeny of *Osborn* and *McCulloch* launched a tradition in which no state law became certainly effective until after prolonged delay and district court review. George Mason's fear that the federal courts would "tend to impair and ultimately destroy . . . the legislation of the state governments,"[79] began to be realized.

THE FRAMING OF THE FOURTEENTH AMENDMENT

Although recent Supreme Court rhetoric would make it appear that the Fourteenth Amendment was intended to end any separation between federal and state interests and to work a permanent subordination of state authority, the history and purposes of the amendment suggest otherwise. In fact, the amendment was an expedient resorted to by the Radical Republicans in 1866 when they realized that their preferred solution—full enfranchisement of southern blacks—could not command a two-thirds majority in Congress. Since the self-protection of political rights and the franchise could not be secured for southern blacks, Congress sought to confer on them, by enactment of the Civil Rights Act of 1866 and the Fourteenth Amendment designed to render it permanent, the civil rights that otherwise would have accrued to blacks by reason of their enfranchisement.

As introduced in the House following enactment of the Civil Rights Act, the amendment contained no self-enforcing provision but contained the provisions now embodied as sections 2 and 5 of the Fourteenth Amendment for reduction in the representation of states disenfranchising portions of their citizens and for Congressional enforcement of provisions relating to privileges and immunities and equal protection. Congressman Kelley explained, "When all men not disqualified by crime or pauperism shall be entrusted with the ballot they can protect their own rights and will need no Congressional guardianship and when the states recognize the equality of all their people before their laws they will have no cause to dread Congressional censorship."

Thaddeus Stevens explained that the purpose of the amendment was "simply to provide that where any state makes a distinction in the same law between different classes of individuals, Congress shall have power to correct such discrimination and inequality." When asked whether the amendment would authorize Congress to invalidate discrimination against married women, he stated, "When a distinction is made between two married people or two femmes sole, then it is unequal legislation, but where all of the same class are dealt with in the same way, then there is no pretense of inequality." Congressman Bingham gave his assurance that "under no possible interpretation can it ever be made to operate in the State of New York while she occupies her present proud position."[80] Congressman Hale of New York, a moderate Republican, declared that the Civil War was produced "by constructions of courts [by which] slavery was cut loose from this confinement by state laws and connected with the federal government as a national institution . . . it was a departure from the spirit of the constitution when it was held that Congress had the power to legislate upon the subject of the rendition of fugitive slaves," a somewhat dubious interpretation as to the fugitive slave provisions, though not as to *Dred Scott*. Opposing the amendment, he further alluded to "the inevitable tendency of power to always augment itself."

Congressman Woodbridge construed the privileges and immunities provision as conferring only rights to visitors to a state "extended to other citizens of the state." Congressman Bingham, closing, gave support to the views of later incorporationists by declaring that the amendment was designed "to arm the Congress with the power to enforce the bill of rights as it stands in the constitution today. It hath that extent—no more." Asked about alien property laws, he declared that matters respecting real estate remained "dependent on the state law except when granted by the United States." Finally Congressman Hotchkiss, in a decisive intervention, urged that the amendment be rendered self-executing so "that legislation cannot override."[81]

When the amendment returned to the House with the self-executing Section 1 added, Congressman Stevens explained that "whatever law punishes a white man for a crime shall punish the black man precisely in the same way and to the same degree." He further explained that "we shall not approach the measure of justice until we have given every adult freedman a homestead on the land where he was born and suffered and toiled. Forty acres of land and a hut would be more valuable to him than the immediate right to vote." He regretted the absence also of a guarantee of the right to vote, but stated that he viewed the second section, providing for proportionate reduction of representation and ultimately a dead letter, as "the most important. It fixes the basis of representation." Congressman (later President) Garfield deplored the fact that the amendment did not provide "the plain, unanswerable proposition that every adult, intelligent citizen of the United States,unconvicted of crime, shall enjoy the right of suffrage," and quoted John Stuart Mill: "the ballot is put into the hands of men, not so much to enable them to govern others as that he may not be misgoverned by others." He went on: "Suffrage is the shield, the sword, the spear and all the panoply that best befits a man for his own defense."[82]

In the course of debate in the Senate, Senator Howard of Michigan, a member of the committee reporting the amendment, declared that it "abolishes all class legislation in the states and does away with the injustice of subjecting one caste of persons to a code not applicable to the other . . . the states are not yet prepared to sanction so fundamental a change as would be the concession of the right of suffrage to the colored race." Senator Stewart of Nevada also urged, "the negro must have the ballot or have no friends . . . give him the ballot and he will have plenty of white friends." Senator John Henderson, a Missouri Republican, in the most notable and prophetic speech in the debate, observed:

> At an earlier day, I offered . . . a constitutional amendment in three lines. It prohibited the states, in prescribing the qualifications of voters, from discriminating against the negro on account of his color. Had this been adopted . . . there would then have been no necessity for declaring who are citizens of the United States, for every freeman would have worn the honored badge of citizenship. . . . It would have been superfluous to interdict the states from taking life, liberty or property from the citizen without due process of law; for liberty first being given, the citizen can protect his own life and property. The provision securing equal protection of the laws against inimical state legislation might then be dispensed with as wholly unnecessary. These few words would have accomplished directly what this proposes to accomplish indirectly after years of political strife, in which truth and conscience and patriotism are too often sacrificed to the attainment of success. . . . The validity of all laws must depend at last upon human judgment. Judges, even in the highest courts, are but mortals. Should the Supreme Court of the United States affirm the judgment of these inferior tribunals, the present period would be no better for the rights of the negro than that when the Supreme Court once before supposed he had no rights which the white man was bound to respect.[83]

Senator Yates concurred, expressing the view that suffrage is "the only thing that can divide the South or introduce a loyal element there that will be a counterbalancing force."

The radicals were not able to secure a two-thirds majority for the Fifteenth Amendment until 1869, and it was not ratified until 1870. Even then, language that would have forbidden voting disqualifications on grounds of nativity, property, or education were stricken in order to secure ratifications.[84] The total thrust of Reconstruction remained as before, given the absence of effective enforcement mechanisms in the Fifteenth Amendment: "limitations on states rather than enhancement of national duties."[85]

CASE LAW FOLLOWING THE RECONSTRUCTION AMENDMENTS

The aberrations of subsequent case law have been well summarized by Professor Currie: "I have trouble believing that the Constitution somewhere .

. . granted a right to travel, that due process limited substantive legislative powers." "The requirement that nonracial classifications be reasonable crept into the law without ever having been discussed. It seems less than clear that the Court's conclusion that racial distinctions are sometimes permissible will work in the long run to the benefit of those it was intended to help.[86] . . . The more serious question is whether, in light of the generally accepted purposes of the first amendment, purely commercial speech should have been held to be protected at all." "I may have a right to keep a burglar out of my house, the Court seemed to be saying, but once he gets inside I must invite him to dinner." "No doubt it was a little late by the time the gender cases were decided to limit the clause once again to race, but that does not make any less regrettable the Court's original failure to justify turning what might have been a firm guarantee against racial discrimination into a flexible tool for striking down any laws found unreasonable by five unelected judges." "In *Wickard v. Filburn*, a congressional limitation of the wheat a farmer could plant for his own use was upheld under the commerce clause, even though the transaction was neither interstate nor commerce." "The activism of the Warren years spawned occasional excesses. In such cases as *Bolling v. Sharpe*, *Reitman v. Mulkey*, *Watkins v. United States*, *Slochower v. Board of Regents*, *Griffin v. Illinois*, *Miranda v. Arizona* and *Robinson v. California*, the Court's zeal may have gotten the better of its judgment. The most egregious example..is the famous 1965 decision in *Griswold v. Connecticut* . . . strik[ing] down a law forbidding the use of contraceptives.[87] . . . The difficulty was that it seemed to offend nothing in the Constitution." "The court in Lemon seemed close to holding that sometimes the state not only might but must treat those who practiced their faith less favorably than those who did not. . . . [Tlhe Burger court . . . by its expansive interpretation of the terms 'property' and liberty, constitutionalized much of administrative procedure."[88]

CONCLUSION

Libraries have been written about the American Constitution. This short addition to them is prepared in the belief that recent scholarship and decision making, centering as they do almost entirely on the Bill of Rights and its supposed emanations, fails to see the woods for the trees. The result is a constitution that is all anchor and no sail—directly contrary to the intentions of the framers. The result also is a judicial micromanagement of all social institutions. It is no accident that every major American reform movement has had to move to curtail "government by injunction"—the Jeffersonians through the Eleventh Amendment and the Anti-Injunction Act; the Populists and Progressives through the Johnson Act, the Three-Judge Court Acts, the Tax Injunction Act and the Clayton and Norris-La Guardia acts; and the New Deal through various procedural changes and the abortive court-packing scheme. It is also useful to be reminded of the case in favor of Senate confirmation and against bloated White House staffs; of the reasons for indirect selection of presidents, senators, and judges; of the importance of state control over the criminal law; of the hostility of the framers to the sort of coercion of the states that today is commonplace and of their preference for direct federal action; of their assumptions concerning the religion clauses and the need for civic virtue; and of their belief in institutional rather than parchment guarantees of the economic order.

The blunt fact is that the Bill of Rights was conceived as a relatively minor appendage to the Constitution. As Professor Currie has summarized:

> Some serious thinkers believed that no Bill of Rights was needed at all, for the structure of government had been carefully designed to protect liberty. Democratic elections reduce the likelihood of oppression because the people are not likely to oppress themselves. Federalism reduces the power of any one government to infringe individual rights. Separation of legislative, executive and judicial powers requires three independent branches to concur before a person may be deprived of life, liberty, or property. Checks and balances such as the veto power, impeachment, and the requirement of Senate consent to treaties and appointments reinforce these safeguards by giving one branch the affirmative power to inhibit arbitrary action by another. Even unpopular minorities are protected by tying their fate to that of everyone else; if a dominant faction can limit the freedom of others only by restricting its own, it is unlikely to do so without a pretty convincing reason only when all these indirect safeguards fail must we fall back on the direct guarantees of the Bill of Rights.

A rejoinder would doubtless stress the judiciary's contribution to free political discussion and to racial equality. It does not denigrate that contribution to say that it is not so great as popularly supposed.

As Madison recognized, the free speech clause was likely to be an ineffective barrier to majority sentiment. "When freedom of expression was endangered by popular hysteria during the First World War, the Court went along without a murmur; when the problem recurred after the Second World War, it protested cautiously and then withdrew from the field."[89] Its contributions, as Madison foresaw, are twofold: It has helped educate the public to tolerance (with the powerful aid of minority or overruled opinions such as that of Holmes in *Abrams* and Hand in *Masses* and of extrajudicial speeches, such as those of Hughes for the New York socialists and Hand during the McCarthy period), and it has been able to protect speech against unpopular national governments(as with the Pentagon Papers) or a minority of state governments (as with the rights of civil rights demonstrators in the South). The cost of this has been a focus on constitutional protection to the exclusion of all else; the concentration of the American media has been allowed to proceed to a point at which discussion in it is far less free and diverse than in the British media, which enjoy only parliamentary protection.

As with the press, so with racial equality. There has been a tendancy to forget that the negative commands of the Fourteenth Amendment were accepted as a third-best solution during Reconstruction, after realization of a social and economic agenda in favor of the freedmen was forestalled and after it became plain that no constitutional majority existed for the full enfranchisement of the blacks under federal authority. It was not until that enfranchisement took place a century later that blacks made truly significant gains, and on any fair view the effects of the Voting Rights Act have been far more beneficient and significant than those of the Supreme Court's adventures in the fields of educational desegregation and employment discrimination. One effect of the continued fixation on Fourteenth Amendment litigation has been to place virtually any proposed change in the education or welfare system under threat of judicial veto; another has been to exclude professions other than the bar from full participation in public discourse and policy making.

The danger of judicial review on the American pattern, as a British commentator, Peter Calvocoressi, observed forty years ago, is that it can become a vehicle for "making the law so much more inflexible as to deflect it from the service of society to the service of a class." On any fair view that has now happened, in consequence of the extension of the First Amendment to commercial speech, the enlargement of constitutional definitions of liberty and property, the invention of privacy and travel rights, the judicial scrutiny of nonracial classifications, the tortured construction of the Establishment Clause and its application against the states, and the misuse of the federal injunction to coerce state governments. The result is a state of political stasis, in which privileges are enjoyed by special classes at the expense of basic rights of self-government. Americans must accordingly decide whether they want a charter for upper-Bohemian lifestyles or rather what was originally intended, a political constitution.

NOTES

1. Burke, *Reflections on the Revolution in France* (Anchor ed. 1973), 90.

2. G. Wood, *Creation of the American Republic* (1969), 562.

3. *Report of the Conference of State Chief Justices on Federal-State Relations as Affected by Judicial Decisions* (1958).

4. Id. at 476.

5. Id. at 513.

6. Id. at 543.

7. *Madison's Debates*, in *Documents Illustrative of the Formation of the Union of the American States*, 69th Congress, 1st Session (House Document 398) (1927) (hereafter "*Madison's Debates*"), 126-27.

8. Id. at 136.

9. Id. at 147.

10. Id. 423. Gerry declared in this, the second debate on the issue, that he "relied for his part on the representatives of the people as the guardians of their rights and interests."

11. Id. at 147.

12. Id. at 147.

13. Id. at 149. Id., 423.

14. 1 Tocqueville, *Democracy in America* (Reeve trans. (1945)) at 142. "[T]he desire to be re-elected is the chief aim of the President . . . the whole policy of his administration, and even his most indifferent measures, tend to this object; and . . . especially as the crisis approaches, his personal interest takes the place of his interest in the public good."

15. Madison's Debates, supra. at 135.

16. Id. at 457.

17. Id. at 613.

18. Id.at 577.

19. Id.at 577.

20. Id. at 590.

21. Id. at 616.

22. Id. at 726.

23. Id. at 716.

24. Id. at 739.

25. J. Elliot, *Debates in the Several State Conventions on the Adoption of the Federal Constitution* (2d ed.1836) (hereafter "Elliot's Debates"), vol. 2, 58.

26. Id. at 197.

27. Id., vol. 2, 214.

28. Id., vol. 2, 233.

29. Id., vol. 4, 162.

30. Id., vol. 4, 160.

31. Id., vol. 2, 268.

32. Id., vol. 2, 355.

33. Id., vol. 4, 219.

34. Id., vol. 2, 362. On the dominant role of the states with respect to the criminal law, see also the *Federalist*, no. 45 (Madison). On the roots of the fear of standing armies and of a large federal role in defining the criminal law, see I. Macaulay, *History of England from the Accession of James II*: "While the Houses were exercising their

authority thus it suddenly passed out of their hands. It had been obtained by calling into existence a power which could not be controlled. . . . In the summer of 1647, about twelve months after the last fortress of the Cavaliers had submitted to the Parliament, the Parliament was compelled to submit to its own soldiers."

35. Id., vol. 2, 26.

36. Id., vol. 2, 469, 487.

37. Id., vol. 4, 209.

38. Id., vol 2, 46 (Ames), vol. 2, 26 (Parsons)., vol. II, 199 (Hancock).

39. Id., vol. 2, 281, 46.

40. Id., vol. 2, 175-76.

41. Id., vol. 2, 196-97.

42. Id., vol. 4, 295-96.

43. Id., vol. 3, 394.

44. Id., vol. 2, 147.

45. Id., vol. 2, 301.

46. Id., vol. III, 303.

47. Id., vol. 2, 438.

48. Id., vol. 2, 491.

49. Id., vol. 3, 247.

50. Id., vol. 3, 330.

51. Id., vol. 2, 202.

52. Id., vol. 3, 204.

53. Id., vol. 4, 196.

54. Id., vol. 4, 194.

55. Id., vol. 3, 93.

56. Id., at vol. 2, 40-41.

57. Id., vol. 2, 108.

58. Id. vol. 2, 115.

59. Id. vol. 2, 452.

60. Id., vol. 2, 286.

61. Id. vol. 2, 67.

62. Id. vol. 2, 200.

63.Id. vol. 2, 171.

64. Id., vol. 2, 433.

65. Id. vol. 3, 238.

66. See 5 J. Hunt (ed.), *Writings of Madison* (1900-10), 389-90; *Annals of Congress*, lst Congress, lst Session, vol. 1, 435-36.

67. The instruments of ratification and accompanying resolutions are set out in *Documents*, supra, note 7, at 1009-59.

68. *Annals of Congress*, vol.1, 757-58; 1 D.Currie: *The Constitution in the Supreme Court: The First Hundred Years* (1985) (hereafter 1 Currie), 341 n.12; P. Kurland, T*he Origin of the Religion Clauses of the Constitution*, 27 Wm. & Mary L. Rev. 839 (1986).

69. R. Rutland, *The Birth of the Bill of Rights, 1776-1791* (1955), 212.

70. *Annals of Congress*, lst Congress, lst Session, 755; Rutland, supra, 208.

71. Rutland, supra, at 212.

72. Jefferson to Admiral John Paul Jones, March 23,1789 in 19 Lipscomb (ed.), *The Writings of Thomas Jefferson* (1904), 54.

73. Madison to Jefferson, October 17, 1788, quoted in Rutland, supra 193.

74. Rutland, supra at 193.

75. 1 Currie, 455.

76. *Scott v. Sandford*, 60 U.S. 393 (1857); see 1 Currie 263-73.

77. *Chisholm v. Georgia*, 2 U.S. 419 (1793); see 1 Currie 14-20.

78. *Osborn v. Bank of the United States*, 22 U.S.738 (1824), see 1 Currie 102-08. *McCulloch v. Maryland*, 17 U.S.316 (1819), see 1 Currie 160-68. *Scott v. Sanford*, 60 U.S. 393, 450-52 (1857), see 1 Currie 271-72.

79. Elliot's Debates, supra, vol. 2, 257.

80. *Congressional Globe*, February 27, 1866, H1057, in A. Avins (ed.), *The Reconstruction Amendment Debates* (1967) (hereafter "Avins"), 153; *Congressional Globe*, February 27, 1866, p. 1063, Avins 153. *CongressionalGlobe*, February 27, 1866, p. 1064, Avins 154. *Ccongressional Globe*, February 27, 1866, p. 1065, Avins 155.

81. *Congressional Globe*, February 27, 1866, p.1066, Avins 156. *Congressional Globe*, February 28, 1866, p. 1089, Avins 157. *CongressionalGlobe*, February 27, 1866, p. 1095, Avins 160.

82. *Congressional Globe*, May 8,1866, Avins 212. *Congressional Globe*, May 8, 1866, p. 2462, Avins 213.

83. *CongressionalGlobe*, May 23, 1866, p. 2766, Avins 220. *CongressionalGlobe*, May 24, 1866, p. 2799, Avins.

84. *Congressional Globe*, June 8, 1866, p.3035, Avins 236. Congressional Globe, June 8, 1866, p. 3037, Avins 236. Avins 410; H.Hyman, *A More Perfect Union: The Impact of Civil War and Reconstruction on the Constitution* (1973) (hereafter Hyman), 522.

85. Hyman, supra, 444.

86. 1 Currie 455, see *Crandall v. Nevada*, 73 U.S.35 (1868), see 1 Currie 334-35,355-56; *Edwards v. California*, 314 U.S.160 (1941); *Shapiro v. Thompson*, 394 U.S. 618 (1969). The Rhode Island convention had unsuccessfully sought inclusion in the Bill of Rights of a provision "that Congress have power to establish a uniform rule of inhabitancy, or settlement of the poor of the different states throughout the United States." Documents, supra, 1059; *Hepburn v. Griswold*, 75 U.S. 603, (1870), 1 Currie 320-29, 369-78, and cases cited; *Lochner v. New York*, 198 U.S.45 (1905), 2 Currie 47-48; *Roe v. Wade*, 410 U.S. 113 (1973), 2 Currie 465-75; *Fullilove v. Klutznick*, 448 U.S.448 (1980), 2 Currie 454, 390-91, 487.

87. 2 Currie 518; 2 Currie 504; *Plyler v. Doe*, 457 U.S. 202 (1982); 2 Currie 493-500; 317 U.S. 111 (1942), 2 Currie 308.

88. 2 Currie 458; 2 Currie 528-29; *Lemon v. Kurtzman*, 403 U.S.602 (1971). 2 Currie 538-46; *Slochower v. Board of Education*, 350 U.S. 551 (1956), 2 Currie 386-88; *Goldberg v. Kelly*, 397 U.S. 254 (1970), 2 Currie 539-40.

89. 2 Currie 560, 603.

3

Delegation to Private Parties in American Constitutional Law

INTRODUCTION

In an age in which so much of constitutional litigation involves efforts to apply or expand the "state action" doctrine under the Fourteenth Amendment, it is surprising that so little attention has been paid to a major constitutional weapon of the 1930s: the doctrine of nondelegation to private parties.[1] Since the end of the Depression, comprehensive federal schemes of agricultural or industrial regulation have been undertaken less frequently, and the doctrine has usually found new application only in the states, primarily in zoning cases, cases involving the validity of privately established professional and industrial standards, and decisions relating to local option elections, the creation of special taxing districts, and state resale price maintenance laws.

At the time that professors Jaffe and Hale wrote their surveys of the subject almost forty years ago,[2] the basis for the doctrine seemed much clearer than it does today. Courts could wax vehement (though they did not always do so) when legislative enactments gave individuals the right to control the conduct and action of others. Belief in laissez-faire and the sanctity of property rights could lead courts to overlook the ways in which the defense of private rights could produce results not greatly different from those that obtain as a result of delegation to private persons.

The history is a familiar one. At common law, private coercive power was not sanctioned. Thus the Supreme Court in 1917 readily granted an injunction against mild organizational efforts by a labor union on the basis that the union induced breach of an oral yellow—dog contract and thereby infringed the penumbra of protection cast around private contract rights.[3] And where legislative delegations rather than common law principles were involved, the Court five years earlier, in *Eubank v. City of Richmond*,[4] likewise struck down a zoning law that, by allowing two-thirds of the residents of a street to request establishment of building lines, compelled an owner to remove "an octagon bay window . . . which projected about three feet over the line." "[T]here is control of the property of plaintiff in error by other owners of property exercised under the ordinance. This, as we have said, is the vice of the ordinance."[5]

Given this constitutional background, and the volatile *Schechter*[6] and *Carter Coal*[7] decisions of the 1930s, one might be surprised to discover that more than thirty years has passed since any major Supreme Court decision on the question of delegation to private parties.[8] At first glance, it is tempting to conclude that the doctrine is slumbering in largely deserved desuetude.[9] Yet there are also indications that the doctrine remains with us, masquerading under various aliases—"equal protection" and "due process," to name only two. Consider the following disquieting developments.

First, the nondelegation doctrine still merits sporadic attention in the Supreme Court, although no majority has yet held it applicable. The most conspicuous recent example is the concurring opinion of Justice Brennan, joined in by justices Douglas and Marshall, in *McGautha v. California.*[10] There, the three justices would have invalidated, partly on delegation grounds, a statute permitting a jury to fix the death penalty without guidelines from the legislature.[11] In addition, the resuscitation of Schechter in *National Cable Television Association v. United States*[12] indicates a potential revival of the doctrine at the federal level under proper conditions.

Second, nondelegation remains a vital issue at the state level. *Carter* is still enthusiastically cited by state courts,[13] and the doctrine has played a role in cases involving issues as diverse as public employee labor relations[14] and environmental law.[15]

Third, several recent cases decided on "state action" grounds might just as easily have relied on the delegation doctrine.[16] If certain conduct may be labelled "state action" for purposes of the Fourteenth Amendment, there is often equal room for nondelegation to operate. That courts presently prefer equal protection rationales is no guarantee they will forever continue to do so.

Thus the time has come for a thorough reexamination of the nondelegation doctrine: its scope, applicability, and limitations. This chapter will attempt to demonstrate, first, that a per se doctrine precluding delegation of legislative powers to private persons is not needed and would have unfortunate results; second, that the decided Supreme Court cases do not constitutionally impose such a doctrine; and third, that the numerous decided cases in lower courts demonstrate both the practical nonexistence of a per se rule against such delegations and the undesirability of such a rule. An attempt will be made in conclusion to define the appropriate contours of a more limited nondelegation doctrine.

Structurally, this chapter will follow in part the organization of Professor Jaffe's definitive 1937 work on the doctrine.[17] The goal is to update the analysis of the older cases and to discuss the developments that have transpired in the almost sixty years since Jaffe addressed the subject. Hopefully, the result will be guidance for courts and the bar, who may be forced to reacquaint themselves with an aspect of American constitutional law long thought moribund.

INAPPROPRIATENESS OF AN UNQUALIFIED NONDELEGATION DOCTRINE

The use of "state action" and antitrust doctrines to control concentrations of private power has led both scholars[18] and state courts[19] to view with a jaundiced eye legislative acts that confer additional powers on private persons. Commentators have assured us that the powers wielded by private groups constitute an unprecendented menace to liberty and democracy[20] and have urged new departures in constitutional law as means of controlling these groups.[21]

As mentioned, it is the thesis of this chapter that the revived use of the *Carter* rule is neither demanded by recent developments in "state action" doctrine nor compatible with them. For as Professor Jaffe noted, [P]articipation in lawmaking by private groups under explicit statutory 'delegation' does not stand . . . in absolute contradiction to the traditional process and conditions of law-making; it is not incompatible with the conception of law. . . . [I]t institutionalizes a factor in law-making that we have, eagerly in fact, attempted to obscure."[22]

The "state action" cases reflect an increasing tendency on the part of courts to look at substance rather than form when engaged in preventing the arbitrary and oppressive use of private power. Yet courts still are alarmed by the forms of delegation, no matter how small the potentialities for oppression or abuse. Where statutes delegating power are upheld, courts frequently justify their decisions by maintaining that no power has been delegated or by asserting that the statute was complete when it left the legislature and that the ensuing acts of private parties are merely "but facts in contemplation of which [the statute] was enacted"[23] or by finding that adequate standards exist,[24] even though standards are usually meaningful only as guidelines for a disinterested administrator. But realism demands that courts look in the second case, as in the first, to the nature of the power exercised, the political forces that operate to check its abuse, and the extent to which abuse of the power will oppress the persons on whom it is directly imposed. This is in fact what courts frequently do, but they vindicate unobjectionable statutes by finding that no delegation is present rather than by holding the delegation permissible. There seems little justification in practice for continued adherence to a fictitious per se rule against delegation to private parties. Save where the delegation is so broad that the legislature cannot retrieve what it has delegated,[25] pronouncement upon a delegation question deals with the effects of a legislative act and not any alteration of legislative power.

The action courts take in "state action" (and increasingly in antitrust) cases is limited in scope: They do not condemn as unconstitutional the existence of power in private groups but merely impose upon them duties of fairness consistent with the public function, and have limited themselves in some measure by the traditional canons of judicial restraint that also govern their willingness to invalidate statutes. Courts have proved willing to invalidate statutes (and find state action) in First Amendment cases where the continuance of the political process is itself thought to be in danger[26] and to act to preserve traditional guarantees of fair trial and fair procedure.[27] The disenfranchisement of minorities has more recently supplied another justification for judicial unwillingness to defer to the political will as reflected in legislative act or legislative inaction.[28] Beyond this courts have been loath to go. Economic due process continues to slumber[29]; despite the urgings of some, constitutional guarantees have not been applied to significantly limit the acts of corporations[30] and labor unions.[31]

Delegation cases, unlike "state action" cases, moreover, involve not legislative inaction but a clear policy choice by the legislature; courts may thus properly display greater reluctance to restrict private power that exists as a result of legislative choice, as has long been manifest in connection with delegation of powers not legislative in character. Legal historians remind us of the long-standing delegations of eminent domain powers[32] and of the use of tax powers for the benefit of private individuals.[33] The "public use" limitation has been all but read out of the Fifth Amendment,[34] while the recent rash of local industrial development authorities[35] reminds us that the day of *Loan Association v. Topeka*[36] is no more. Despite Adam Smith,[37] the Constitution, unlike those of many states, contains no interdiction against state-created monopolies,[38] as the rhetoric of the court in the *Noerr*[39] case under the antitrust laws reminds us, nor, indeed, does it prohibit delegations of legislative power. The restrictions, such as they are, on delegations to administrative agencies stem from notions relating to separation of powers not necessarily relevant where a delegation is to private groups.[40]

This is not to say that scope may not remain for circumspect use of the nondelegation doctrine. But its use should be restricted to the three great areas where the judicial activism inherent in declarations of unconstitutionality has most frequently been exercised. Where a delegation by virtue of its content or breadth calls into question the future operation of the political process, judicial scrutiny seems warranted. Also, where it relates to powers not legislative but judicial and thus trenches on historic notions of fair hearing and fair trial, scrutiny seems warranted, particularly since judicial and licensing determinations are not readily subject to legislative correction. Finally, there may be scope for condemnation of delegations that operate against the interest of minorities disenfranchised in respect of the election of the legislature that authorized the delegation, though this limitation ought not to inspire acquiescence in the extravagant rhetoric of those who speak in terms of "disenfranchised" consumers[41] and thus render nugatory canons of restraint.

The principle relating to breadth of delegations has been most actively delineated in the present federal law relating to delegations of rulemaking power to public bodies,[42] though the absence of the checks supplied by the appropriation and appointment powers and the lack of the self-imposed restraint resulting from public officers' oaths may be thought to justify a more rigorous application of the doctrine so as to confine to narrower limits the scope of powers conferrable upon private persons. Yet many of the vices thought to be inherent in delegation to private groups constitute violations of express constitutional mandates—particularly the requirements of due process and equal protection. Reliance on a general nondelegation principle to remedy all such violations would be inappropriate, but the proximity of the nondelegation principle to other constitutional safeguards deserves examination.

Historic notions of fairness and the difficulty of legislative correction may seem to justify a per se rule against delegation of judicial or licensing powers,[43] at least where inadequate review is provided. But the applicable constitutional provision here is the due process clause, not a vague "nondelegation" doctrine. Disqualification for pecuniary bias has at times been used as a substitute for a doctrine barring delegation of judicial powers[44] however, the "rule of necessity" may frequently operate to render this solution inadequate.[45] Controversies in this area thus do and should turn on where the line between judicial and legislative function falls.[46]

The fact that every delegation of legislative authority involves a nexus with state power may justify application of equal protection standards to the content of rules made by private parties when the courts are invoked to enforce these rules: "Jurisdiction always is jurisdiction only to decide constitutionally."[47] If delegation of judicial powers to private parties is to be barred, application of equal protection standards to delegated legislation would seem warranted, since the equal protection clause, taken in its narrowest meaning,[48] may be regarded as a prohibition against adjudication under the guise of legislation somewhat akin to the constitutional prohibition against bills of attainder.[49]

HISTORICAL QUALIFICATIONS OF THE NONDELEGATION DOCTRINE

The zoning intervention case of *Eubank v. City of Richmond*, already described,[50] was shortly followed by *Thomas Cusack Co. v. City of Chicago*.[51] There the Court, under the influence of traditional property law concepts, upheld a similar state statute phrased in terms of consent rather than objection, declaring that the provision allowing lifting of the zoning prohibition by consent "is not a delegation of legislative power, but is . . . a familiar provision affecting the enforcement of laws and ordinances."[52] Here, the inroad upon the doctrine was perceived as shielded by tradition. The vitality of the nondelegation doctrine per se was later attested to, however, by the subsequent invalidation of a similar consent ordinance in the *Roberge*[53] case, where the Court observed, "There is no provision for review under the ordinance . . . [the neighbors'] failure to give consent is final. They . . . are free to withhold consent for selfish reasons or arbitrarily. Cusack was distinguished on the basis that "the [prohibited uses] . . . were liable to endanger . . . safety and decency."

The vehement rhetoric in the Schechter case directed at the specific delegations to code authorities gave the doctrine added force: "But would it be seriously contended that Congress could delegate its legislative authority to trade or industrial associations or groups so as to empower them to enact the laws they deem to be wise and beneficent for the rehabilitation and expansion of their trade or industries? . . . The answer is obvious. Such a delegation of legislative power is unknown to our law and is utterly inconsistent with the constitutional prerogatives and duties of Congress."[54] In *Schechter*, however, the Court did admit the possibility of some lawful delegations to private persons. The opinion distinguished "[i]nstances . . . in which Congress has availed itself of such assistance; as e.g., in the exercise f its authority over the public domain, with respect to the recognition of local customs or rules of miners as to mining claims, or, in matters of a more or less technical nature, as in designating the standard height of drawbars."[55]

The decisive factor for Justice Cardozo, whose concurring opinion has probably better stood the test of time, was the presence of "an attempted delegation not confined to any single act nor to any class or group of acts identified or described by reference to a standard. Here in effect is a roving commission to inquire into evils and upon discovery correct them."[56] Narrower delegations to private groups would apparently be valid, at least if subject to presidential approval an approval that Cardozo recognized would be formal at best. Delegation in such circumstances is born of the necessities of the occasion. . . . Nor is the substance of the power changed because the President may act at the instance of trade or industrial associations having special knowledge of the facts. Their function is strictly advisory; it is the imprimatur of the President that begets the quality of' law."[57] But imprimatur and authorship are very different things.

This isolated grappling with real issues had little influence on the Supreme Court's later delegation decisions. In *Carter v. Carter Coal Co.*[58] a federal statute making maximum hours and minimum wages agreed upon by a majority of miners and producers of two-thirds of the annual national tonnage of coal binding on the remainder was held invalid, the delegation doctrine serving as an alternate ground: "The power conferred upon the majority is, in effect, the power to regulate the affairs of an unwilling minority. This is legislative delegation in its most obnoxious form; for it is not even delegation to an official or an official body, presumptively disinterested, but to private persons whose interests may be and often are adverse to the interest of others in the same business."[59] The ban on delegation sprang from the Fifth Amendment due process clause[60] and not, as Justice Harlan was later to assume,[61] from abstract doctrines about the vesting of legislative power having their source in Article I.

The Court in *Carter* thus may have departed somewhat from its earlier position in *Schechter,* where it laid stress upon "the prerogatives and duties of Congress." It may also have departed from its position in *Booth v. Indiana.*[62] In that case, a state statute requiring coal operators to install washrooms upon the request of twenty or more employees was held valid against delegation challenge, the Court observing that "[t]he Supreme Court of the State decided that the law could be called into operation by petition, and in the decision no Federal question is involved.[63] The choice of the Fifth Amendment due process clause in *Carter* might suggest that Article I notions impose no per se ban on federal delegations to private parties, which are to be judged by the more flexible criterion of due process. But *Carter* may also suggest that such constitutional restrictions as may exist apply equally to the states by virtue of the Fourteenth Amendment, results that would not obtain if the prohibition found its source in Article I.

Since the Fifth Amendment was used, the restriction on delegation in federal statutes may be thought less severe than it otherwise could be. However, the Court cited *Schechter*, *Eubank*, and *Roberge* and observed that "it is unnecessary to do more than refer to decisions of this court which foreclose the question."[64] The concurring opinion of Chief Justice Hughes appeared to find limitations on delegation in Article I as well as the Fifth Amendment: "Such a provision, apart from the mere question of the delegation of legislative power, is not in accord with the requirement of due process of law which under the Fifth Amendment dominates the regulations which Congress may impose."[65]

The fiction of nondelegability was adhered to in the *Old Dearborn* case,[66] where the Court, influenced again by familiar property and contract doctrines, upheld the provision of the Illinois Fair Trade Act requiring persons with notice of manufacturer-retailer price maintenance contracts to adhere to the prices established in them, even where such persons did not assent to the terms of the contracts—a form of delegated rulemaking power. The Court distinguished *Eubank*, *Roberge*, and *Carter*: In those cases the property affected had been acquired without any preexisting restriction in respect of its use or disposition. . . . Here, the restriction, already imposed with the knowledge of appellants, ran with the acquisition and conditioned it.[67] Mr. Justice Jackson, among others, was to be puzzled by the differing results reached by Justice Sutherland and in *Carter* and *Old Dearborn*. "Taken together, the decisions suggest that the labor provisions of the Coal Act were 'obnoxious' not so much to the Constitution as to the judicial sense of what was good for the business community.[68]

In *Highland Farms Dairy, Inc. v. Agnew*,[69] the Court declined to make clear whether a state statute delegating rulemaking power could be invalidated on the basis of the nondelegation doctrine. There a Virginia statute set up a state milk marketing board with authority to fix minimum rates. The Court, echoing *Booth,* emphatically rejected the challenge to this delegation. "The statute challenged as invalid is one adopted by a state. This removes objections that might be worthy of consideration if we were dealing with an act of Congress."[70] But the statute also provided for cancellation of minimum price regulations upon petition of a majority of the producers affected. As to this power to repeal, the Court was more ambivalent.

Delegation to official agencies is one thing, there being nothing in the concept of due process to require that a particular agency shall have a monopoly of power; delegation to private interests or unofficial groups with arbitrary capacity to make their will prevail as law may be something very different! . . . Without acceptance or rejection of the distinction in its application to this statute, we think it is enough to say that the power of cancellation has not been exercised or even threatened.[71]

In *Currin v. Wallace,*[72] decided in 1939, the Supreme Court upheld a statute empowering the Secretary of Agriculture to establish markets for the inspection and certification of tobacco, no such market to be established "unless two-thirds of the growers, voting at a prescribed referendum, favor it.[73] The Court, citing Cusack, observed that "Congress has merely placed a restriction upon its own regulation by withholding its operation as to a given market unless two-thirds of the growers voting favor it."[74] *Carter* was distinguished as a case "where a group of producers may make the law and force it upon a minority,"[75] while *Roberge* was disposed of largely on the basis that the zoning regulation there was beyond the police power: "[A] prohibition of an inoffensive and legitimate use of property . . . imposed not by the legislature but by other property owners."[76]

Similar conclusions were reached in the case of *United States v. Rock Royal Co-operative, Inc.*[77] The Court followed *Currin v. Wallace* in upholding the statute and was undisturbed by the fact that a single cooperative league, empowered to vote on behalf of its members, was able to cast over half the votes counted in the referendum: "[I]n as much as Congress could place the order in effect without any vote, it is permissible for it to provide for approval or disapproval in such way or manner as it may choose."[78]

In *Sunshine Anthracite Coal Co. v. Adkins,*[79] the Court upheld, on the authority of *Currin v. Wallace*, a statute setting up industry boards each empowered "on its own motion or when directed by the [public] Commission" to propose minimum prices which "may be approved, disapproved, or modified by the Commission. "The prices thus set were applicable to code members alone, but tax was imposed on noncode members. The opinion of Justice Douglas took the view that "[t]he members of the code function subordinately to the Commission. . . . Since law-making is not intrusted to the industry, this statutory scheme is unquestionably valid.“[80] The Court did not rely on the facade of voluntarism that the option of paying the tax in place of price regulation might have been thought to supply.

In *Parker v. Brown,*[81] it was not felt necessary even to discuss the delegation problem when the Court upheld a California statute, the effectiveness of which was conditioned on both initiation of action by private persons and a referendum of producers following pro forma approval by the state, thus reducing the *Carter* doctrine to a hollow shell. Yet this result was achieved without once directly questioning the proposition that legislative power could not be delegated to private persons, and later cases have likewise upheld delegations sub silentio.[82]

SPECIFIC EXAMPLES OF THE DOCTRINE

Statewide Referenda and Local Option

The conception of delegation of legislative power has been applied in a large number of cases involving statewide referenda and local option elections. The cases do so largely under the compulsion of state court precedents, which in turn follow the remarkable early Delaware case of *Rice v. Foster*.[83] These the court observed:

[O]ur republican government was instituted by the consent of the people. The characteristic which distinguishes it from the miscalled republics of ancient and modern times, is, that none of the powers of sovereignty are exercised by the people; but all of them by separate, co-ordinate branches of government in whom those powers are vested. . . . These co-ordinate branches are intended to operate as balances, checks and restraints, not only upon each other, but upon the people themselves; to guard them against their own rashness, precipitancy, and misguided zeal; and to protect the minority against the injustice of the majority.[84]

But what of the tyranny of legislative majorities, chosen by the same electors that vote in a proposed referendum? To this question, the court rejoined in the language of Burke's Address to the Electors of Bristol: "The representative owes to his constituents, not only his industry, but his judgment: and he betrays, instead of serving them, if he sacrifices it to their opinions.[85] This proposition is clearly unexceptionable. But the court went further, for the act in question involved a prohibition statute. Might not a conscientious representative, without violating Burke's precepts, conclude that the desirability of the statute was itself a function of the public's attitude toward it? Later experience attests to the wisdom of such a view, yet the court declined to permit the statute to be conditioned on popular acceptance. "The sovereign power . . . of this State, resides with the legislative, executive, and judicial departments. Having thus transferred the sovereign power, the people cannot resume or exercise any portion of it."[86]

It was of this case that Justice Holmes was to write, in a dissenting opinion taking the opposite view,

The question is not whether the people of their own motion could pass a law without any act of the Legislature. That no doubt, whether valid or not, would be outside the Constitution. So perhaps might be a statute purporting to confer the power of making laws upon them. But the question . . . is whether an act of the Legislature is made unconstitutional by a proviso that, if rejected by the people, it shall not go into effect. If it does go into effect, it does so by the express enactment of the representative body. . . . I agree that the discretion of the Legislature is intended to be exercised. I agree that confidence is put in it as an agent. But I think that so much confidence is put in it that it is allowed to exercise its discretion by taking the opinion of its principal if it thinks that course to be wise. . . . The contrary view seems to me an echo of Hobbes's theory that the surrender of sovereignty by the people was final. I notice that the case from which most of the reasoning against the power of the Legislature has been taken by later decisions states that theory in language which almost is borrowed from the Leviathan. . . . Hobbes urged his notion in the interest of the absolute power of King Charles, and one of the objects of the Constitution of Massachusetts was to deny it.[87]

Statewide Referenda. At the time that Professor Jaffe wrote in 1937, the majority of courts persisted in a refusal to allow legislatures to condition the passage of laws on statewide referenda,[88] though a number of states took Holmes's view. But practical needs led a large number of states to refuse to follow the early Delaware court in disallowing local option elections[89] indeed, three states had been led to overrule earlier holdings in order to validate such local referenda.[90] And this was so even though from a purely formal standpoint there is less justification for delegation by a legislature to voters of a county than there is for delegation to the voters of a state. The second group, Jaffe points out, has constitutional significance; the first does not.[91] Indeed, the Delaware court found an anomaly in allowing state law to be modified "by the will of a majority of the citizens who voted in [a] county, although it might be against the will of a majority of the citizens of the State."[92]

Since Jaffe's article, developments in this branch of the doctrine have been laggard. The Supreme Court of Wisconsin reaffirmed its adherence to the minority view upholding statewide referenda.[93] The Arkansas court upheld a statewide referendum by analogy to the local option cases, thus joining the minority states.[94] In addition, a number of other states have begun whittling away at the majority rule although continuing to pay lip service to it.[95] In Oregon, the legislature has been allowed to make the effectiveness of an act contingent upon the rejection of another act at a referendum.[96] In Kentucky, where the issuance of bonds is constitutionally subject to public approval, the court has allowed a referendum on an act removing the interest limitation on an issue of unsold bonds, pointing to the fact that the question would not have arisen but for the public approval of the bond issue itself.[97] The Supreme Court of Alabama had reaffirmed its adherence to the majority view, which applies in that state to tax questions only.[98] However, Alabama has more recently taken a stance similar to Oregon's in upholding a statute whose effectiveness was contingent upon the adoption of a related constitutional amendment; the latter required voter approval.[99] Most telling is the recent decision of the Supreme Court of the United States in *James v. Valtierra*,[100] with its ringing dictum that "[p]rovisions for referendums demonstrate devotion to democracy, not to bias, discrimination, or prejudice." *Valtierra* may well have sounded the final doom of the *Rice v. Foster* doctrine.

Local Option Laws. Virtually all state courts now recognize the validity of local option laws. In addition to the six states listed by Professor Jaffe,[101] nineteen other states have squarely upheld the validity of such acts.[102] The willingness of the courts to uphold the local option is founded on what is perceived to be a practical need for local approval of liquor and tax laws, the courts taking the view that "the constitution itself does not require the impracticable or impossible."[103] In the language of an early New Jersey case, "It has always been recognized as a legitimate part of the legislative function, as well as a duty in harmony with the spirit of our institutions, to enable the people, in whom all power ultimately resides, to control the police powers in communities for themselves."[104]

There are still some limitations on local option elections, however. The election acts are usually upheld on the theory that they are complete statutes, the execution of which merely happens to be contingent on a local event. Where, by an accident of draftsmanship, approval of the act itself is made contingent on local acceptance, the courts may follow the example of a Rhode Island decision that invalidated an act that "in its present form does not purport to be a completed act by the legislature in performance of its legislative function under the constitution."[105]

In addition, some courts, such as those of Tennessee, invalidate acts that depend on a single election for effectiveness, holding that the act of a legislature is not complete unless it retains continuing validity regardless of immediate approval.[106] By contrast, a Missouri court upheld an enactment on the basis that "the statute does not delegate to the people the power to discontinue and recreate the separate officers of recorder at pleasure, but only permits them to vote on the question of joining the two officers; and when there has been such joinder it would seem the voting power of the people under the section is exhausted."[107]

Some traces of the earlier position remain. Thus a North Carolina court invalidated a statute that allowed the voters of a town to authorize a municipal racing commission to establish a racetrack outside the town, the statute being regarded as an imposition on the residents of the outlying district.[108] But if the earlier reasoning is rejected, it should not apply to this sort of case either, since a legislature in which residents of the outlaying district are represented has determined that the construction of the track would not offend state policy and has merely conditioned its approval on ratification by the persons who are to put up the funds. No licensing function is involved; if delegation questions are made to run on the distinction between rulemaking and adjudication, statutes that merely require popular assent to legislative acts ought not to fall.

Creation of Special Districts

Many American statutes allow property owners to petition and vote for the creation of special taxing districts, the boundaries of which are defined by the petition. Districts of this sort are created for a variety of reasons.[109] The special taxing district is a flexible device and can be used to cut across municipal lines that would otherwise inhibit the development of integrated services. In recent years, it has found increasing use in more developed regions as a means of evading statutory or constitutional municipal debt limits.

Where the districts are created by the act of a legislature, they are constitutionally unassailable, even though the legislature may be giving mere pro forma approval to proposals by private parties. Where, however, the petition/referendum device is authorized by statute, courts have been concerned with protecting dissenting property owners within the proposed district. Both due process and nondelegation doctrines have been invoked to require that a hearing be given to dissenting property owners and that an official be vested with discretion to reject districts that would be of no benefit to dissenting property owners' lands. The Supreme Court in 1926 required such a procedure for due process reasons:

> Where a local improvement territory is selected, and the burden is spread by the legislature . . . the owners of property in the district have no constitutional right to be heard on the question of benefits. . . . But it is essential to due process of law that such owners be given notice and opportunity to be heard on that question where, as here, the district was not created by the legislature, and there has been no legislative determination that their property will be benefited by the local improvements.[110]

The decision whether a particular landowner's property is to be included within a district is thus properly regarded by the courts as action partaking of the character of an adjudication, rather than an exercise of rulemaking power, where the determination is made by neighbors rather than by the representatives of the public at large.[111]

Though in early years courts were sometimes willing to uphold the creation of special districts without a hearing when tax rates charged in them were nominal,[112] this course of action has been foreclosed by other decisions.[113] Courts thus consistently strike down the creation of districts when no safeguards are present.[114] But when provision for hearing and discretionary disapproval is made, courts have consistently upheld the creation of new districts.[115] The sole concern of the courts in most cases has been the protection of dissenting property owners; considerations of general public policy rarely enter into decisions.[116] This approach seems appropriate in the light of the analysis of the delegation doctrine developed above.

It might seem appropriate for courts to use substantive due process doctrines to hold that the general enabling statutes must direct the courts to make some inquiry into the bona fides of a district as a political organ, as well as into whether the use of district funds will benefit the total area encompassed within a district, for in many cases the creation of special districts has been approved even though the use of the device may be oppressive to the interests of future residents and bondholders.[117] In approaching the problems presented by new districts, courts frequently assume attitudes redolent of the spirit of the old frontier. The special district is viewed as a form of social contract that enables neighbors on the isolated prairie to unite for the common good.[118] The recent proliferation of special districts created to support activities ranging from tourist promotion to weather control calls the accuracy of this earlier view into question. Without provision in enabling acts for some judicial scrutiny, the use of tax district funds to engage in promotional advertising and to finance business enterprises will merely become a means of permanently placing tax burdens upon large stretches of land regardless of any benefits accruing to future residents. Collective bargaining agreements with taxing districts might also be thought to raise problems,[119] though the issues in this area are not different from those which arise in the law of municipal corporations generally. And controls over the capacity of taxpayers to prejudice other residents or bondholders also seem indicated.[120] But again it may be doubted that the nondelegation doctrine is the appropriate means through which to impose controls. Indeed, judicial checks would seem inappropriate for many of the same reasons that judicial checks on government expenditures and monetary policy are inappropriate. The burden of dispensations in favor of special districts falls, at least in the first instance, on the public at large.

Restrictions on the Use of Property

The confusion of thought prevalent in this area of the law is nowhere more apparent than in the cases relating to the imposition and removal of zoning restrictions. The history is a familiar one. The three leading Supreme Court cases have generated much subsequent confusion. In *Eubank v. City of Richmond,*[121] decided in 1912, the Court invalidated a statute allowing two-thirds of the residents of a street to require revisions in a building line. Five years later, in *Thomas Cusack Co. v. City of Chicago,*[122] the Court upheld a statute requiring written consent from the owners of the greater part of the frontage on a street as a prerequisite to the erection of billboards. The Court distinguished between the imposition and the lifting of restrictions: "The plaintiff in error cannot be injured, but obviously may be benefited by this provision, for without it the prohibition of the erection of such billboards in such residence sections is absolute. He who is not injured by the operation of a law or ordinance cannot be said to be deprived by it of either constitutional right or of property." Finally, in *Washington ex rel. Seattle Title Trust Co. v. Roberge,*[123] the Court struck down an act requiring consent of two-thirds of the owners of neighboring property to authorize the construction of an old-age home. The Court distinguished the *Cusack* case on the basis that the billboards were recognized as a nuisance, whereas the old-age home was not.

It is easy to scoff at the Supreme Court's distinctions, and many commentators have indulged in this obvious pleasure.[124] It has been said of *Eubank* and *Cusack*, that "[i]n either case, the action or non-action of the property owners would be the chief factor in determining whether or not the building line should be established. . . . [The difference] is a matter of mathematics rather than of legal principle."[125] Commentators have had an easier time in squaring *Roberge* and Cusack: Since *Village of Euclid v. Ambler Realty Co.*[126] used a nuisance criterion to measure the validity of zoning ordinances, the provision in *Roberge* may have been invalid because it undertook to prohibit nonnuisances, not because it allowed exemptions to the prohibition by the consent of neighbors. Yet the vindication in *Cusack* of a statute allowing neighbors to consent to nuisances may still seem a paradox: "Shall the owner of an isolated apartment house be permitted to erect and maintain a fire-trap with the consent of his tenants? Shall a grocer be allowed to sell deleterious foods with the consent of his customers? . . . Merely to ask such questions is to answer them."[127]

The vindication of consent statutes may be due to the judicial indulgence toward the dispensing power manifest in other contexts.[128] It may seem justified, too, to those who take the view that "it is difficult to imagine a more appropriate use of the police power, than that which imposes a limitation upon the use of property for the protection of community property values."[129] The courts have not purported to sustain zoning statutes on this basis,[130] though perhaps they should have done so. If this view of the zoning function is taken, the *Eubank*-*Cusack* distinction can be rationalized: "In the Eubank Case there seems to have been more of an attempt to invest property owners with powers similar to those of an administrative board. In the cases where the question is strictly one of consent of property owners expressed by action, it is clearer that they are merely permitted to waive a statutory right passed chiefly for their protection."[131]

But one need not go on with attempts at distinctions. For the purposes of this analysis, these statutes are all of a piece. Many state courts, despite *Cusack*, have invalidated consent statutes even where possible nuisances are not involved.[132] Their hostility— and the hostility of the Supreme Court to delegation in *Eubank* and perhaps that in *Roberge* rests on considerations foreign to distinctions between prohibitory and consent statutes or between nuisances and innocent uses. The hostility rests rather on dislike of delegation of powers of an essentially judicial character. Since zoning statutes, unlike statutes of the type sustained in *Jackman v. Rosenbaum Co.*,[133] are thought to rest on the police power rather than on "the community's understanding of the reciprocal rights and duties of neighboring landowners,"[134] delegation of their detailed administration to private groups raises problems akin to those presented by private licensing schemes. Laws which so literally make persons go as supplicants to their neighbors may thus seem especially unattractive to the courts.

Hence, many courts and writers have been concerned with the evil of purchased consents.[135]

> You cannot with a yard stick decide whether the location of [a] saloon would be an injury. It may or may not be an injury. . . . But if you give power to every person within twenty-five feet of every proposed liquor store, to determine that question for himself, you put into his hands a great power which he is likely to abuse. . . . To give a neighboring real estate owner an uncontrollable right to object may . . . be giving him the whip hand over the applicant for a license; and it will depend entirely upon the character of him who holds that whip, whether this instrument of castigation be used for the owner's protection or be applied in securing unjust booty. The existing law was put on the statute book with no view of limiting in number the licenses granted, or of enhancing the value of one man's real estate at the expense of another. It was put there

as a shield for property owners against what might be an injury to them. . . . [I]t was not designed to be used as a sword. But when you give the absolute right to object, you have put into the hands of men an irresistible weapon.[136]

Thus it can be suggested that the validity of zoning consent statutes ought to turn on the extent to which the statutes encourage the twin evils of ad hominem determinations and purchased consents. Where a statute permits landowners over a reasonably wide area to legitimize otherwise forbidden uses, the determination made, if not limited to a specific case, is legislative rather than essentially judicial in character. Validation of such statutes is not inconsistent with the thesis tendered here, even though the area of the referendum may not encompass whole townships so as to come under the rule of the local option cases. But the ordinary ordinance requiring consent of neighbors would properly seem to be more vulnerable to challenge, unless the view of the *Rosenbaum* case is taken.

Other courts have followed no consistent patterns in upholding or invalidating consent provisions. Statutes have been invalidated where consent was required to operate schools,[137] gin mills,[138] and filling stations,[139] but validated where commercial enterprises,[140] used auto lots,[141] liquor licensees,[142] taxi stands,[143] and, more recently, "adult" theaters[144] were made subject to the requirement. A statute limiting a zoning board's discretionary power to grant zoning variances to cases where variances were requested by two-thirds of the residents of a district was invalidated,[145] a surprising result in light of *Cusack* since the petition did not bind the zoning board and was hence equivalent to only a consent provision. Another court upheld a statute providing that zoning variances required a three-fourths instead of majority vote by a board vested with discretionary powers when a protest petition signed by 20 percent of area residents was filed against a zoning change.[146] This result seems consistent with *Cusack,* since this is only an elaborate consent provision.

The courts have not even been consistent in cases involving petitions rather than consent provisions, despite the *Eubank* case. A North Carolina court upheld a statute giving the owners of property at an intersection the power (but not the duty) to compel rezoning of their property when the municipality rezones two other corners at the same intersection.[147] The court took the view that the statute was valid since it merely prescribed the conditions under which the zoning power was to be exercised. By contrast, the Illinois Supreme Court invalidated a statute making changes in street names mandatory when petitioned for by 60 percent of the residents of a street.[148] This case would seem to be de minimis even under the *Eubank* rule. It is doubtful whether the interest of dissenting property owners in the present street name can supply the basis of a constitutionally noticeable deprivation of right.

Determination of Professional and Industrial Standards

The frequent legislative adoption of privately sponsored professional and industrial standards represents another area in which the courts have had occasion to invoke the nondelegation doctrine.

Statutes Adopting Preexisting Lists and Codes. The adoption of privately formulated lists and codes has not troubled the courts when the legislative act adopts a private code in the form in which it stood at the time that the legislation was passed. This result is clearly sound. The *Noerr* and *Pennington* decisions[149] serve to remind us that freedom for private groups to seek their legislative ends is itself constitutionally protected. The fact that a legislature adopts, by name, a private code rather than enacting a detailed bill drawn up by the same interest group is scarcely of constitutional significance. And the acceptance of a rule that would not distinguish between the legislative effusions of a small parochial interest group and a private organization like the American Law Institute would seem clearly untenable. Though courts have occasionally been troubled by such legislation by reference, the public filing of the code coupled with the principle that "that is certain which can be made certain" has usually proved sufficient to allay their misgivings.

Educational Accreditation Statutes. The adoption of future standards promulgated by private groups has understandably given the courts greater difficulty. One major battleground has involved the adoption of classifications of professional schools issued by medical and bar associations. Graduation from a privately accredited school has frequently been made a prerequisite to the obtaining of a license to practice. The early appeal of this legislation derived from the view that professionals themselves were better qualified to gauge the quality of professional education than any legislative committee or administrative board could be. Thus it is not surprising that a Kansas court, writing shortly after the beginning of the reform movement in medical education initiated by the Flexner Report,[150] strongly upheld a statute requiring graduation from a medical school on the "A" or "B" list issued by the American Medical Association, "the membership of which and the purpose of which are not disclosed, but which we may presume to consist of eminent men in the medical profession who are prompted by a laudable desire to elevate the standard of their profession and the standard of medical schools."[151]

The more restrictive practices adopted by professional accrediting agencies[152] coincided with a more skeptical attitude on the part of the courts toward the legislative adoption of their private lists. Though a Florida court upheld a statute requiring veterinarians to be graduates of approved schools, the opinion did not squarely meet the delegation question, declaring only that the statute was "reasonable under the police power."[153] The same court, in two prior cases, had upheld similar statutes by construing the word "accredited" to mean that the school in question was accredited at the time the legislation was enacted,[154] following the example of a Rhode Island court.[155] But the Florida court took a more indulgent view of an adoption of a bar association list. There the word "accredited" was construed to mean that the school in question was currently approved by the association,[156] members of the bar apparently being considered above suspicion.

The newer attitude toward professional association lists is probably most accurately reflected in a more recent District of Columbia Circuit decision[157] subjecting decisions of accrediting agencies to review under the due process clause. The decision may, despite the deferential standard applied by the court, portend a new attitude.

The lack of administrative or economic checks on the capacity of professional associations to restrict members and the importance of the right to practice to those excluded from a profession has understandably tempted the courts to use the nondelegation doctrine to invalidate statutes requiring graduation from approved schools. Yet the use of the doctrine in this context raises problems under our analysis, problems similar to those raised by Joint Anti-Fascist Refugee Committee v. McGrath..[158] The power to designate approved schools may be thought to operate as a rulemaking rather than a licensing power when individual doctors themselves make complaint about the statute, since it is, in form, a licensing power only in relation to the schools themselves. The view here taken stresses the corrective forces that operate upon abuses of rulemaking powers; abuses of rulemaking powers are more visible, fall on and thus give rise to reaction by the community at large, and may more readily be redressed after the event. Licensing powers, by contrast, bear more heavily on particular individuals, while abuses of them are less likely to be brought to public view or be susceptible of easy correction. It is clear under this view that the schools have reason to complain of the delegation, and it may be thought reasonable to allow their graduates to complain on their behalf where the accrediting system was not in operation at the time of the applicant's enrollment. Where it was in operation when the applicant enrolled, more difficult problems are presented. The widespread use of a statutory requirement of graduation from an "accredited" college or university suggests that it would be highly awkward to adopt a blanket rule of invalidity. Thus it is by no means clear that delegations to professional groups of power to generate standards (number of books, of instructors, etc.) that schools must meet to be licensed ought to be considered invalid per se merely because they may be restrictive. Where the standards are arbitrary the delegation, at least in its exercise, may fail on equal protection grounds; had the celebrated pre–World War II refusal to charter foreign medical schools been implemented by rule it might still have been vulnerable in this respect.[159]

Health and Safety Standards. The several cases invalidating the incorporation into building codes of future electrical wiring standards formulated by associations of insurance underwriters[160] do not raise the analytical problems suggested by the medical accreditation cases. The wiring cases seem incorrect under our analysis, since they involve mere rulemaking powers. The fact that the economic interests of insurance companies may point to the maintenance of unworkably high safety standards does not justify invalidation on delegation grounds. And though privately enforced standards have been met with suspicion in antitrust cases where formulated in part by competitors of persons against whom they are enforced,[161] it may be suggested under our analysis that this sort of bias in rulemaking (apart from the equal protection problems its results may raise) ought not to raise delegation problems when the rules are regularly enforced through the courts. Enforcement of privately formulated standards by private boycott involves a licensing as well as a rulemaking function not present where the rules are enforced at law. Though the Sherman Act boycott cases clearly rest on antipathy toward "private government"[162] and not on economic effects alone, their lessons are not clearly applicable to delegation cases involving rulemaking functions only.

Judicial suspicion of electrical wiring codes has not extended to legislative adoption of the pharmacopoeia compiled by the United States Pharmacopoeial Convention,[163] an organization composed of federal agencies, national medical and pharmaceutical associations, and schools of medicine and pharmacy.[164]

Prevailing Wage Laws. In the cases involving "prevailing wage" statutes a number of judges have likewise taken an indulgent view. Courts have had little difficulty in rejecting contentions that statutes directing administrative commissions to determine and pay prevailing local wages to state employees constitute an unconstitutional delegation to the commissions.[165] Where statutes provide for the payment of prevailing union wage rates, courts have been sharply split. In 1922, the Supreme Court of Wisconsin divided four to three in invalidating a statute that would have required a city council to pay wages equal to those "paid to members of any regular and recognized organization of . . . skilled laborers."[166] The court read the statute as imposing a purely ministerial duty on the council to accept any union wage scale.

In 1953, the Illinois Supreme Court, without discussion, invalidated a similar "union wage" statute.[167] A Kentucky court four years before, however, upheld a statute requiring the payment of the prevailing rates as set in union collective bargaining contracts, "if there are such agreements . . . in the locality applying to a sufficient number of employers to furnish a reasonable basis for considering those rates to be the prevailing rates in the locality."[168] The fact that the delegated power was subject to market control thus legitimized the statute. The rationalization that such statutes are valid because the private actions were legislatively noticed "facts" may not be fictitious in "prevailing wage" cases. More recently, a South Dakota court struck down a similar statute directed at Sioux Falls firemen, finding, as did the Wisconsin court in 1922, that "neither the city commission nor any agency thereof retains any power or discretion to ascertain or determine what are prevailing wages. . . . The trade unions and private contractors . . . absolutely fix the same."[169] On the other hand, the New Jersey Supreme Court found no difficulty in sustaining that state's prevailing wage statute.[170]

Union and Company Rules. The recognition by unemployment insurance appeal boards of union rules limiting allowable periods of employment of members as good cause for relinquishing employment has troubled some courts. An Ohio court invalidated such a course of action,[171] while a New York court upheld it only after noting that the board had discretion to reject unreasonable rules.[172] Judicial hostility to the use of such rules probably derives from doubts as to their wisdom as a matter of public policy rather than from views as to procedural unfairness. For here again, the delegation, if any, would seem to involve the power to make rules rather than the power to adjudicate rights. Where the effect of the use of a rule is significantly to increase a former employer's insurance premiums (as opposed to state contributions), the employer may, however, be thought under this formula to possess an interest that the delegation doctrine should protect, if the union rule in question applies to that employer's employees alone and not to members of the union employed elsewhere. However, it may be significant in this connection that "company rule" tort doctrines have little troubled the courts, though rules of such limited scope may be thought in effect to amount to adjudications of the rights of those subject to them. Their validity may be saved by the fact that they appear in a contractual setting. Since the existence of the employment relationship is voluntary on both sides, both union rules and company rules may be thought not to raise delegation problems, since those subject to them can readily remove themselves from their scope.[173]

Resale Price Maintenance

The doctrine forbidding delegations to private parties has achieved its greatest importance in recent years in connection with state court decisions invalidating the so-called nonsigner clauses of state resale price maintenance statutes. The high courts of sixteen states, including the important commercial states of California, Illinois, New Jersey, and New York, have upheld the statutes. The highest courts of twenty-five states, including those of Massachusetts, Pennsylvania, North Carolina, and Michigan, have invalidated the statutes.[174] In addition, "new type" statutes proceeding on an implied contract theory making receipt of goods prima facie evidence of agreement to adhere to price conditions have been upheld by the Supreme Court of Virginia[175] and by a controlling minority of the Supreme Court of Ohio,[176] while a statute providing for resale price maintenance by notice attached to the goods was upheld in New Jersey in an early case.[177]

Many of the state court decisions invalidating price maintenance statutes have rested in whole or in part on nondelegation grounds.[178] A number of courts have also declared that all delegations to private parties are forbidden, regardless of standards or safeguards which may be present,[179] one court distinguishing between delegations to private and public bodies in this respect.[180] Other courts, adopting a restrictive view of legislative power, take the position that the legislature may not forbid one who has acquired a commodity to determine its resale price, absent a substantial "public interest."[181] Still others, despite requirements of "free and open competition" in the acts, invalidated the statutes for want of standards.[182] Some pointed to the lack of safeguards such as hearing and judicial review.[183] At least one court invalidated an act on the basis that, by creating an antitrust exemption, the act would allow private parties to repeal a law; but the court would presumably have been satisfied with the act if no antitrust prohibition existed.[184] Finally, a number of courts, engaging in formal distinctions between delegation of power to make law and delegation of power to apply it, have condemned the acts on the curious ground that no duty exists to set a resale price.[185] To these courts, mandatory price maintenance, such as that provided in the liquor trade in some states, stands on a better footing than purely permissive legislation, despite the fact that the available economic checks are less significant.

The courts that have upheld the acts against challenge on delegation grounds have utilized varied reasoning. Some, following the federal *Old Dearborn* case,[186] take the view that the acts merely protect the continuing property of a manufacturer in his trademark. Others take the view that the actions of private parties authorized by the statutes do not involve the exercise of legislative power at all, since the legislature could not itself constitutionally establish the price of a particular branded article, as distinct from a commodity.[187] Similar reasoning appears to lie behind the decisions upholding newer statutes on the basis that the acts merely alter private commercial law.[188] Other courts find in the "free and open competition" clause an adequate statutory standard, even though such standards guide only courts and not the rulemakers where acts of private parties (as opposed to public agencies) are at issue.[189] A federal court, in the second *Schwegmann* case, found adequate safeguards in the operation of market forces.[190] A number of early courts upheld the nonsigner clauses by analogy to *Lumley v. Gye*.[191] This analogy on its face is not invalid where a manufacturer may restrict his distribution to signers of contracts.[192] But later antitrust decisions made it doubtful that he might lawfully do so,[193] while some courts refused to protect price maintenance contracts against induced breach even where distribution was thus limited.[194] Finally, there are, as might be expected, courts that upheld the statutes after hewing to formal distinctions between the delegation of power to make a law and the delegation of power to apply it.[195]

It is thus apparent that considerable confusion of thought has accompanied judicial consideration of the delegation problem presented by these former statutes. This confusion has been particularly apparent in connection with efforts to induce federal courts to invalidate state legislation on nondelegation grounds, since, as discussed above, it is not clear which provision of the federal constitution operates to restrict the delegation of legislative power by state governments.[196] Similar observations can be made as to challenge of federal enabling acts on delegation grounds, since these acts can be questioned only on the dubious basis that they delegate power to repeal federal statutes, not on the basis that they empower private parties to legislate in regard to the conduct of other individuals.[197]

Most of the cases embodying such arguments do little more than announce conclusions.[198] The cases upholding the statutes on the basis that the power delegated was one the legislature could not itself directly exercise are made of more substantial stuff, in the light of suggestions by some scholars that the inability of a legislature to regulate in detail may justify greater breadth of delegation.[199] But this too does not reach the central question if the nondelegation doctrine is to be viewed primarily as an aspect of procedural rather than substantive due process.[200]

Even if scope is left for a rule against delegation of rulemaking powers, there is no reason to believe that the statutes should have fallen, for the breadth of the delegation at issue is far narrower than that of those condemned in the *Schechter* and *Carter* cases: each delegate was accorded power to regulate the prices of a single trademarked article, not of an industry. Where the market power of a manufacturer is small, the power can scarcely be considered tantamount to a power to license or exclude.[201] Delegations to control persons in a chain of title fall well along the continuum that connects legislation and voluntary contract: Where subjection to a regulation can be avoided at relatively small cost, it may not be altogether fictitious to consider that failure to avoid it may amount to implied assent.[202] The intimate connection between enforcement of price maintenance by legal action and enforcement by individual refusal to deal makes the point clearer.[203] For the purposes of constitutional law, if not of antitrust law,[204] Justice Holmes's dissenting observation in the Beech-Nut[205] case may seem sufficient, at least where the market power of manufacturers is small: "I cannot see how it is unfair . . . to say to those to whom the respondent sells, and to the world, you can have my goods only on the terms that I propose, when the existence of any competition in dealing with them depends on the respondent's will."

This is in accordance with the thesis of this chapter, that delegations to private parties ordinarily become objectionable only where they involve the power to adjudicate, not the power to make rules enforceable by the ordinary processes of law. Of course, the "fair trade" case differs somewhat from the cases where the institution of legal actions to enforce privately formulated rules is left to a public officer.[206] Under most "fair trade" statutes, enforcement was left to actions brought by private persons, thus perhaps opening up possibilities of favoritism and selective enforcement not present where enforcement is vested in public officers. But it may be doubted that this fact enhanced the possibilities of arbitrariness in enforcement: Where private suits are involved, courts are bound by equitable doctrines to refuse or lift injunctions where a showing of uniform enforcement is not made,[207] while public prosecutors are in practice left much greater discretion in bringing enforcement actions discretion limited only by the restraints that *Yick Wo v. Hopkins*[208] imposes on systematic discrimination and not by the purely theoretical "duty to prosecute."[209]

The "fair trade" statutes did not confer on any single delegate the right to deprive another person of the opportunity to pursue a lawful calling, nor did they authorize price maintenance by monopolists or agreements between those to whom power is delegated. Attacks on the statutes for their supposed want of standards or of procedural safeguards such as public hearings and judicial review seem misconceived.[210] Standards are today required, if at all, only as a means of defining the subject matter of the power to be exercised by administrators; they have limited impact on the judgment of either public administrators or reviewing courts in appraising the proper exercise of delegated powers. And there is no constitutional requirement of hearing or review or even of an impartial tribunal when legislation or rulemaking is at issue;[211] to decry the lack of such safeguards is again to confuse legislation with adjudication.[212] The "fair trade" statutes did not resemble licensing statutes in either form or substance. The power delegated was a rulemaking power, and the statutes, whatever their economic merits,[213] did little to restrict vocational opportunities but rather had the opposite purpose and tendency.[214] If the statutes were to be condemned, it is fair to suggest that the condemnation should have proceeded on the basis of the doctrines through which those courts which care to do so have traditionally expressed their notions as to economic policy. The nondelegation doctrine, properly treated, should be preserved to other ends.[215]

Administration of Law and Representation of Interests

The participation of private interests in the choice of members of public boards and the delegation to private associations of authority to administer regulatory schemes have been the subject of much discussion by writers on administrative law.[216] While most courts and scholars would agree with Justice Cardozo's statement in *Schechter* that "when the task that is set before one is that of cleaning house, it is prudent as well as usual to take counsel of the dwellers,"[217] their views on specific problems exhibit little consistency.

Less than seventy years ago, Ernst Freund could observe that "neither in the United States federal service nor in New York are there bodies constituted on the principle of interest representation." Freund went on to make the suggestive comment that

> Altogether, lay co-operation seems to be utilized more in England than in America. Probably this is due to the higher development in England of professionalism in the civil service. Nominally, it is true that ruling powers in England are largely in the hands of politically-constituted officials; but in substance, decisions are inevitably controlled by the professional staff. It serves then to temper the odium of adverse rulings and to remove resulting friction, if a popular element enters into the administration. This consideration was certainly conspicuous in the creation of the English tax commissioners. But in America there is no similar contrast between professionalism and nonprofessionalism. The classified civil service is a relatively recent thing, and not permanent or a career in the English sense. Officials are not as yet a class apart. We accept the jury system but are not inclined to apply a similar idea to the administration. The sporadic instances of lay service in the administration have shown no vitality.[218]

Three types of arrangement generate most of the delegation cases in this field. Under some statutes, private groups are empowered to appoint members of state boards, subject to no requirement of official approval. Other statutes vest in private associations or occupational groups a nominating function or require that members of a public agency be appointed from members of specified groups. Still other statutes accord existing private groups authority to govern certain fields, without formally cloaking them with the mantle of public authority by placing them under oath or providing for their payment.

In considering the way in which courts have dealt with these arrangements, it is best to classify the cases according to the nature of powers delegated, rather than according to the type of body to which they are delegated. It is appropriate to begin with private licensing and disciplinary schemes, before turning to delegations of rulemaking powers and delegations of the power to administer public funds and resources.

Delegation of Judicial and Licensing Powers to Existing Private Ggroups. Courts have demonstrated fairly consistent hostility toward statutes vesting licensing powers in private groups when these groups are not clothed in the raiment of a public board and no review is provided. Two New York cases invalidating statutes vesting licensing powers over harness race starters and horse trainers in private groups such as the New York Jockey Club are typical here.[219] In Pennsylvania, a statute permitting three private organizations to select a near-majority of a committee charged with disbursement of funds collected pursuant to the Harness Racing Act was held invalid.[220] Cases in other states have invalidated statutes requiring the unanimous consent of existing banks in a community as a condition precedent to the licensing of new banks.[221] A New Jersey court invalidated a statute delegating to the State Medical Society power to approve or veto group medical-surgical plans. The court stressed the fact that "the Medical Society . . . has an interest in promoting the welfare of the only existing medical service corporation [Blue Shield] in this State."[222] An accompanying statute denying licenses to medical service corporations in any county in which 51 percent of the practicing physicians were not participating physicians was also invalidated by a divided court.[223]

A number of "automobile anti-bootlegging" statutes generated similar judicial hostility. The statutes limit the sale of new cars to dealers franchised by automobile manufacturers and were enacted at the behest of dealers who feared the competition of "discount houses" selling cars surreptitiously obtained from overstocked franchises.[224] In invalidating such a statute on delegation grounds, a divided Ohio court described it as an unlawful delegation, arguing that "the case at bar is even more emphatic because private automobile manufacturers from out of the state are vested with power to determine who shall sell new cars in this state."[225] A number of other courts have struck down the statutes on equal protection grounds.[226] However, a Louisiana court upheld such a statute with the observation that "[t]he right of the manufacturer to choose its dealers is merely the right of the freedom of contract."[227] An earlier case invalidating the Louisiana Fair Trade Act was unconvincingly distinguished. It seems clear that the court's decision rests on its view that "this business produces more open competition through advertisement, sales promotion and other media than any other that comes to our mind and we think that it is truly representative of free enterprise as practiced in a democracy."[228] Thus the policy-based distinction for a time made by the Supreme Court in the *White Motor*[229] case is translated into state constitutional doctrine. The result seems peculiarly unfitting since the degree of industrial concentration in the auto industry makes any delegation broader in scope than in the ordinary resale price maintenance case and since the power delegated here is, in effect, a licensing power. But the power exercised may, because of the existence of a chain of title, still seem more closely to resemble contract than legislation; taken in this light, the court's result may seem reasonable even if its distinction of the "fair trade" cases does not.

Another provocative decision also dealt with licensing powers thought to have been delegated to a purely private group without provision for judicial review. In *Blumenthal v. Board of Medical Examiners*,[230] the California Supreme Court speaking through Justice Traynor, invalidated on delegation grounds a statute requiring five years experience with a dispensing optician as a condition to licensure. The court observed that the statute "confers upon presently licensed dispensing opticians the unlimited and unguided power to exclude from their profession any or all persons. . . . Delegated power must be accompanied by suitable safeguards to guide its use and to protect against its misuse. . . . the conclusion is inescapable that the experience necessary to qualify a person to dispense optical goods is obtainable in a variety of ways."[231]

This case seems of arguable merit as an application of the nondelegation doctrine. The licensing power here may be too widely scattered for it to be thought that an identifiable private group has been given the power by a single adjudication to dispose of an individual's rights. Thus the case may be one more appropriate for the use of economic due process rather than the delegation doctrine; if the delegation doctrine is used, there is no weighing of interests and no clear stopping place short of the drastic proposition that all mandatory apprenticeship schemes are per se unconstitutional.[232]

The California judges might have done well to remember that medical internship requirements provide another instance of the survival in the professions of mandatory apprenticeship requirements. Their financial aspects have been under fire,[233] and there have also been cases subjecting hospitals to equal protection requirements on the basis that they exercise delegated licensing power,[234] but one would be astonished to see it contended that internship requirements per se are constitutionally impermissible.

It may be true that the contemporary movement, within and increasingly without the traditional professions, has been away from apprenticeship and toward educational requirements and that the latter may seem to partake of a greater objectivity. Learned Hand would have understood these developments well:

As the social group grows too large for mutual contact and appraisal, life quickly begins to lose its flavor and its significance. Among multitudes relations must become standardized; to standardize is to generalize, and to generalize is to ignore all those authentic features which mark, and which indeed alone create, an individual.

[T]he day has clearly gone forever of societies small enough for their members to have personal acquaintance with each other, and to find their station through the appraisal of those who have any first-hand knowledge of them.[235]

An apprenticeship scheme for river pilots, not dissimilar to that involved in the *Blumenthal* case, was vindicated by the Supreme Court against due process challenge in the much disputed case of *Kotch v. Board of River Port Pilot Commissioners*.[236] There the record revealed that the apprenticeship requirements operated to restrict entry to the friends and relatives of present river pilots. "Mark Twain," one critic of the Kotch decision has suggested, "would surely have felt constrained in the most fundamental sense, if his youthful aspiration to be a river-boat pilot had been frustrated by a State-ordained system of nepotism."[237] However, that writer seems in fact to have felt more amused than constrained by the traditional restrictions on river pilotage.[238]

There are, of course, other examples of statutes delegating licensing powers to private groups without provision for review. Perhaps statutes validating marriages performed by church officials fall into the same category. There, however, the licensing power is usually not exclusively conferred on church officials, and such officials are in any case scattered and numerous. Furthermore, the delegation here may be thought to relate to a dispensing power and may be viewed as more immune to attack on that account,[239] while the ministerial as opposed to discretionary character of the determination is also relevant.

It is merely a matter of accepting as authentic an act done under supposedly inherent guarantees of regularity. The practice may involve problems in the way of insuring impartial and reliable certification, and perhaps also service on reasonable terms; it is a compromise arrangement due to expediency or practical necessity; the secularization of marriage in Germany represents a repudiation of the compromise in favor of pure officialism.[240]

No discussion of statutes providing for private adjudication of offenses without review would be complete without mention of *Dr. Bonham's Case*.[241] That case, the first and last British venture into judicial review of legislative acts,[242] held bad a statute allowing the College of Physicians to fine persons practicing medicine in London for more than one month without a license from the college, where half the fine was to go to the college and half to the king. "The censors cannot be judges, ministers, and parties; judges to give sentence or judgment; ministers to make summons; and parties to have the moeity of the forfeiture."[243] Neither that case nor later cases[244] questioned the private licensing arrangement itself where a direct pecuniary interest was not as plainly present, though *Bonham's Case* is memorable not only for Lord Coke's homilies[245] and for what it says about judicial review but also for its recitals of standards for licensing[246] and for its early observations on the tort immunity of quasi-judicial officers,[247] including private persons exercising delegated powers.

Statutes requiring job printing done for government agencies to bear a union label have been invalidated with some consistency,[248] usually on the basis that they violate equal protection or antimonopoly clauses in state constitutions. Such statutes, particularly where they require the label of a named union,[249] could be viewed as delegating an unchecked licensing power, and might perhaps be distinguished from "prevailing union wage" statutes in this respect.[250] But since the time of the Wagner Act, governments have been allowed to afford various degrees of positive aid to the process of unionization.[251] The mere requirement that contractors be engaged in collective bargaining relationships with their employees would not seem to contravene equal protection standards, though requiring a contract with a specific union might do so or might (passing the problem of standing) be viewed as denying procedural due process to contractors by delegating licensing functions.

Courts have generally been willing to vindicate delegation of licensing powers to purely private groups where de novo review is provided in a public agency or in the courts. The best-known example of this willingness is that supplied by the National Association of Securities Dealers. This organization was created pursuant to the Maloney Act of 1938[252] as a body equipped with disciplinary powers over its members, whose determinations are subject to review de novo by the Securities and Exchange Commission, which in turn is subject to a lesser degree of review by the courts. The act so structures the apparatus of securities regulation as to in effect require that all brokers and dealers belong to the NASD. Nonmembers of the group are deprived by statute of the opportunity to participate in important distributions, so that membership is in effect compulsory for persons not members of a stock exchange. The delegation was summarily upheld.[253] Other legislative proposals would have broadened it by allowing NASD orders to become effective without a stay pending appeal to the Securities and Exchange Commission.[254]

The availability of de novo review in the courts has also been the basis on which delegation of disciplinary functions to an "integrated bar" association has been upheld in state courts.[255] It is difficult to say whether de novo review by a public administrative agency subject in turn to some check by the courts is in practice a greater or lesser safeguard than direct de novo judicial review, but both approaches have been upheld where tested.

Cases involving the Railway Labor Adjustment Board supply another instance where de novo review in the courts was thought necessary and sufficient to protect due process where purely private persons were given judicial functions. The Railway Labor Act[256] provides that either party to a grievance dispute may refer it to the National Railway Adjustment Board.[257] The act had been construed to give the board, a group composed of equal numbers of private persons designated by labor and management, exclusive primary jurisdiction over the dispute to the exclusion of any common law remedy available to the employee[258] or the employer.[259] It had been held that due process does not demand that employees be allowed judicial review of board decisions denying claims,[260] even though this result allowed employers, by referring cases to the board, to deprive employees of a common law remedy that would otherwise exist. However, due process had been held to demand that the employer be given a right to judicial review of money judgments against him. The courts, taking note of the private composition of the board, held that nothing less than de novo review is sufficient to preserve the constitutionality of the statute as applied to the employer,[261] though it had been held that this review need not take place until the employee brings a suit to enforce the award and hence that the employer did not have a right to a declaratory judgment as to the award's validity.[262] The denial to the employee of a right to review was presumably justified on the basis that the act itself deprives him of any common law right of action for matters within the exclusive jurisdiction of the board; the board is not held to ordinary due process standards since it can only confer benefits on the employee, not deprive him of extant rights.[263] This justification for denial of review to employees assumes that the Board remedy is exclusive and primary, and that courts are deprived of jurisdiction over claims even though neither party has referred a claim to the board. The fact that a money claim is involved and the holding that the availability of state remedies for railroad labor contract violations is determined by federal law[264] may present Seventh Amendment problems, since the statutory remedy is a direct substitute for one available at common law.[265] Though the act provides only that parties "may" refer disputes to the board, not that they, "shall" refer them there, it has been construed to give the board exclusive jurisdiction (save for wrongful discharge claims).[266] If the act were read more literally, it would in effect delegate to the employer the right to deprive an employee of a claim cognizable at common law by referring a case to the board. But even this delegation might not be thought fatal to the statute, since courts have upheld statutes giving employers the right to deprive employees of common law tort claims by setting up workmen's compensation plans not required of all employers.[267] The delegation to the employer has been thought permissible because of the employee's voluntary entry into the employment contract. The fact that under the Railway Labor Act wrongful discharge claims (as distinguished from grievance claims) initially remained cognizable at common law[268] suggests the extent to which the existence of a contractual or chain-of-title relationship will lead courts to sustain delegations deemed impermissible where such a relationship is absent or has terminated.[269] But since the waiver of common law rights is incorporated by force of law into all contracts in the industry, an "unconstitutional conditions" problem is present that is not present in cases allowing employers the option of divesting employees of common law rights by setting up workmen's compensation plans or allowing a single party to an agreement to bypass the courts by referring a claim to binding arbitration where a contract so provides. It is worth noting that in the recent cases involving the validity as a matter of procedural due process of the delegations to private parties inherent in replevin procedures and cognovit notes, the Supreme Court has distinguished between contracts of adhesion and arm's-length contracts.[270]

Delegation of Judicial and Licensing Powers to To Public Boards Selected From Private Groups. Where the private persons to whom licensing powers are delegated are formally sworn as public officials, the courts have been prone to hold that something less than de novo court review will suffice to sustain the statutory scheme.[271] The fact that members of a board must be appointed from a particular occupational group or from lists furnished by that group ordinarily does not disturb the courts where some judicial review is provided. The Supreme Court in the *Kotch*[272] case made reference to the right of states to chose their own public officers; courts generally have taken the view that the controls imposed by appointment, appropriation, and removal powers and the oaths taken by public officers make adequate a lesser measure of judicial review than that necessary to preserve statutes delegating licensing or disciplinary powers to purely private groups. Thus a Virginia court in 1950 upheld a statute creating a milk marketing board composed of producers, distributors, and consumers.[273] The court emphasized that

> [m]embers of the Commission are appointed by the Governor and subject to removal at his pleasure. . . . To hold the act unconstitutional on the ground that two members of the Commission are interested in the production and distribution of milk would be to apply the same qualifications to members of an administrative agency created by the legislature as is required of judges in trying cases. . . . Any person aggrieved by an order of the Commissions refusing to issue a license . . . is given a right of appeal to this court.[274]

Delegation of Judicial and Licensing Powers to Public Boards Appointed by Private Groups. Statutes that provide for the direct appointment of board members by private groups have received a more hostile reception from the courts, though here too the weight of judicial opinion still seems to favor validity. A Delaware act giving state chairmen of political parties authority to designate members of a county board of elections was invalidated by a divided court, which distinguished cases in which "the appointments are to be made from a list of names which allows the appointing power to exercise some discretion."[275] But older "state action" cases treating political parties as being bound to the standards of conduct required of state agencies cast doubt on whether such statutes do delegate power to private groups." It may also be urged that the board serves an adversary and mediatory rather than judicial function and that group representation is proper since "[t]o insure honest elections it is essential that the county board be made up at least by the choice of both powerful political parties."[276]

Legislative acts permitting private groups to name members of various public boards cannot be cavalierly dismissed as efforts by narrow-minded occupational groups to insulate themselves from public regulation or scrutiny. For enactments of this sort frequently arise from a felt need for professional expertise or, more frequently, from a desire to insulate a particular governmental function from "politics" in its invidious sense. The statute relating to the selection of the New

York City Board of Education sustained in *Lanza v. Wagner*[277] probably falls into this category. That statute and others founded on similar political premises have not met with uniform acclaim. The perennial and protracted controversy over the so-called Missouri Plan for the selection of judges and the role accorded bar associations under it[278] sheds light upon the political issues that lurk in this field a field where the advocates of a greater measure of professional power and responsibility stand opposed to the contemporary representatives of the Jacksonian strain in American political thought. The merits of such controversies need not be discussed here, beyond observing that committing their resolution to democratic legislatures hardly seems to do violence to democratic ideals.

Denunciations of state statutes creating industry-dominated state boards sometimes proceed from a dislike of the policy objectives that such state boards frequently foster—the protection of small, local businesses and the prevention of innovation and change.[279] In creating such boards, legislators cannot be unaware of the nature of the policies that they prospectively ratify. Dislike of policy cannot justify constitutional invalidation. Economic folly and social wisdom may at times go hand-in-hand[280]; and more than one modern judge would remind us that "[a] motive to build up through legislation the quality of men may be as creditable in the thought of some as a motive to magnify the quantity of trade. Courts do not choose between such values in adjudging legislative powers. They put the choice aside as beyond their lawful competence."[281]

But this is not to say that some of the statutes considered above may not be challenged on procedural grounds. Adjudication or licensing by a board of interested tradesmen does raise questions of bias and lack of fairness,[282] even when the board members are sworn as public officials and subject to political controls. Such actions are open to objections to which private rulemaking and rate-fixing are not subject. For denial of a license or application of a sanction bear more heavily on particular individuals than does the announcement of general rules, even when these rules are aimed at a particular group or particular manner of doing business. Moreover, arbitrariness and unfairness in rulemaking and rate-fixing is readily susceptible to legislative detection and control, whereas unfairness in consideration of a particular application or offense is unlikely to be brought to public view and even when disclosed may be explained away on the basis of particular facts or may be found difficult of redress or correction.

Courts, however, ought not go so far as to accept as a constitutional requirement a recent suggestion for legislative reform of the licensing field:

> The legislature could . . . provide for registration of all who wished to be licensed. . . . Then, in order to maintain high levels of rectitude, provision could be made for a decree of suspension or revocation upon a finding, after suitable judicial proceedings, that the licensee had misrepresented his skill or training, had demonstrated his incompetence, or had engaged in dishonorable conduct relevant to his occupation. This proposal envisages the creation of an appropriate administrative agency . . . to initiate actions in court by the filing of duly detailed complaints.[283]

It is clear, as those making such proposals would concede, that a number of occupations are not suited to such loose control. Medicine is, no doubt, the most obvious case in point. It likewise seems clear that any professional regulatory board will, whether deliberately so designed or not, tend to contain members of the affected profession. One might suggest that courts are usually unsuited to the making of judgments as to which occupations do and which do not require licensing or regulation. One might further suggest that judicial control over occupational licensing boards is best achieved by focusing on their functions rather than on their composition. Where the function of the board is merely to make rules, the composition of the board would seem quite irrelevant. The Constitution does not demand that legislators be unbiased or that their lives be free of conflicting interests when they pass on legislation; there is no reason to impose more onerous requirements on administrators performing legislative functions. Any cure for arbitrariness or invidious discrimination on the part of regulatory boards should find its source in the doctrines of equal protection that likewise limit the actions of legislatures.

Delegation of Rulemaking Powers. The delegation to private groups of rulemaking powers has ordinarily met with more gentle treatment at the hands of the courts, notwithstanding *Carter* and *Schechter*. Where an arrangement requires the assent of a large percentage of producers or where it is based upon arrangements negotiated by them (even though these arrangements may have been negotiated in contemplation of the statutory scheme), both the temptations of the market and political exigencies impose important checks.[284] Nor are abuses under such schemes unlikely to be perceived and corrected by the public.

These considerations may account for the vindication by the Supreme Court and by state courts of marketing schemes, both agricultural and industrial, whose differences from that condemned in the *Carter* case are more formal than real. Thus, statutory schemes requiring programs initiated by public authorities to be approved by a referendum of producers have been sustained,[285] as have schemes that cannot operate until initiated by a specified number of producers.[286] State courts have bridled where power is delegated to private groups to fix prices[287] or the hours of operation of independent businesses[288] without any formal checks by public officers, but this hostility is not as apparent where the power delegated relates to the hours and conditions of work of employees[289]— throwback, perhaps, to the days prior to *Nebbia v. New York*.[290]

The courts have ordinarily had little difficulty with statutes delegating rulemaking or price-fixing powers to boards made up of members of an industry.[291] The 1953 California case of *State Board of Dry Cleaners v. Thrift-D-Lux Cleaners, Inc.*[292] announced a different rule, condemning a statute allowing a board "made up of six active members of the industry, and one member of the public at large" to set minimum rates.[293] A strong dissenting opinion by Justice Traynor emphasized the fact that "[t]he members of the State Board of Dry Cleaners are appointed by the Governor and approved by the Senate. They are officials of the state, paid by the state for administering the law, and their acts are reviewed by the judiciary."[294] This emphasis on the political checks inherent in the appointment and confirmation of public officials is of even greater validity as applied to statutes thatwhich confer a removal power upon a state governor. In addition, the oaths of office taken by board members may have some restraining influence.[295] As noted above, however, a different attitude may be proper where licensing or adjudicatory functions are at issue.[296] In 1972, California adhered to the *Thrift-D-Lux* rule in *Allen v. California Board of Barber Examiners*,[297] invalidating a law that permitted the board, composed primarily of members of that profession, to set minimum barbershop prices. The intermediate court found the act was a "delegation of a power to fix prices, holding *Thrift-D-Lux* squarely applicable."[298] It should be noted that the board possessed the enforcement power of license revocation.

Similarly, the making of criminal legislation by private delegates may be constitutionally objectionable. Since violation of such legislation carries about it a moral stigma, it may not be inappropriate to insist that its enactment be reserved to the legislature or some other body fully representative of the sense of the community at large. This view has been apparent in some of the cases involving delegation to private parties[299] as well as in the early reluctance,[300] since overcome, to allow public administrative bodies to promulgate penal regulations and in the continuing reluctance to allow the size of penalties to be set by private groups. Similar thoughts may underlie the recent invalidation on procedural due process grounds of state replevin statutes.[301]

Delegation of Administrative Powers. Another important class of delegations are those that might be denominated delegations of administrative powers—powers that do not involve the making of rules enforced and enforceable in the ordinary courts and yet do not in their exercise bear so heavily on particular persons as to constitute licensing or adjudication.[302] Such delegations are often little noted in the reported cases. One student of this area has called for "an emphasis on administration as distinguished from administrative law. Law can promote but it can also impede. The ultimate answers to our besetting problems . . . are not to be found in judicial utterances, for they are essentially the problems of laymen in fields calling for more than what mere law has to offer."[303]

Delegations to private parties of the character here under consideration take place when the legislature entrusts the management of public functions to private institutions or significantly supports such institutions in their activities. The litigation surrounding such delegations usually concerns the duties of the delegates under the equal protection clause rather than the validity of the delegation itself. Where litigation does take place under the doctrine, the delegations are usually upheld. Thus an Illinois court, in an opinion by Justice Schaefer, upheld a statute providing that a railroad terminal authority could, by contract, vest in a committee "including but not limited to" interested railway companies authority to supervise and manage terminal facilities.[304] The court observed that the statute allowed the authority to "avail itself of the services of those who are presumably most familiar with the problems involved. To this extent it contemplates that delegation of administrative duties, but in this we see no constitutional violation. . . . If this sensible and apparently harmless provision should be abused, a question not now presented would arise."[305] The court did not make clear the constitutional basis of its reservations. Likewise, a federal court sustained a statute vesting in private banks the trusteeship of funds belonging to certain Indian tribes.[306] The court, citing *Berman v. Parker*,[307] noted that the powers involved were essentially managerial in character. A statute delegating to a quasi-public corporation the power to provide recreational facilities was upheld with the explanation that provision of recreational facilities was not a purely municipal function.[308] Similarly, the familiar sort of statute vesting various powers in a volunteer fire department was upheld in a Wisconsin decision against challenge on nondelegation grounds.[309] A Wyoming court has upheld a municipal employment bargaining law, including a compulsory arbitration clause, against a nondelegation challenge.[310]

It may be noted that there has been little litigation concerning the validity of statutes according private police degrees of immunity from suit and rights of a nature similar to those accorded public officials.[311] It would not be difficult to equate the powers typically accorded such police with adjudicatory powers, the delegation of which has traditionally been condemned, since extrajudicial exercises of the powers of police impinge on the rights of particular individuals and cannot easily be equated merely with rulemaking. However, the courts have generally given effect to the immunities extended to private policemen.[312] Since the end of the days of groups like the Pennsylvania Coal and Iron Police,[313] the subject has not been a live issue, though statutes authorizing "industrial police" survive in some states. It has been made plain that the acts of the remaining "private police" constitute "state action" subject to the Fourteenth Amendment equal protection guarantees.[314] The absence of litigation contesting the validity of "industrial police" laws has made it unnecessary for the courts to consider the reach, if any, of Justice Jackson's dictum[315] about the state's monopoly on violence as applied to legislative grants of powers of arrest and immunities like those available to police or to consider the source in the constitution of any limitations upon such grants. It was, fittingly, Justice Frankfurter who called a halt in two of the mass-picketing cases[316] to expansion even of the techniques used by the labor and civil rights movements: "It must never be forgotten . . . that the Bill of Rights was the child of the Enlightenment. Back of the guaranty of free speech lay faith in the power of an appeal to reason by all the peaceful means of gaining access to the mind. It was in order to avert force and explosions due to restrictions upon rational modes of communication that the guaranty of free speech was given a generous scope."[317]

Legislation has again focused attention on the problems surrounding government use of private groups to administer its programs. Various antipoverty measures and the recent welfare reform legislation contain provisions for the channelling of funds through private organizations, thus again proving, if proof were needed, that institutions commonly thought to be "vested interests" are not the sole beneficiaries of the governmental delegations here considered. Recent education bills contain extensive provisions for aid to private and parochial institutions, while direct grants-in-aid to private colleges are a commonplace. On the one hand, administration of public programs through private groups makes possible a greater variety of approaches, promotes diversity by offsetting the effect on private activities of universal taxation, and makes it possible for the government to aid programs assumed to be beneficial that it would not be thought proper for the government to administer directly.[318] It makes possible the use for government purposes of existing private institutions and provides leverage to induce change in those institutions—including such institutions as the church and the family. It also can provide means of bypassing other publicly responsible agencies at state and local levels through creation of and assistance to new private groups. Contrariwise, administration through private groups can be viewed as destructive of their autonomy,[319] or as a deleterious means of allowing the government to avoid accountability for its actions, or as promotive of an excessive amount of separatism and segregation: economic, racial, or religious (the latter charge is frequently levelled at programs for aid to private and religious education and may perhaps, with equal justice, be levelled at many means-tested programs).[320] It also may be viewed as aggrandizing the power of aggregates, whether governmental or private, at the expense of the individual.[321]

These conflicts arising in respect to any transfer of governmental powers or resources to private groups have long been at the center of the controversies surrounding the meaning and scope of the Establishment clause—itself a prohibition of one form of delegation. It has been suggested above that one standard for determining the permissibility of delegations should be whether the powers delegated to private groups are legislative in character or judicial: greater safeguards may be required in the latter case than in the former. Many of the most important objections to government aid to private groups, as *Lemon* v. *Kurtzman*[322] makes clear, center on the extent to which government aid may destroy the autonomy of private institutions or the extent to which inadmissible favoritism toward particular political or religious groups, classes, or persons may be practiced. Most distributions of government largesse, since they depend on appropriations and taxation falling on the community at large, do not merit judicial review since the operative political checks are sufficient. The same may be said even if, as is highly unlikely, the suggestions of professors Corwin,[323] Jaffe,[324] and Reich[325] are accepted and all or nearly all government disbursements or allocations are made potentially subject to judicial review on broader constitutional grounds, such as equal protection. The canons of restraint that remain relevant continue to relate to the distinction between legislation and adjudication. If the legislature determines that a broad class of beneficiaries be aided and if the beneficiaries and amounts of benefits are defined according to a limited number of objective standards so that only ministerial tasks need be carried out by the government, then the delegation in all its implications would seem a delegation subject to adequate political checks, and judicial invalidation would be inappropriate. If, on the other hand, the effect of the delegation is to leave government officials broad powers to choose among prospective private recipients, then many of the dangers giving rise to the existing constitutional bars to specific types of delegations are present, political checks are less adequate, and judicial invalidation of the totality of the delegation as well as of its implementation may be more appropriate.[326] Perhaps two specific examples may point the moral. In two Establishment clause cases the Maryland Court of Appeals respectively invalidated state grants to certain named religious colleges[327] and yet sustained tax exemptions in favor of churches and church-run educational institutions.[328] In justification of the disparity in results, the court was able to advance only a historical justification: Logically both forms of grant were "establishments," but "logic is a minion of the law, not its master."[329] Under the Maryland court's reasoning, the New York "scholar-incentive" plan, based on direct grants to students coupled with added grants to the institutions they elect to attend, would also be invalid unless partially upheld on the perhaps somewhat disingenuous basis that it aids the student and not the institution.[330] Yet surely tax exemptions to religious and charitable institutions, tax credits for tuition, and direct grants to students or per capita to the institutions they attend are not subject to many of the objections to which direct grants to named colleges are subject or to which federal research grants in varying amounts to specific universities are subject.[331] Where blanket per capita grants or tax exemptions are given to a wide class of institutions, the dangers of favoritism, destruction of the autonomy of private groups, or aggrandizement of powers of the government that are among the principal bases of the Establishment clause and similar "public use" provisions are not present in anything like the same measure.

CONCLUSIONS

What conclusions may be drawn from this protracted review of the history in our law of the notion that "delegations to private parties are invalid"?

The first conclusion is a negative one: that the nondelegation doctrine, in its commonly expressed form, is nonsense. As to this we may refer to the words of John Chipman Gray: "Especially valuable is the negative side of analytic study. On the constructive side it may be unfruitful; but there is no better method for the puncture of windbags. Most of us hold in our minds a lot of propositions and distractions which are in fact identical, or absurd or idle, and which we believe, or pretend to ourselves to believe, and which we impart to others as true and valuable. If our minds and speech can be cleared of these, it is no small gain."[332]

The second conclusion is that it is a pernicious notion that private rights can only be contracted and not be expanded[333] and that a wide scope can and does remain for government conferral of power on private groups and individuals, particularly where the powers conferred are not judicial or licensing powers or are subject to public review. As to this and as to the related questions presented by the growth of the "state action" doctrines, we may refer to the timely cautionary words of Alexander Pekelis:

> Plato, who knew how to be consequent and Socrates, who knew how to choose his interlocutors, clearly saw the links between unity of a society and the total destruction of the element of arbitrariness in all human relations, beginning with the relations between man and wife, parent and child. If we try to match their intellectual courage, we shall concede that unless a certain element of capriciousness and arbitrariness is introduced in the world, unless differences which are in a sense arbitrary, nonrational differences are admitted, preserved, and protected, unless our society is a society of societies, a community of communities, real freedom cannot be achieved. . . .
>
> . . . The more unisonal harmony of which Aristotle speaks is attempted in the American system through the peculiarity of a constitutional control which is not dissimilar to the judge's control of a jury. It leaves ample room for nonrational, intuitional, experimental, and arbitrary elements. It renounces, by definition, the idea of perfection, makes justice a question of degree, and is satisfied with keeping the juror's whim or discretion and the several governments' discretion or whim within the minimum limits of reason, and thus to reconcile diversity with equality and the rule of law with the freedom of men.[334]

The third conclusion relates to the appropriate standards for testing the validity of statutes assailed as violative of the nondelegation doctrine. Among the factors that should be weighed are the following:

1. Does the statute confer upon private delegates the power not only to make rules but also to apply the law to particular individuals?

2. Are the actions of private delegates subject to no further public or judicial review, or to review only upon attenuated standards such as the substantial evidence rule?

3. Are the private delegates chosen by a process involving public consent, as by nomination or confirmation by elected officials?

4. Are the private delegates sworn to oaths of office?

5. Do the private delegates have pecuniary interests in the determinations to be made?

6. Is a power to define criminal acts or impose penal sanctions delegated?

7. Is the delegation one of powers threatening the state's monopoly of violence, or one of a breadth and scope threatening the ultimate corrective powers of the legislature?

8. Is the delegation, if one of administrative powers or financial resources, one in which the delegates and their powers are defined according to a limited number of objective standards, or is it rather one that accords the government broad powers to pick and choose among prospective delegates?

Consideration of these questions will, it is believed, serve to clarify if not to resolve most of the issues raised by the nondelegation doctrine in its contemporary applications.

The final conclusion is that the distinction—now so eroded—between legislative and judicial functions[335] is more relevant in resolving these problems of delegation than many have been prone to assume. There is still merit in Mr. Justice Jackson's familiar proposition:

> Procedural fairness, if not. all that originally was meant by due process of law, is at least what it most uncompromisingly requires. Procedural due process is more elemental and less flexible than substantive due process. It yields less to the times, varies less with conditions, and defers much less to legislative judgment. Insofar as it is technical law, it must be a specialized responsibility within the competence of the judiciary on which they do not bend before political branches of the Government, as they should on matters of policy which comprise substantive law.[336]

Of course, insistence on procedural fairness has implications for the substance of legislation.

> [P]leadings must be filed and evidence presented before a judgment could be had; cause must be shown, forms filled out, compliance with license conditions proved, before executive or administrative action. Herein the effect of the law's formality was similar to that of the law's insistence on generalizing (abstracting) from particulars. In both respects the availability of legal process encouraged men to increase their awareness of relationships among things and events and thereby to sharpen their eyes to the existence of gains and costs and the sources of gain or cost.[337]

Indeed, nothing dramatizes this more than the far-reaching effects of much recent legislation of a procedural character—the National Environmental Policy Act,[338] for example. The answer to the political needs and forces giving rise to delegations is not to be found in blanket condemnation of delegation nor in a constitutionally compelled unitary state. It is rather to be found in focusing on the difference between rulemaking and adjudication and in insistence that delegations in the latter category be subject to adequate judicial or public review. Only thus can we, in dealing with this limited but important congeries of problems, live up to Whitehead's reminder that "[t]he art of free society consists first in the maintenance of the symbolic code; and secondly in fearlessness of revision, to secure that the code serves those purposes which satisfy an enlightened reason;"[339] a definition that demands that we be prepared, in Holmes's words, "to learn to transcend our own convictions and to leave room for much that we hold dear to be done away with short of revolution by the orderly change of law."[340]

NOTES

1. "[T]he majority rule is that the power to legislate may not be delegated by the legislature to the people." 1 J. Sutherland, *Statutes and Statutory Construction* 306 (3d ed., F. Horack, Jr. ed., 1943).
"Legislation may be held invalid if it empowers private persons to decide either what the law shall be or when a law shall be effective." 1 C. D. Sands [Sutherland] *Statutes and Statutory Construction* § 4, 11 (4th ed., 1972) (footnote omitted).

The present article, in concerning itself with delegation to private parties, is confined to an analysis of the cases passing upon legislative delegations. No effort is made here to consider the constitutional consequences of transfer of functions to private individuals by branches of the government other than the legislature, nor the doctrines that operate (or once operated) to restrict legislative delegations to administrative agencies. A recent work on numerous aspects of the doctrine is S. Barber, *The Constitution and the Delegation of Congressional Power* (1975).

2. Jaffe, *Law Making by Private Groups*, 51 Harv. L. Rev. 201 (1937) ; Hale, *Our Equivocal Constitutional Guaranties*, 39 Colum. L. Rev. 563 (1939). See also S. Barber, *The Constitution and the Delegation of Congressional Power* 72-107 (1975).

3. *Hitchman Coal & Coke Co. v. Mitchell*, 245 U.S. 229 (1917), discussed in Jaffe, supra, note 2, at 215-16.

4. 226 U.S. 137 (1912).

5. Id. at 144.

6. *A.L.A. Schechter Poultry Corp. v. United States*, 495, 551 (1935) ("Here . . . is an attempted delegation not confined to any single act nor to any class or group of acts identified or described by reference to a standard," Cardozo, J., concurring).

7. *Carter v. Carter Coal Co.*, 298 U.S 238, 311 (1936) ("This is legislative delegation in its most obnoxious form; for it is to private persons whose interests may be adverse to the interests of others in the same business").

8. But see note 82 infra. *Parker v. Brown*, 317 U.S. 341 (1943), appears to be the most recent case to extensively discuss the issue. On the Parker "state action" exception to the antitrust laws, see Verkuil, *State Action, Due Process and Antitrust: Reflections on Parker v. Brown*, 75 Colum. L. Rev. 328 (1975). See also *Goldfarb v. Virginia State Bar*, 95 S. Ct. 2004 (1975); *New Mexico v. American Petrolfina, Inc.*, 501 F.2d 363 (9th Cir. 1974); *United States v. Oregon State Bar*, 385 F. Supp. 507 (D. Ore. 1974).

9. See, e.g., Jaffe, *An Essay on Delegation of Legislative Power*, 11, 47 Colum. L. Rev. 561, 581 (1947) ("Were the country to enter a new depression or become committed to general planning, insistence on the doctrine of the *Schechter* case might again provoke a constitutional crisis." "Realistically considered *Schechter* has been put in the museum of constitutional history."). See also *Yakus v. United States*, 321 U.S. 414, 452 (1944) (Roberts, J., dissenting), where it was said that the delegation holding of the *Schechter* case has been effectively overruled. The decision of course involved a wartime statute. The majority, in *Yakus*, however, in distinguishing *Schechter*, observed that in that case "[t]he function of formulating the codes was delegated, not to a public official responsible to Congress or the Executive, but to private individuals engaged in the industries to be regulated." Id. at 424. *Schechter* was relied upon in the dissenting opinion of Justice Harlan in *Arizona v. California*, 373 U.S. 626 (1963). It was approvingly referred to in *National Cable Television Ass'n v. United States*, 415 U.S. 336, 342 (1974), for the proposition that Congress should not be presumed to have delegated the taxing power

conferred on it by U.S. Const. art. 1, § 8, cl. 1. See also *United States v. Mazurie*, 419 U.S. 544, 556 (1975), permitting a delegation to Indian tribal councils of authority to enact ordinances, subject to approval of the Secretary of the Interior, excluding certain transactions between Indians and non-Indians from a federal criminal statute. The limitations on delegation were held to be "less stringent in cases where the entity exercising the delegated authority itself possesses independent authority over the subject matter."

The delegation doctrine has also occasionally been involved in cases where criminal prosecutions are at issue. See *United States v. Sharpnack*, 355 U.S. 286, 298 (1958) (Douglas, J., dissenting); *Watkins v. United States*, 354 U.S. 178 (1957) ; see also Bickel, *Foreword: The Passive Virtues*, 75 Harv. L. Rev. 40, 69-71 (1961), and notes 336-37 infra. See also *United States v. Robel*, 389 U.S. 258, 275 (1967) (Brennan, concurring); *McGautha v. California*, 402 U.S. 183, 272 nn.21-22 (1971) (Brennan, dissenting),citing a number of cases,and Jaffe, supra note 2, for the proposition that "due process places limits on the manner and extent to which a state legislature may delegate to others powers which the legislature might admittedly exercise itself." The opinion, purportedly relying on K. Davis, *AdministrativeLaw Treatise*, §§ 2.00 to 2.00-6 (Supp. 1970), further asserts a new form of "incorporationist" doctrine—that "precisely the same functions are performed by the Due Process Clause" of the Fourteenth Amendment with respect to the states as are performed by the constitutional separation of powers and the due proces clause of the Fifth Amendment with respect to the federal government. 402 U.S. at 273 n.23. It should be noted that *McGautha*, *Louisiana v. United States*, 380 U.S. 145 (1965), and *Giaccio v. Pennsylvania*, 382 U.S. 399 (1966), involved delegation of adjudication or licensing powers, and not delegation of rulemaking powers. Cf. *Ward v. Village of Monroeville*, 409 U.S. 7 (1972); cf. also Justice Marshall's concurring opinion in *FPC v. New England Power Co.*, 41-; U.S. 345, 352 (1974).

10. 402 U.S. 183, 248, 272 (1971).

11. Id. at 272 n.22; see note 9 supra.

12. 415 U.S. 336 (1974).

13. *Corning Glass Works v. Ann & Hope, Inc.*, 294 N.E.2d 354, 361 (Mass. 1973) (nonsigner clause) ; *Bayside Timber Co. v. Board of Supervisors*, 20 Cal. App. 3d 1, 13, 97 Cal. Rptr. 431, 439 (1971); *General Elec. Co. v. Wahle*, 207 Ore. 302, 296 P.1-d 635 (1956) (nonsigner clause). See also *Bulova Watch Co. v. Brand Distribs., Inc.*, 285 N.C. 467, 206 S.E.2d 141 (1974). See notes 174-215 infra & text accompanying.

14. See note 119 *infra.*

15. *Bayside Timber Co. v. Board of Supervisors*, 20 Cal. App. 3d 1, 97 Cal. Rptr. 431 (1971) (statute delegating to timber owners power to formulate forest practice rules with force of law an unlawful delegation).

16. The distinctions between a deprivation of due process or equal protection and an unlawful delegation of legislative power are often obscure. Thus it is not surprising that the Court in *Carter* held that the Bituminous Coal Conservation Act of 1935 contained an improper delegation of legislative power, and as such deprived petitioners of "rights safeguarded by the due process clause of the Fifth Amendment." 298 U.S. at 311.

The shift in the focus of concern regarding state-sanctioned concentrations of private power is nothing short of astonishing. In 1961, objection was voiced over such matters as compulsory union membership, the Agricultural Marketing Agreement Act of 1937, 7 U.S.C. § 608 (1970) (exempting certain marketing agreements and concomitant price-fixing from antitrust scrutiny), and nonsigner clauses sanctioned by various fair trade laws.

Hanslowe, *Regulation by Visible Public and Invisible Private Government*, 40 Texas L. Rev. 88, 101, 103, 110 (1961).

More recently, well-known developments in constitutional law have shifted attention to state-sanctioned power vested in creditors, public utilities, and the like. Based upon decisions such as *Sniadach v. Family Fin. Corp.*, 395 U.S. 337 (1969), and *Fuentes Shevin*, 407 U.S. 67 (1972), several lower courts were prepared to hold that all prejudgment seizures or suspensions of property interests violated the due process clauses of the fifth and Fourteenth Amendments. See, e.g., *Adams v. Egley*, 338 F. Supp. 614 (S.D. Cal. 1972); Collins v. Viceroy Hotel Corp., 338 F. Supp. 390 (N.D. Ill. 1972); *Tones Press, Inc. v. Motor Travel Servs., Inc.*, 286 Minn. 205, 176 N.W. 2d 87 (1970). But see *Mitchell v. W.T. Grant Co.*, 416 U.S. 562 (1974); see also 35 La. L. Rev. 221 (1974). Of course, a basic problem in any of these cases is a finding of "state action." Some courts held that statutory authorization of certain practices such as self-help repossession constituted sufficient state action in itself, even though no state official was directly involved in the seizure or retention. See, e.g., *Adams v. Department of Motor Vehicles*, 11 Cal. 3d 146, 520 P.2d 961, 113 Cal. Rptr. 145 (1974) (statute authorizing garageman's liens). Clearly, if courts are willing to find state action under such circumstances, definite parallels to the former abuses of the delegation doctrine exist. It may not be too much to say that the Due Process and Equal Protection clauses have in recent years been doing some of the work formerly done by the delegation doctrine. For a characterization of one theory of state action in terms of delegation, see Clark & Landers, *Sniadack, Fuentes and Beyond: The Creditor Meets the Constitution*, 59 Va. L. Rev. 355, 377-83 (1973). Cf. 2 F. Pollack & F. Maitland, *The History of English Law* 574-78 (2d ed. 1968). Cf. also *City of Amsterdam v. Helsby*, 79 Misc. 2d 676, 362 N.Y.S.2d 698 (Sup. Ct 1974); City of *Warwick v. Warwick Regular Firemen's Ass'n*, 106 R.I. 109, 256 A.2d 206 (1969); Comment, *Collective Bargaining for Public Employees and the Prevention of Strikes in the Public Sector*, 68 Mich. L. Rev. 260, 284-85 (1969).

In Verkuil, *State Action, Due Process and Antitrust: Reflections on Parker v. Brown*, 75 Colum. L. Rev. 328, 330-31 n. 14 (1975), the author contrasts the meaning of "state action" in antitrust and Fourteenth Amendment contexts.

For a discussion of the relationship between the delegation doctrine and the Equal Protection clause, see notes 47-49 infra & text accompanying.

17. Jaffe, *Law Making by Private Groups*, 51 Harv. L. Rev. 201 (1937) (hereinafter cited as Jaffe).

18. See Wirtz, *Government by Private Groups*, 13 La. L. Rev. 440 (1953); Hanslowe, supra, note 16; Conant, *Resale Price Maintenance: Constitutionality of Nonsigner Clauses*, 109 U. Pa. L. Rev. 539, 545-50 (1961); cf. *Lathrop v. Donohue*, 367 U.S. 820, 878 n.1 (1961) (Douglas, J., dissenting).

19. See generally 1 K. Davis, *Administrative Law Treatise* § 2.14 (1958) and cases there cited.

20. E.g., Wirtz, supra, note 18; Hanslowe, supra, note 16.

21. Wirtz, supra, note 18, at 132-35. For a discussion of the relationship between state action in recent due process and equal protection cases and in the delegation doctrine, see note 16 supra.

22. Jaffe at 220-21.

23. *WECO Prod. Co. v. Reed Drug Co.*, 2-15 Wis. 474, 484, 274 N.W. 426, 430 (1937) (Wisconsin Fair Trade Act "complete" on leaving legislature).

24. Note, *Delegation of Power to Private Parties*, 37 Colum. L. Rev. 447, 453 (1937). See *City of Biddeford v. Biddeford Teachers Ass'n*, 304 A.2d 287 (Me. 1973). Cf. H. Friendly, *The Federal Administrative Agencies: The Need for Better Definition of Standards* 21-22 (1962); Landis, *Book Review* (of Friendly, op. cit. supra.), 30 U. Chi. L. Rev. 597 (1963).

25. Cf. *A.L.A. Schechter Poultry Corp. v. United States*, 295 U.S. 495 (1935); Ehmke, *Delegata Potestas Non Potest Delgari: A Maxim of American Constitutional Law*, 47 Cornell L.Q. 50 (1961). See also *Amalgamated Meat Cutters & Butchers Workmen of N. America v. Connally*, 337 F. Supp. 737 (D.D.C. 1971). It could scarcely be asserted that delegations to private groups are, for constitutional purposes, not subject to revocation. That view might have found favor in the Dartmouth College case and in other early decisions under the contract clause; other cases are emphatic in stressing the inalienability of the police power. See *Norman v. Baltimore & O.R.R.*, 294 U.S. 240 (1935); *Home of the Friendless v. Rouse*, 75 L7.S. (8 Wall.) 430 (1869).

26. E.g., Marsh v. Alabama, 326 U.S. 501 (1946); but see *Lloyd Corp. v. Tanner*, 407 U.S. 551 (1972); *Associated Press v. United States*, 326 U.S. 1 (1945).

27. Cf. *Silver v. New York Stock Exch.*, 373 U.S. 341 (1963); *Fashion Originators' Guild of America v. FTC*, 312 U.S. 457 (1941). See also cases cited note 16 supra; see also note 162 infra & text accompanying.

28. *Shelley v. Kraemer*, 334 U.S. 1 (1948); *Smith v. Allwright*, 321 U.S. 6-49 (1944) see note 16 supra. That Shelley is an equal protection and not a nondelegation case is made plain by the fact that the Court did not dispute that restrictive convenants utilizing nonprohibited classifications remain enforceable save as prohibited by statute. See *Bell v. Maryland*, 378 U.S. 226, 329 (1964) (Black, J., dissenting). Cf. Comment, *Validity Rules Concerning Public Zoning and Private Covenants: A Comparison and Critique*, 39 S. Cal. L. Rev. 409 (1966).

29. Cf. McCloskey, *Economic Due Process and the Supreme Court: An Exhumation and Reburial*, 1962 Sup. Ct. Rev. 34. Cf. also *Dandridge v. Williams*, 397 U.S. 471 (1970).

30. Miller, *The Constitutional Law of the "Security State,"* 10 Stan. L. Rev. 620 (1958). But cf. note 16 supra.

31. Wellington, *The Constitution, the Labor Union, and Governmental Action*, 70 Yale L. J. 345 (1961).

32. See generally J. Hurst, *Law and the Conditions of Freedom in the Nineteenth Century United States* 63-66 (1956) and authorities there cited. Cf. the early statutes allowing mill owners to flood neighboring lands upon payment of compensation to landowners, collected and upheld in *Head v. Amoskeag Mfg. Co.*, 113 U.S. 9 (1885); *Georgia R.R. & Banking Co. v. Smith*, 128 U.S. 174 (1888) (upholding grant of eminent domain powers to railroads); *Berman v. Parker*, 348 U.S. 26 (1954) (upholding use of eminent domain powers where land conveyed to private developers). In the last case, the Court declared: "Once the object is within the authority of Congress, the means by which it will be attained is also for Congress to determine. Here one of the means chosen is the use of private enterprise for redevelopment of the area. Appellants argue that this makes the project a taking from one businessman for the benefit of another businessman. The public end may be as well or better served through an agency or private enterprise than through a department of government or so the Congress might conclude." Id. at 33-34. Cf. *Lathrop v. Donohue*, 367 U.S. 740 (1961), *IAM v. Street*, 367 U.S. 740 (1961); *Louisville Joint Stock Bank v. Radford*, 295 U.S. 596, 602 (1935; *Pennsylvania Coal Com.*

v. Mahon, 260 U.S. 393 (1922).

33. See C. Jacobs, *Law Writers and the Courts* (1954): McAllister, *Public Purpose in Taxation*, 18 Calif. L. Rev. 137, 241 (1930); McBain, *Taxation for a Private Purpose*, 29 Pol. Sci. Q. 185 (1914); Virtue, *The Public Use of Private Capital: A Discussion of Problems Related to Municipal Bond Financing*, 35 Va. L. Rev. 235 (1949). Leading cases include *Carmichael v. Southern Coal Co.*, 301 U.S. 495 (1937); *Cochran v. Louisiana State Bd. of Educ.*, 281 U.S. 370 (1930); *Green v. Frazier*, 253 U.S. 233 (1920); *Jones v. City of Portland*, 245 U.S. 217 (1917). Since taxation, like the regulation of money and credit, is felt by the community at large, there is more reason to believe that political checks will be adequate to control it than exists in the case of eminent domain or even in the case of ordinary exercises of the police power. See Pinsky, *State Constitutional Limitations on Public Industrial Financing: An Historical and Economic Approach*, 111 U. Pa. L. Rev. 265, 307 (1963).

34. See *Berman v. Parker*, 348 U.S. 26 (1954); Dunham, *Griggs v. Allegheny County in Perspective: Thirty Years of Supreme Court Expropriation Law*, 1962 Sup. Ct. Rev. 63.

35. A representative enabling statute is the Indiana Local Industrial Development Act, IND. ANN. STAT. §§ 18-7-14-1 to -10 (Code ed. 1974).

36. 87 U.S. (20 Wall.) 655 (1873) (invalidating as outside the powers of the legislature under the Kansas constitution a statute empowering a municipal authority to issue bonds in aid of manufacturing concerns).

37. A. Smith, *The Wealth of Natioms*, ch. 10 (1776), is of course the classic denunciation of state monopoly grants. This antipathy did not always exist at the time the Constitution was framed. See *American Fed'n of Labor v. American Sash & Door Co.*, 335 U.S. 538, 543 n.1 (1949) (Frankfurter, J., concurring), and the works there cited. The only reference to monopolies in the federal Constitution is that in art. 1, § 8, cl. 8, empowering Congress "to promote the Progress of Science and useful Arts, by securing for limited Times to Authors and Inventors the exclusive Right to their respective Writings and Discoveries. . ." Since this clause is supplemented by the commerce power, it does not operate as a restriction on federal power to grant monopolies other than patents and copyright. It may, however have a negative thrust against state legislation in areas closely related to patent and copyright, at least where such legislation can be viewed as conflicting with federal patent and copyright statutes enacted pursuant to the constitutional authorization. See *Sears, Roebuck & Co. v. Stiftel Co.*, 376 U.S. 225 (1964). The above abortive efforts of several states to amend the commerce clause prior to its ratification to forbid congressional grants of monopolies are briefly discussed in F. Frankfurter, *The Commerce, Clause Under Marsja; Taney and Waite* 12-13 (1937). On monopolies and the Fourteenth Amendment, see the *Slaughterhouse* cases, 83 U.S. (16 Wall.) 36 (1873) (including the dissenting opinion of Justice Field), and their sequel, *Butchers' Union Co. v. Crescent City Co.*, 111 U.S. 746 (18M) (involving the same slaughterhouse monopoly). See generally C. Fairman, *Mr. Justice Miller and The Superme Court* ch. 8 (1939).

38. But cf. *Morey v. Doud*, 354 U.S. 457 (1957), where the Equal Protection Clause was perhaps used for a similar purpose. See L. Hand, *The Bill of Rights* 46-47 (1958). Cf. *H.P. Hood & Sons, Inc. v. Du Mond*, 336 U.S. 525, 545 (1949) (Black, J., dissenting); *Willson v. Black Bird Creek Marsh Co.*, 27 U.S. (2 Pet.) 245 (1829), for the rejection of what might have been efforts to use the Commerce Clause to invalidate state monopoly grants. Cf. *Gibbons v. Ogden*, 22 U.S. (9 Wheat.) 1 (1824).

It seems well established that the Equal Protection Clause imposes few barriers in the way of monopoly grants through the device of "grandfather clauses." See *Brooks v. State*

Bd. of Funeral Directors & Embalmers, 233 Md. 98, 195 A.2d 728 (1963), and cases there discussed. Cf. also *United States v. Maryland Sav. Share Ins. Corp.*, 400 U.S. 4 (1970); *Wampler v. Lecompte*, 282 U.S. 172 (1930). One commentator, at least, would have it do so. See Sharp, *The Old Constitution*, 20 U. Chi. L. Rev. 529, 534 (1953). Cf. *In re Norwalk Call*, 62 Cal. 2d 183, 397 P.2d 426, 41 Cal. Rptr. 666 (1964). Any requirement of uniformity of application will of course impair the political feasibility of innovation, legislative or judicial. See *Johnson v. New Jersey*, 384 U.S. 719 (1966).

39. *Eastern R.R. Presidents Conf. v. Noerr Motor Freight, Inc.*, 365 U.S. 127, 135, 136-37 (1961), discussed at note 149 infra & text accompanying. But cf. *Continental Ore Co. v. Union Carbide & Carbon Corp.*, 370 U.S. 690, 707 (1962).

40. Perhaps the language of Justice Cardozo in another context is pertinent to a discussion of the doctrine: "Appeal is vaguely made to some constitutional immunity, whether expressed or implied is not stated with distinctness. . . . If the immunity vests upon some express provision of the Constitution, the opinion of the Court does not point us to the article or section." *Jones v. SEC*, 298 U.S. 1. 32-33 (1936) (Cardozo, J., dissenting).

41. E.g., McCloskey, *Economic Due Process and the Supreme Court: An Exhumation and Reburial*, 1962 Sup. Ct. Rev. 34; Reich, *The Public and the Nation's Forests*, 50 Calif. L. Rev. 381 (1962). Compare the more robust view taken in K. Llewellyn, *Jurisprudence* 241-42 (1962): "When action by the specialists on a point of constitutional change pinches the personal toes of Albert Jones too sharply, Albert is likely to react as he does to less fundamental change of similar effect. . . . If only one of an unorganized class or ruck, he groans and gets nowhere, unless the pressure is painful and sustained enough to lock his fellows and himself together into an interested group."

42. See 1 K. Davis, *Administrative Law Treatise* § 2.15, at 150-51 (1958). There are no significant constitutional requirements as to procedure in rulemaking: "In absence of statutory requirement of hearing, and in absence of a dispute of adjudicative facts, the case law ordinarily does not require either a speech-making hearing or a trial-type hearing for rule making." Id. § 6.12, at 405.

43. One may surmise that even now the most perceptive courts are motivated much more by the degree of protection against arbitrariness than by the doctrine about standards that they write about in their opinions. By and large, the safeguards required for adjudication are greater than those required for general rulemaking. Id. § 215, at 151.

"The lawyer's chief concern with 'the rule of law' was earlier considered to be that of setting out procedural safeguards to insure non-arbitrary solution to the problems of the individual. . . . When a city council, nominally a legislative body, passes zoning regulations, grants variations therefrom, provides for slum clearance, and does numerous other acts which affect directly individuals, it affects them in much the same way that an administrator does. The courts do often indiscriminately apply the same rules when both of these categories of actions are questioned, but speak in different terms when general ordinances affecting all persons in the area are considered." J. Winters, *State Constitutional Limitations on Solutions of Metropolitan Area Problem*, 147 (1961) (footnote omitted).

44. E.g., *Smith v. Department of Regis. & Educ.*, 412 111. 332, 106 N.E.2d 722 (1952).

45. 2 K. Davis, supra, note 42, § 12.04.

46. Cf. F. Hayek, *The Constitution of Liberty* 209 (1960); quoted in Kurland, of Church and State and the Supreme Court, 29 U. Chi. L. Rev. 1, 5 (1961): "[C]lassification in abstract terms can always be carried to the point at which . . . the class singled out

consists only of particular known persons or even a single individual . . . [N]o entirely satisfactory criterion has been found that would always tell us what kind of classification is compatible with equality before the law. Compare *Peery v. Virginia Bd. of Funeral Directors & Embalmers*, 203 Va. 161, 123 S.E.2d 94 (1961), with *In re Mayor of New York*, 246 72 [In re Elm St.] 158 N.E. 24 (1927) (Cardozo, C.J.).

47. Hart, *The Power of Congress to Limit the Jurisdiction of Federal Courts: An Exercise in Dialectic*, 66 Harv. L. Rev. 1362, 1402 (1953), reprinted in P. Bator, P. Mishkin, D. Shapiro, & H. Wechsler. Hart and Wechsler's The Federal Courts and The Federal System 330, 360 (2d ed. 1973). Cf. *Moose Lodge No. 107 v. Irvis*, 407 U.S. 163, 177-79 (1972).

48. Note the conflicting views taken in the opinions in *Douglas v. California*, 372 U.S. 353 (1963); cf. Wechsler, *TowardNeutralPrinciplesofConstitutionalLaw*, 73 Harv. L. Rev. 1 (1959).

49. See *City of Amsterdam v. Helsby*, 79 Misc. 2d 676, 362 N.Y.S.2d 698 (Sup. Ct. 1974). Cf. *Hurtado v. California*, 110 -U.S. 516, 535-36 (1984): "Law is something more than mere will exerted as an act to power. It must not be a special rule for a particular person or particular case . . . thus excluding, as not due process of law, acts of attainder, bills of pains and penalties, acts of confiscation, acts reversing judgments, and acts directly transferring one man's estate to another, legislative judgments and decrees, and other . . . arbitrary exertions of power under the forms of legislation." It may be noted that for Justice Frankfurter many cases which for others involved problems under substantive clauses resolved themselves into questions of procedural due process. See *Kedroff v. St. Nicholas Cathedral*, 344 U.S. 94, 121 (1952) (Frankfurter, J., concurring) *United States v. Lovett*, 323 U.S. 303, 322, 328-29 (1946) (Frankfurter, J., concurring); F. Frankfurter, Of Law and Men 14-15 (1956).

50. See text accompanying notes 4-5 supra.

51. 242 U.S. 526 (1917).

52. Id. at 531.

53. *Washington ex rel. Seattle Title Trust Co. v. Roberge*, 278 U.S. 116, 122 (1928).

54. *A.L.A. Schechter Poultry Corp. v. United States*, 295 U.S. 495, 537 (1935).

55. Id. (footnotes omitted). The missing statute referred to was the Act of July 26, 1866, ch. 262, 14 State 251. It had been upheld by way of dictum in *Butte City Water Co. v. Baker*, 196 U.S. 119, 126 (1905). The railroad drawbar statute was the Act of Mar. 2, 1893, ch. 196, 27 Stat. 531. It had been applied and by inference upheld in *St. Louis & Iron Mt. & So. Ry. v. Taylor*, 210 U.S. 281, 286 (1908).

56. 295 U.S. at 551 (Cardozo, J., concurring). See *Amalgamated Meat Cutters & Butchers Workmen of N. America v. Connally*, 337 F. Supp. 737 (D.D.C. 1971).

57. 295 U.S. at 552 (Cardozo, J., concurring). Justice Cardozo at this point in his opinion cited *Doty v. Love*, U.S. 64, 71 (1935), where the Court, speaking through Cardozo, upheld a Mississippi statute empowering a state superintendent of banks, with court concurrence, to reopen closed banks where 75 percent of the depositors had signed "freezing-of-deposits agreements" providing for deferred return of their deposits. Cf. *United States Mortgage Co. v. Matthews*, 293 U.S. 232 (1934), rejecting a challenge under the Equal Protection Clause to a statute requiring the assent of 25 percent of mortgage holders to obtain a summary foreclosure decree.

58. 298 U.S. 238 (1936).

59. Id. at 311. One commentator has contended that the delegation holding rested on "the indefiniteness of the group" to which power was delegated and that its sweeping language is "dictum." Note, *The Disqualification of Administrative Officials*, 41 Colum. L. Rev. 1384, 1398 n.79 (1941).

60. See Jefferson, *The Supreme Court and State Separation and Delegation of Powers*, 44 Colum. L. Rev. 1 (1944).

61. *Lathrop v. Donohue*, 367 U.S. 820 , 855 (1961) (concurring opinion).

62. 237 LT.S. 391 (1915).

63. Id at 397. It is usually thought that, subject to the limitations imposed by procedural due process, the states may distribute their powers among public bodies as they see fit. *Mayor of Philadelphia v. Educational Equality League*, 415 U.S. 605, 615 n.13 (1974); *McGautha v. California*, 402 U.S. 183, 272 n.21 (1971) (Brennan, J., dissenting); *Sweezy v. New Hampshire*, 354 U.S. 234, 255 (1957); *Crowell v. Benson*, 285 U.S. 22 57 (1932) (dictum); *Dreyer v. Illinois*, 187 U.S. 71 (1902); *Forsyth v. Hammond*, 166 U.S. 506 (1897).

64. 298 U.S. at 311.

65. Id. at 318.

66. *Old Dearborn Distrib. Co. v. Seagram-DistillersCorp.*, 299 U.S. 183 (1936). A number of commentators have asserted that the *Old Dearborn* case, on its facts, did not uphold a "nonsigner clause" since the defendant there had signed a contract, though the court treated it as ineffective. Id. at 187. It is sufficient to observe that no contract was present in the companion cases of *McNeil v. Joseph Triner Corp.*, 299 U.S. 183 (1936), and *Pep Boys, Inc. v. Pyroil Sales Co.*, 299 U.S. 198 (1936).

67. 299 U.S. at 194. Cf. *O'Gorman & Young, Inc. v. Hartford Fire Ins. Co.*, 282 U.S. 251 (1931).

68. R. Jackson, *The Struggle for Judicial Supremacy* 164 (1941).

69. 300 U.S. 608 (1937).

70. Id. at 612.

71. Id. at 614.

72. 306 U.S. 1 (1939).

73. Id. at 6.

74. Id. at 15.

75. Id.

76. Id. at 16.

77. 307 U.S. 533 (1939).

78. Id. at 578. "Of 38,627 votes counted as valid in the referendum, 33,663 or 87.1 percent were in favor of the issuance of the Order and 4,964 or 12.9 percent were opposed. Of the favorable votes, the League cast 22,287." Id. at 557. See also *H.P. Hood & Sons, Inc. v. United States*, 307 U.S. 588 (1939); *Salyer Land Co. v. Tulare Lake Basin Water Storage Dist.*, 410 U.S. 719, 735 (1973) (Douglas, J., dissenting) ("J.G. Boswell Co. commands the greatest number of votes, 37,825, which are enough to give it a majority of the board of directors."). In upholding such distributions of voting power in water districts, the Supreme Court noted in a companion case: "We cannot agree with the dissent's intimation that the Wyoming Legislature has in any sense abdicated to a wealthy few the ultimate authority over land management in that State. The statute authorizing the establishment of improvement districts was enacted by a legislature in which all of the State's electors have the unquestioned right to be fairly represented. Under the act, districts may be formed only as subdivisions of soil and water conservation districts. .

. . And a precondition to their formation referendum is a determination by a board of supervisors of the affected conservation district, popularly elected by both occupiers and owners of land within the district, that the watershed improvement district is both necessary and administratively practicable." *Associated Enterprises v. Toltec Watershed Improvement Dist.*, 410 U.S. 743, 744-45 (1973). In the *Salyer* case, supra, it was noted that the scheme there at issue required the concurring approval of the state treasurer, the state Department of Water Resources, a majority of landowners voting in an unweighted election, and a weighted majority.

79. 310 U.S. 381 (1940).

80. Id. at 399.

81. 317 U.S. 341 (1943). The statute was upheld against challenges based on the Sherman Act and Commerce Clause. See *Florida Lime & Avocado Growers v. Paul*, 373 U.S. 132, 176 n.19 (1963); *United States v. Borden Co.*, 308 U.S. 189, 199 (1939). In *West Coast Hotel Co. v. Parrish*, 300 U.S. 379 (1937), the Court upheld a Washington minimum wage statute under which wage scales could be promulgated by a public board only after recommendations by a conference constituted on a principle of interest representation. See also *Opp Cotton Mills v. Administrator*, Wage & Hour Div., 312 U.S. 126 (1941).

82. Thus in *Kotch v. Board of River Port Pilot Comm'rs*, 330 U.S. 332 (1947), the Supreme Court upheld a statute vesting licensing powers in a board consisting entirely of river pilots and providing that the board should license only persons who had served a six month apprenticeship as river pilots. Four judges dissented on equal protection grounds. A newer challenge to the statute involved in *Kotch* was similarly unsuccessful. See *Brechtel v. Board of Examiners of Bay Pilots*, 230 F. Supp. 18 (D. La. 1964); accord, *Register v. Milam*, 188 So. 2d 785 (Fla. 1966).

Another indication of the shifting scope of the doctrine is illustrated by the fate of *Kesler v. Department of Pub. Safety*, 369 U.S. 153, 181 (1962), sustaining as not in conflict with the federal bankruptcy act a state statute allowing judgment creditors of motorists involved in automobile accidents to initiate the suspension and consent to the restoration of drivers' licenses. *Kesler* was overruled in *Perez v. Campbell*, 402 U.S. 637, 651-52 (1971); see *Bell v. Burson*, 402 U.S. 535 (1971), invalidating a related provision on procedural due process grounds.

An amusing sidelight to the delegation cases is provided by *Helvering v. Lerner Stores Corp.*, 314 U.S. 463, 468 (1941). There the court sustained a statute allowing taxpayers to choose between alternate tax bases, holding it was not a delegation since "Congress has fixed the criteria in light of which the choice is to be made [by the taxpayer]." In *Duhame v. State Tax Comm'n*, 65 Ariz. 268, 179 P.2d 252 (1947), a similar provision was upheld on the basis that the taxpayer "applied" the law rather than made it. Surely the obvious observation to make in these cases is that the taxpayer is not delegated the right to regulate anyone's conduct but his own.

83. Del. (4 Harr.) 479 (1847).

84. Id. at 487.

85. 2 E. Burke, *Works* 89, 96 (7th ed. 1881), quoted in id. at 490.

86. 4 Del. (4 Harr.), at 488. Compare the similar Hobbesian view of the court in *Serrano v. Priest*, 5 Cal. 3d 584, 487 P.2d 124, 96 Cal. Rptr. 601 (1971), with its proposition that a state cannot by delegating taxing and spending powers to local governments produce results that it could not validly achieve through its own direct measures. But cf. *San Antonio Ind. School Dist. v. Rodriguez*, 411 U.S. 1, 54 n.110 (1973).

87. *Opinions of the Justices*, 160 Mass. 586, 593, 594-95 [In re Municipal Suffrage to Women], 36 N.E. 488, 491-92 (1894) (Holmes, J., dissenting).

88. Cases from Alabama, California, Illinois, Iowa, Louisiana, Massachusetts, New Hampshire, and Texas. Contra, cases from Georgia, Michigan, Vermont, and Wisconsin (dictum). See Jaffe at 222 nn.45 & 46.

89. Valid: California, Illinois, Indiana, Massachusetts, New York, Pennsylvania. Void: Delaware, Iowa, Texas. Jaffe at 223 n.47.

90. Id. The states were California, Indiana, and Pennsylvania.

91. Id. at 224.

92. *Rice v. Foster*, 4 Del. (4 Harr.) 479, 491 (1847). See also Holmes, J., dissenting, in *Opinions of the Justices*, 160 Mass. 586, 594 [In re Municipal Suffrage to Women], 36 N.E. 488, 492 (1894): "The objection [to constitutionality], if sound, would seem to have equal force against all forms of local option. But I will consider the question when it arises. The difference is plain between that case and one where the approval required is that of the sovereign body."

93. *State ex rel. Broughton v. Zimmerman*, 261 Wis. 398, 52 N.W.2d 903 (1952).

94. *Fulkerson v. Refunding Bd.*, 201 Ark. 957, 147 S.W.2d 980 (1941).

95. *Busch v. Turner*, 26 Cal. 2d 817, 161 P.2d 456 (1945); cf. *Geiger v. Board of Supervisors*, 48 Cal. 2d 832, 313 P.2d 545 (1957); *Application of Oklahoma Building Bonds Comm'n*, 410 P.2d 521 (Okla. 1966); *Application of Oklahoma Indus. Fin. Auth.*, 360 P.2d 720 (Okla. 1961).

96. *Marr v. Fisher*, 182 Ore. 383, 187 P.2d 966 (1947).

97. *Walton v. Carter*, 337 S.W.2d 674 (Ky. App. 1960).

98. *In re Opinions of the Justices*, 232 Ala. 56, 166 So. 706 (1936).

99. *Opinion of the Justices*, 287 Ala. 326, 251 So. 2d 744 (1971).

100. 402 U.S. 137, 141 (1971).

101. See note 89 supra.

102. See 16 C.J.S. *Constitutional Law* § 142 n.93 (1956) and cases there cited; id., Supp. 1974; 2 E. McQuillin *The Law of Municipal Corporations* § 4.08-10 (3d ed., F. Ellard ed., 1966).

103. See *Reynolds v. Dallas County*, 203 S.W.2d 320 (Tex. Civ. App. 1947).

104. *Paul v. Gloucester County*, 50 N.J.L. 585, 600, 15 A. 272, 280 (Ct. Err. & App. 1888).

105. *Opinion to the Governor*, 62 R.I. 316, 328, 6 A.2d 147, 153 (1939).

106. *Halmontafler v. City of Nashville*, 206 Tenn. 64, 332 S.W.2d 163 (1960) (holding single elections invalid).

107. *State ex inf. Crain ex rel. Peebles v. Moore*, 339 Mo. 492, 501, 99 S.W.2d 17, 22 (1936).

108. *State ex rel. Taylor v. Carolina Racing Ass'n*, 241 N.C. 80, 94 S.E. 2d 390 (1954).

109. See M. Peck, *Independent Special Districts: A Solution to the Metropolitan Area Problem* (1962); Willoughby, *The Quiet Alliance*, 38 S. Cal. L. Rev. 72 (1965).

110. *Browning v. Hooper*, 269 U.S. 396. 405-06 (1926). See *Embree v. Kansas City & Liberty Blvd. Road Dist.*, 240 U.S. 242 (1916).

111. Cf. text accompanying note 73 supra.

112. *Davis v. State*, 141 Ala. 84, 37 So. 454 (1904) (fencing district).

113. *Summerville v. North Platte Valley Weather Control Dist.*, 170 Neb. 46, 101 N.W.2d 748 (1960) (holding district invalid for lack of hearing though only one mill tax). Cf. *Syfie v. Tri-County Hosp. Dist.*, 186 Neb. 478, 184 N.W.2d 398 (1971).

114. Id. See also *State ex rel. Jones v. Brown*, 338 Mo. 448, 92 S.W.2d 718 (1936); *Anderson v. Carlson*, 171 Neb. 741, 107 N.W.2d 535 (1961) (due process grounds).

115. See, e.g., *Millerv. Ryan*, 54 So. 2d. 60 (Fla. 1951) (advertising district); *Dortch v. Lugar*, 255 Ind. 545, 266 E.2d 25 (1971); *Martin v. Ben Davis ConservancyDist.*, 238 Ind. 502, 503 N.E.2d 125 (1958) (conservation district); *Evans v. West Norriton Twp. Mun. Auth.*, 370 Pa. 150, 87 A.2d 474 (1971) (pure stream authority); *Branch v. Salt Lake County Serv. Area No. 2-Cottonwood Hts.*, 23 Utah 2d. 181, 460 P.2d 814 (1969) (County Service Area Act). In *Kriz v. Klingensmith*, 176 Neb. 205, 125 N.W.2d 674 (1964), discretion in the county board to reject a district was held sufficient to sustain the statute, though no notice or hearing was provided for. The court held that no hearing was requisite until an actual assessment was sought to be imposed.

116. But see *State ex rel. Attorney General v. County School Bd.*, 181 Miss. 818, 181 So. 313 (1938) (rights of citizens outside district to convenient schools must be found not impaired).

117. But cf *In re Arch Hurley ConservancyDist.*, 52 N.M. 34, 191 P.2d 338 (1948) (court must find that all of district will benefit). Concern for the welfare of future citizens was advanced as a ground for judicial intervention some time ago in Reich, The Public and the Nation's Forests, 50 Calif. L. Rev. 381 (1962). For a discussion of the use of the generations-yet-to-come argument in traditional and current environmental thought, see Meyers, *An Introduction to Environmental Thought: Some Sources and Some Criticisms*, 50 Ind. L.J. 426, 450 (1975).

118. The classic approach is that of Cooley: "As the burdens of municipal governent must rest upon [the corporators'] shoulders, and especially as by becoming incorporated they are held, in law, to undertake to discharge the duties the charter imposes, it seems eminently proper that their voice should be heard on the question of their incorporation." T. Cooley, *ConstitutionalLimitations* 129 [*118] (3d ed., 1874); id. at 236 (8th ed., 1927) (citing cases).

119. See K. Hanslowe, *The Emerging Law of Labor Relations in Public Employment* 21-24 (1967). Certain courts have held that it would be an impermissible delegation of legislative power to allow teachers to bargain collectively with school boards. *Fellows v. LaTronica*, 151 Colo. 300, 377 P.2d 547 (1962); accord, *Rockey v. School Dist. #11*, 32 Colo. App. 203, 508 P.2d 796 (1973). See *Board of Educ. v. Scottsdale Educ. Ass'n*, 17 Ariz. App. 504, 498 P.2d 578 (1972) (rev'g trial ct.), trial ct. reversal sustained on other grounds, 109 Ariz. 342, 509 P.2d 612 (1973); *Schryver v. Schirmer*, 84 S.D. 332, 171 N.W. 2d 634 (1969); *Joint School Dist. v. WisconsinEmp. Rel. Bd.*, 37 Wis. 2d 483, 155 N.W 2d 78 (1967) (dictum); Annot., 31 A.L.R.2d 1142, 1170 (1953), and cases therein cited.

The issue of delegation in collective bargaining can sometimes be profitably considered as a matter of subdelegation— that is, whether the state had delegated to the school board or municipality the powers it was seeking to subdelegate (by bargaining). Cf. Ind. Ann. Stat. § 20-7.5-1-1(d) (Code ed. 1975). In most states, school boards exercise only those powers specifically delegated to them by the state legislature; see, e.g., *Gary Teachers Union, Local 4, AFT v. School City*, 132 Ind. App. 591, 294 N.E.2d 108 (1972). Subdelegation problems always involve initial questions of whether the subdelegating body possessed the powers it sought to delegate away. This inquiry is a matter of statutory construction, as it must be where municipal powers arise solely from statute, and the charge is that the city acted ultra vires. Ultra vires resolution, being statutory, is preferable to resolution by recourse to the delegation doctrine, which is a constitutional argument. For cases applying (and attempting to distinguish) both ultra vires and delegation doctrines, see *City & County of San Francisco v. Cooper*, 13 Cal. 3d 898, 334 P.2d 403, 120 Cal. Rptr. 707 (1973); *Jefferson Elementary School Dist. v. Bent*, 41 Cal. App. 3d 962, 116 Cal. Rptr. Z-34 (1974).

Similar delegation problems arise where municipalities or school boards agree to settle impasses in bargaining by arbitration (interest arbitration). Comment, *Collective Bargaining for Public Employees and the Prevention of Strikes in the Public Sector*, 68 Mich. L. Rev. 260, 281-88 (1969). Cf. *Gary Teachers Union, Local 4, AFT v. School City*, 152 Ind. App. 391, 284 N.E.2d 108 (1972) (grievance arbitration). The mandatory interest arbitration provisions of Maine's teacher bargaining law survived attack against a charge of unconstitutional delegation, lacking enforceable standards, where it was argued that legislative policymaking would be delegated to the arbitrators required to be used in the event of impasse. *City of Biddeford v. Biddeford Teachers Ass'n*, 304 A.2d 287 (Me. 1973) (evenly divided court) (citing and discussing delegation cases in the field of public employment labor relations), construed in *Finks v. State Highway Comm'n*, 328 A.2d 791, 795 n.2 (Me. 1974).

120. Jaffe at 226 and cases there cited. Cf. Application of *Johnston*, 69 Idaho 139, 204 P.2d 434 (1949).

121. 121 226 U.S. 137 (1912). Cf. *Gorieb v. Fox*, 274 U.S. 603 (1927).

122. 242 U.S. 526, 530 (1917), discussed in text accompanying notes 50-53 supra.

123. 278 U.S. 116 (1928), discussed in text at note 53 supra.

124. E.g., Freund, *Some Inadequately Discussed Problems of the Law of City Planning and Zoning*, 24 Ill. L. Rev. 135, 142-44 (1929), Havighurst, *Property Owners' Consent Provisions in Zoning Ordinances*, 36 L.Q. 175 (1930); McBain, *Law-Making by Property Owners*, 36 Pol. Sci. Q. 617 (1921); Jaffe at 226-28.

125. McBain, supra, note 124, at 637 n.4. Of course, there may be differences in the amount of social confict generated by the two types of provisions. It might also be argued that a purchaser of land subject to a consent statute takes subject to the restriction, but since the market may discount in advance the imposition or removal of a restriction there is little difference between the *Eubank* and *Cusack* statutes in this respect.

126. 272 U.S. 365 (1926).

127. McBain, supra, note 124, at 637.

128. Compare the law relating to government gratuities summarized in 4 K. Davis, *Administrative Law Treatise*, ch. 28 (19-58).

129. McBain, supra, note 124, at 639.

130. In the *Euclid* case, 272 U.S. at 387-88, the Court observed: "The ordinance must find [its] justification in some aspect of the police power. . . . [Tlhe law of nuisances . . . may be consulted, not for the purpose of controlling, but for the helpful aid of its analogies in the process of ascertaining the scope of the power."

131. Havighurst, supra, note 124, at 181.

132. The cases in this area are collected in A. Rathkopf, *Law of Zoning and Planning*, ch. 29 (3d ed., 1956 & Supp. 1974).

133. 260 U.S. 22 (1922) (sustaining a statute immunizing a person reconstructing a party wall from liability to his neighbor for incidental damages).

134. 2 P. Freund A. Sutherland, M. Howe, & E. Brown, *Constitutional Law: Cases and Other Problems* 1336-37 (2d ed., 1961).

135. *Doane v. Chicago City Ry. Co.*, 160 111. 22, 45 N.E. 507(1895), is a leading early case invalidating purchased consents. Of course, a purchased consent may be regarded as a private substitute for compensation in eminent domain, but the cost of the consent will be more related to benefit than damage and the prospects for inequities as between neighbors will be much greater. Similar problems arise under private leases requiring landlord consent to alterations. In *Gorleb v. Fox*, 274 U.S. 603 (1927), the Supreme Court sustained a statute requiring new houses to conform to the setback lines established by houses on the same street at the time of the enactment of the statute. Compare *Sierra Constr. Co. v. Board of Appeals*, 12 N.Y.2d 79, 187 N.E.2d 123, 236 N.Y.S.2d 53 (1962), where the court, in a 4-3 decision, sustained an ordinance requiring setback lines of new houses to conform to those established by houses on the same street which were themselves built after enactment of the ordinance. The decision seems correct; the houses were not built for the purpose of regulating the conduct of the later builder, nor are there possibilities of ad hominem determinations and purchased consents under such an ordinance.

136. Argument of Louis D. Brandeis, on behalf of the Massachusetts Protective Liquor Dealers' Ass'n, before the Joint Comm. on Liquor Law of the Massachusetts Legislature, Feb. 27, 1891, reprinted in I Hearings on the Nomination of Louis D. Brandeis before a Subcomm. of the Senate Comm. on the Judiciary 1057, 1065 (1916).

137. *Yanow v. Seven Oaks Park, Inc.*, 18 N.J. Super. 411, 87 A.2d 454 (Ch. Div. 1952), rev'd in part, 11 N.J. 341, 94 A.2d 482 (1953).

138. *Wilcher v. Sharpe*, 236 N.C. 308, 72 S.E.2d 662 (1952).

139. *Willis v. Town of Woodruff*, 200 S.C. 266, 20 S.E. 2d 699 (1942). Cf. *Niggel v. City of Columbia* , 254 S.C. 19, 173 S.E.2d 136 (1970).

140. *Leighton v. City of Minneapolis*, 16 F. Supp. 101 (D. Minn. 1936); *O'Brien v. City of St. Paul*, 285 Minn. 378, 173 N.W.2d 462 (1969).

141. *People v. Gottlieb*, 337 Mich. 276, 39 N.W.2d 289 (1953).

142. *Beacon Liquors v. Martin*, 279 Ky. 468, 131 S.W.2d 446 (1939).

143. *In re Petersen*, 51 Cal. 2d 177, 331 P.2d 24 (1958) (abutting property).

144. *Nortown Theatre, Inc. v. Gribbs*, 373 F. Supp. 363, 368-69 (E.D. Mich. 1974) (citing *Cusack*).

145. *State ex rel. Foster v. City of Minneapolis*, 255 Minn. 249, 97 N.W. 2d 273 (1959). Cf. *O'Brien v. City of St. Paul*, 285 Minn. 378, 173 N.W. 2d 462 (1969) (sustaining a consent ordinance). A result similar to the result in the *Foster* case was reached in *Marta v. Sullivan*, 248 A.2d 608 (Del. 1968).

146. *Herrington v. County of Peoria*, 11 Ill. App. 3d 7, 295 N.E.2d 731 (1973). See also *Farmer v. Meeker*, 63 N.J. Super. 56, 163 A-2d 729 (L. Div. 1956).

147. *Marren v. Gamble*, 237 N.C. 680, 75 S.E.2d 880 (1953). Cf. *Zopfi v. City of Wilmington*, 273 N.C. 430, 160 S.E.2d 325 (1968).

148. *People ex rel. Chicago Dryer Co. v. City of Chicago*, 413 Ill. 315, 109 N.E.2d 201 (1952).

149. *Eastern R.R. Presidents Conf. v. Noerr Motor Freight, Inc.*, 365 U.S. 127 (1961); *UMW v. Pennington*, 381 U.S. 657 (1965). Cf. *Continental Ore Co. v. Union Carbide & Carbon Corp.*, 370 U.S. 690 (1962). See Costilo, *The Scope of the Noerr - Pennington Doctrine*, 34 Antitrust L.J. 141 (1967). It is not without significance that the Noerr doctrine has been held partly inapplicable in the context of judicial as distinct from

legislative action. *California Motor Transp. Co. v. Trucking Unlimited*, 404 U.S. 508 (1972).

One court has intimated the unconstitutionality of such a statute. *Costanzo v. New Jersey Racing Comm'n*, 126 N.J. Super. 187, 313 A.2d 618 (App. Div. 1974).

150. A. Flexner, *Medical Education in the United States and Canada* (1910).

151. *Jones v. Kansas State Bd. of Medical Regis. & Educ.*, 111 Kan. 813, 814, 208 P. 639 (1922); accord, *Ex parte Gerino*, 143 Cal. 412, 77 P. 166 (1904). See also *Hewitt v. Charier*, 33 Mass. (16 Pick.) 353 (1835), typical of the nineteenth century cases.

152. See Jaffe at 230; cf. Quirin, *Physician Licensing and Educational Obsolescence: A Medical-Legal Dilemma*, 36 Albany L. Rev. 503, 505-07 (1972).

153. State ex rel. *Kaplan v. Dee*, 77 So. 2d 768 (Fla. 1955).

154. *Attwood v. State ex rel. Newman*, 53 So. 2d 825 (Fla. 1951); *Spencer v. Hunt*, 109 Fla. 248, 147 So. 282 (1933).

155. *Allen v. State Bd. of Veterinarians*, 72 R.I. 372, 52 A.2d 131 (1947). Cf. *State v. Hynds*, 61 Ariz. 281, 148 P.2d 1000 (1944), where the court upheld a statute requiring graduation from an approved school of chiropody, without construing the statute, noting only that it did not delegate power to an association.

156. *Ex parte State Bd. of Law Examiners*, 141 Fla. 706, 193 So. 753 (1940).

157. *Marjorie Webster Junior College v. Middle States Ass'n of Colleges & Secondary Schools*, 432 F.2d 650 (D.C. Cir.), cert. denied, 400 U.S. 965 (1970). In *People v. Barksdale*, 8 Cal. 3d 320, 337, 503 P.2d 257, 269, 105 Cal. Rptr. 1, 13 (1972), there are dicta to the effect that "reliance upon the standards of professional accrediting bodies is not an unconstitutional delegation of governmental power if it is neither arbitrary, unreasonable, nor discriminatory." Cf. Kessel, *Price Discrimination in Medicine*, 1 J.L. & Econ. 20, 27 (1958). Statutes that merely provide for education in a school maintaining standards equal to those prevailing in approved schools do not disturb the courts. See *State ex rel. Beck v. Gleason*, 148 Kan. 1, 79 P.2d 911 (1938). For an earlier view, see E. Freund, *Administrative Powers Over Persons and Property* 47 (1928): "In attempting to secure desirable standards, the legislature may deem it advisable not to establish such standards directly by law or even by administrative regulation, but to rely upon parties to put their own house in order. . . . [A] form of such utilization is the official employment of organizations having a recognized monopoly of representation of interests. This type is found in the regulation of professions. It was formerly common, but is somewhat inconsistent with modern principles of public law. New York dropped the systern in 1910, but it still survives to some extent in England (Royal College of Veterinary Surgeons)."

158. 341 U.S. 123 (1951). Cf. *Barrows v. Jackson*, 346 U.S. 249 (1953); *Pierce v. Society of Sisters*, 268 U.S. 510 (1925).

159. See Note, *The State Courts and Delegation of Public Autthority to Private Groups*, 67 Harv. L. Rev. 1398 (1954). The accreditation of hospitals by the Joint Commission on Accreditation of Hospitals raises similar delegation problems. Worthington & Silver, *Regulation of Quality of Care in Hospitals: The Need for Change*, 35 Law & Contem. Prob. 305, 320 n.68 (1970).

160. Such statutes were invalidated in *City of Tucson v. Stewart*, 45 Ariz. 36, 40 P.2d 72 (1935) (here the approved methods were made only prima facie evidence); *Agnew v. City of Culver City*, 147 Cal. App. 2d 144, 304 P.2d 788 (1956); *State v. Crawford*, 104 Kan. 141, 177 P. 360 (1919); *Hillman v. Northern Wasco County People's Util. Dist.*, 213 Ore. 264, 323 P.2d 664 (1958). However, a more recent case upheld a similar statute

against attack on delegation grounds, finding no actual delegation. *Kingery v. Chapple*, P.2d 831, 836-37 n.13 (Alaska 1972).

161. Cf. *Radiant Burners, Inc. v. Peoples Gas Light & Coke Co.*, 364 U.S. 656, 659 (1961), where a boycott by public utilities of persons using gas burners failing to conform to American Gas Association standards was held a per se violation of the Sherman Act. The association consisted of utilities, manufacturers of gas burners, and pipeline companies. In a suit brought against the association by a manufacturer of unapproved burners, the Court observed that the association's "tests are not based on objective standards, but are influenced by respondents, some of whom are in competition with petitioner, and thus its determinations can be made arbitrarily and capriciously." It is not clear that the result in this case rests on the participation of competitors in the association. See Bird, *Sherman Act Limitations on Non-Commercial Concerted Refusals to Deal*, 1970 Duke L.J. 247; Comment, *Use of Economic Sanctions by Private Groups: Illegalityunder the Sherman Act*, 30 U. Chi. L. Rev 171 (1962). Cf. *Roofire Alarm Co. v. Royal Indem. Co.*, 202 F. Supp. 166 (E.D. Tenn. 1962), aff'd, 313 F.2d 635 (6th Cir.), cert. denied, 370 U.S. 949 (1963), holding that a primary boycott by a testing association, none of whose members were in competition with the plaintiff, was not actionable under the Sherman Act.

162. The antipathy toward "private government" is reflected in many Sherman Act cases and, of course, plays a prominent role in that Act's folklore. See, e.g., T. Arnold, *The Bottlenecks of Business* (1940). In *Addyston Pipe & Steel Co. v. United States*, 175 U.S. 211, 242 (1899), it was said that the condemned violation "trenches upon the power of the national legislature and violates the statute." In *Fashion Originators' Guild of America v. FTC*, 312 U.S. 457, 465 (1941), it was said that the combination is in reality, an extra-governmental agency, which prescribes rules for the regulation and restraint of interstate commerce, and provides extra-judicial tribunals for determination and punishment of violations." See also *Associated Press v. United States*, 326 U.S. 1, 19 (1943). But cf. *Sugar Institute v. United States*, 297 U.S. 553, 598 (1936): "Voluntary action to end abuses and to foster fair competitive opportunities in the public interest may be more effective than legal processes. And cooperative endeavor may appropriately have wider objectives than merely the removal of evils which are infractions of positive law." Cf. also the curious decision in *Silver v. New York Stock Exch.*, 373 U.S. 341 (1963) (holding that the availability to a private group of a statutory exemption from the antitrust laws was dependent upon the extent of the hearing the private group accorded to nonmembers), construed in *Gordon v. New York Stock Exch.*, 422 U.S. 659 (1975).

It is significant that the references to "private goverrunent" rarely occur in the context of simple price-fixing, where the price-fixing is unaccompanied by elements of boycott. It has been suggested that there are even limitations on the per se illegality of boycotts, some commentators finding these in noncommercial purpose. See Coons, *Non-Commercial Purpose as a Sherman Act Defense*, 56 N. W. U.L. Rev. 705 (1962); Cf. *Klor's Inc. v. Broadway-Hale Stores*, 359 U.S. 207, 213 n.7 (1959). Others hold that the per se prohibition extends only to secondary, as opposed to primary, boycotts. See Comment, *Use of Economic Sanctions by Private Groups: Illegality Under the Sherman Act*, 30 U. Chi. L. Rev., 171 (1962). For a classic attack on boycotts as a form of private government, see Stephen, *On the Suppression of Boycotting*, 20 The Nineteenth Century 765 (1886). See generally Posner, *Exclusionary Practices of the Antitrust Laws*, 41 U. Chi. L. Rev. 506 (1974).

163. Such statutes were upheld in the cases of *White v. State Bd. of Pharmacy*, 285 App. Div. 486, 138 N.Y.S.2d 448 (1953); and *State v. Wakeen*, 263 Wis. 401, 37 N.W.2d 364 (1953). For a similar view, see *Osco Drug, Inc. v. Pharmacy Exam. Bd.*, 61 Wis. 2d 689, 695, 214 N.W.2d 47, 50 (1974) (Hansen, T., dissenting).

164. For a description of the organization, see Note, *State Regulation of Drugs: Who May Sell "Patent and Proprietary" Medicines*, 63 Yale L.J. 550, 552 n.10 (1954).

165. See generally Annot., 18 A.L.R.3d 944, 965-69 (1968), and cases there cited. Criminal statutes of this type can raise void-for-vagueness problems. See *Connally v. General Constr. Co.*, 269 U.S. 385 (1926). The federal Davis-Bacon Act, 40 U.S.C. § 276a (1970), and Walsh-Healey Act, 41 U.S.C. § 35 (1970), embody similar standards.

166. *Wagner v. City of Milwaukee*, 177 Wis. 410, 411, 188 N.W. 487 (1922).

167. *Bradley v. Casey*, 415 111. 576, 114 N.E.2d 681 (1953).

168. *Baughn v. Gorrell & Riley*, 311 Ky. 537, 540, 224 S.W.2d 436, 438 (1949) (quoting the statute).

169. *Schryver v. Schirmer*, 84 S.D. 352, 171 N.W.2d 634, (1969). A possible distinction from prior cases was articulated by the court: "We see very little or no similarity between the character of the work performed by city firemen and that of the . . . tradesmen designated in the ordinance." Id. at 637. A statute that set a wage rate for municipal employees based on that in a neighboring municipality was upheld in *Kugler v. Yocum*, 69 Cal. 2d 371, 445 P.2d 303, 71 Cal. Rptr. 687 (1968).

170. *Male v. Ernest Renda Contracting Co.*, 64 N.J. 199, 314 A.2d 361 (1974).

171. *Chambers v. Ohio Bureau of Unemp. Comp.*, 15 Ohio Supp. 106, 30 Ohio Op. 1 (C.P. 1944), rev'd, sub nom. *Chambers v. Owens-Ames-Kimball Co.*, 44 Ohio L. Abs. 146, 62 N.E.2d 496 (Ct. App. 1945), rev'd, 146 Ohio St. 559, 33 Ohio Op. 60, 67 N.E.2d 439 (1946).

172. *In re Fiol*, 279 App. Div. 963, 111 N.Y.S.2d 288, appeal denied, 280 App. Div. 901, 115 N.Y.S.2d 311 (1952), remanded, 305 N.Y. 264, 112 N.E.2d 281 (1953), on remand, 284 App. Div. 519, 132 N.Y.S.2d 533 (1954), aff'd, 309 N.Y. 661, 128 N.E.2d 317 (1955).

173. As to conformity with "company rules" as evidence of due care in negligence actions, see C. Gregory & H. Kalven, *Cases and Materials on Torts* 143-43 (2d ed. 1969). See also Jaffe at 113-49. On the reach of corporate bylaws, see A. Dicey, *Introduction to The Study of the Law of the Constitution* 71-77 (10th ed., 1960); 3 R. Pound, *Jurisprudence* 652-54 (1959).

174. The cases are collected in 2 *Trade Reg.* Rep. para. 6021. See *Bulova Watch Co. v. Brand Distribs., Inc.*, 283 N.C. 467, 206 S.E.2d 141 (1974).

175. *Standard Drug Co. v. General Elec. Co.*, 202 Va. 367, 117 S.E.2d 289 (1960), appeal dismissed, 368 U.S. 4 (1961).

176. *Hudson Distribs. v. Upjohn Corp.*, 174 Ohio St. 487, 190 N.E.2d 460 (1963), aff'd, 377 U.S. 386 (1964).

177. *Ingersoll & Bro. v. Hahne & Co.*, 88 N.J. Eq. 222, 101 A. 1030 (Ch. Ct. 1917).

178. E.g., *Corning Glass Works v. Ann & Hope, Inc.*, 294 N.E.2d 354 (Mass. 1973); *Bulova Watch Co. v. Brand Distribs., Inc.*, 285 N.C. 467, 206 S.E.2d 141 (1974).

179. E.g., *Bissell Carpet Sweeper Co. v. Shane Co.*, 237 Ind. 188, 143 N.E.2d 415 (1957). But see *Louisiana Motor Vehicle Comm'n v. Wheeling Frenchman*, 235 La. 332, 103 So. 2d 464 (1958).

180. *General Elec. Co. v. Wahle*, 207 Ore. 30, 296 P.2d 635 (1956).

181. This may well be the modern view. See *Bulova Watch Co. v. Brand Distribs., Inc.*, 285 N.C. 467, 206 S.E.2d 141 (1974).

182. E.g., *Miles Laboratories v. Eckerd*, 73 So. 2d 680 (Fla. 1954).

183. E.g., *American Home Prods. Corp. v. Homsey*, 361 P.2d 297 (Okla. 1961).

184. *McGraw Elec. Co. v. Lewis & Smith Drug Co.*, 159 Neb. 703, 68 N.W. 2d 608 (1955).

185. E.g., *General Elec. Co. v. Whale*, 207 Ore. 302, 296 P.2d 635 (1956).

186. *Old Dearborn Distrib. Co. v. Scagram-DistillersCorp.*, 299 U.S. 183 (1936). On the willingness of courts to authorize delegations when linked to familiar categories of property or contract, see Note, *The State Courts and Delegation of Public Authority to Private Groups*, 67 Harv. L. Rev., 1398 (1954). Cases at common law not involving constitutional questions have occasionally authorized what are in effect "delegations," by analogy, to equitable servitudes on land. Cf. Chafee, *Equitable Servitudes on Chattels*, 41 Harv. L. Rev. 945 (1928). Of course, even land servitudes may be viewed as "delegations." Perhaps their respectability derives from the fact that they have been traditionally recognized at conunon law. That only underlines the fact that the nondelegation doctrine rests largely on a confusion of the familiar with the necessary. For suggestions that decisions in this area should turn on the extent to which survival outside the contract is feasible, see Chafee, *The Internal Affairs of Associations*, 43 Harv. L. Rev. 993, 1021-23 (1930).

187. *Scovill Mfg. Co. v. Skaggs Payless Drug Stores*, 45 Cal. 2d 881, 291 P.2d 936 (1955). See Hale, *Our Equivocal Constitutional Guaranties*, 39 Colum. L. Rev. 563, 576 (1939): "It is . . . seldom recognized that when the state is enforcing contract and property rights at common law it is using its compulsory powers to effectuate the wills of private persons, and doing so in a manner which forces other private persons to forego the exercise of liberties which the state could not constitutionally deny them in furtherance of any legislative policy of its own other than that of enforcing contracts or protecting property." Pushed to its extreme, the nondelegation doctrine could be viewed as precluding any public protection or recognition of private property rights, cf. Cohen, *Property and Sovereignty*, 13 Cornell L.Q. 8 (1927), or at least any legislative extension or enforcement of them that goes beyond the "common law." Cf. *Bell v. Maryland*, 378 U.S. 226, 286, 304 (1964) (Goldberg, J., concurring); *Katzenbach v. Morgan*, 384 U.S. 641, 657 (1966) (emphasis added) : "The principle that calls for the closest scrutiny of distinctions in laws denying fundamental rights . . . is inapplicable for the distinction challenged by appellees is presented only as a limitation on a reform measure." See also *San Antonio Ind. School Dist. v. Rodriguez*, 411 U.S. 1, 54-55 (1973); *Macmillan v. Board of Educ.*, 430 F.2d 1145 (2d Cir. 1970).

188. A trial judge upheld the "implied contract" provision of the Virginia act by analogy to contracts of adhesion in insurance law. See Brief for Appellant at 3-4, *Standard Drug Co. v. General Elec. Co.*, 368 U.S. 4 (1961).

189. See, e.g., *Corning Glass Works v. Dichter*, 102 N.H. 505, 161 A.2d 569 (1960). Cf. *Vornado, Inc. v. Corning Glass Works*, 255 F. Supp. 216 (D.N.J. 1966).

190. *Schwegmann Bros. Giant Super Mkts. v. Eli Lilly & Co.*, 205 F.2d 788, 792 (5th Cir.), cert. denied, 346 U.S. 856 (1953): "It was, we think, within the province of the legislature to assume that economic laws constitute a sufficient restraint against capricious or arbitrary price fixing by the producer. As pointed out long ago by Louis D. (later Mr. Justice) Brandeis, the producer establishes his price at his peril the peril that if he sets it too high, either the consumer will not buy or, if the article is, nevertheless, popular, the

high profits will invite even more competition." Cf. *Daniel v. Famlly Sec. Life Ins. Co.*, 336 U.S. 220, 225 n. 5 (1949).

191. 2 El. & B. 216, 118 Eng. Rep. 749 (Q.B. 1853). See *Max Factor & Co. v. Kunsman*, 3 Cal. 2d 446, 55 P.2d 177, aff'd. 299 U.S. 198 (1936). Cf. *Bissell Carpet Sweeper Co. v. Shane Co.*, 237 Ind. 188, 143 N.E. 415 (1957), where the nonsigner clause was upheld insofar as it codified this doctrine.

192. Where distribution was thus restricted, it could be presumed that any nonsigner selling goods had induced the breach of a signer's contract. See *Sunbeam Corp. v. Payless Drug Stores*, 113 F. Supp. 31 (N.D. Cal. 1953). This doctrine, in more highly developed form, supplies the basis of resale price maintenance in Germany, where actions against nonsigners are not expressly provided by statute. See Schapiro, *The Gernan Law against Restraints of Competition: Comparative and International Aspects*, 62 Colum. L. Rev. 1, 201, 207 (1962).

193. *United States v. Bausch & Lomb Optical Co.*, 321 U.S. 707 (1944). Cf. *Copper Liquor, Inc., v. Adolph Coors Co.*, 506 F.2d 934, 946 (5th Cir. 1975).

194. See, e.g., *Sunbeam Corp. v. Masters of Miami*, 225 F.2d 191 (5th Cir. 1955). But see *Staufier Chem. Co. v. Allied Gas & Chem. Co.*, 328 F. Supp. 785 (S.D. Iowa 1971).

195. E.g., *Eli Lilly Co. v. Saunders*, 216 N.C. 163, 4 S.E.2d 528 (1939); , 225 Wis. 474, 274 N.W. 426 (1937). But cf. *Corning Glass Works v. Ann & Hope, Inc.*, 294 N.E.2d 354, 362 (Mass. 1973).

196. See the concurring opinion of Justices Harlan and Frankfurter in *Lathrop v. Donohue*, 367 U.S. 820, 855 (1961) (emphasis in original): "Moreover, it is by no means clear to me in what part of the Federal Constitution we are to find the prohibition of state-authorized self-regulation of and by an economic group that the Schechter case found in Article I as respects the Federal Government. Is state-authorized self-regulation of lawyers to be the occasion for Judicial enforcement of Art. IV § 4, which provides that 'The United States shall guarantee to every state in this union a Republican form of government . . .'?" Justice Douglas, dissenting, was able only to observe that "[a] self-policing provision whereby lawyers were given the power to investigate and disbar their associates would raise under most, if not all, state constitutions the type of problem posed in [Schechter]." 367 U.S. at 878 n.1. See generally D. McKean, The Integrated Bar (1963).

197. Cf. *Thomas Cusack Co. v. City of Chicago*, 242 U.S. 526 (1917). But see *Railway Employees Dep't, AFL v. Hanson*, 351 U.S. 225 (1956), where closed shop contracts were held to constitute state action since a federal enactment removed barriers to their validity imposed by state law. Even this rule would not necessarily extend to conduct legitimized by a federal enactment that removes barriers to validity imposed by federal law. See *United States v. National Ass'n of Sec. Dealers*, 422 U.S. 694 (1975). There might also be a paradox in holding, first, that the acts of price-maintaining manufacturers are "legislative," so as to run afoul of the delegation doctrine, and, second, that such acts are private acts so as to require special federal antitrust immunity despite the rule of *Parker v. Brown*, 317 U.S. 34.1 (1943). See Rahl, *Resale Price Maintenance, State Action, and the Antitrust Laws*, 46 Ill. L. Rev. 349 (1951). See also Rahl, *Control of an Agent's Prices: The Simpson Case—A Study in Antitrust Analysis*, 61 NW. U.L. Rev. 1 (1966).

198. There is merit in Justice Hughes' remark in Carter that this approach "would remove all restrictions upon the delegation of legislative power, as the making of laws could thus be referred to any designated officials or private persons whose orders or agreements would be treated as 'events,' with the result that they would be invested with the force of law having penal sanctions." 298 U.S. at 318.

199. Jaffe, *An Essay on Delegation of Legislative Power*, 47 Colum. L. Rev. 561 (1947). Resale price maintenance in the book trade has been defended on this basis. *In re Net Book Agreement*, I W.L.R. 1347 (R.P.C. 1962); *In re Associated Booksellers of New Zealand*, [1962] N.Z.L.R. 1057 (Trade Prac. App. Auth.). The copyright monopoly has been similarly defended. Chafee, *Reflections on the Law of Copyright, I*, 45 Colum. L. Rev. 503, 519 (1945).

200. See Note, *The State Courts and Delegation of Public Authority to Private Groups*, 67 Harv. L. Rev. 1398 (1954).

201. Of course, critics of the legislation frequently contend that the power to impose price conditions is equivalent to the power to exclude. But courts, paradoxically, have frequently viewed statutes that require manufacturers to set resale prices with greater indulgence than statutes that merely permit them to do so. Cf. *Allied Properties v. Department of Alcoholic Beverage Control*, 53 Cal. 2d 141, 130, 346 P.2d 737, 741-42 (1959), where it was observed: "One of the new features is that the Alcoholic Beverage Control Act requires, rather than permits, producers and wholesalers to set retail prices. This fact, however, does not render the function of the producer or wholesaler legislative in character but, to the contrary, decreases his discretion since he is not free to determine whether fair trading should occur. While mandatory fair trading means that retailers cannot obtain merchandise free from price restrictions, this is due to the determination of the Legislature, not the action of the producers and wholesalers." See also *Schenley Affil. Brands Corp. v. Kirby*, 21 Cal. App. 3d 177, 98 Cal. Rptr. 609 (1971).

202. This was the view of the *Old Dearborn* case, 292 U.S. at 192.

203. See Levi, infra note 204. Cf. Bork, *The Rule of Reason and the Per Se Concept: Price Fixing and Market Division* 2, 75 Yale L.J. 373 (1966); Bork, *A Reply to Professors Gould and Yamey*, 76 Yale L.J. 731 (1967); Bork, *Resale Price Maintenance and Consumer Welfare*, 77 Yale L.T. 950 (1968).

204. It was suggested at an earlier time that individual refusals to deal were themselves constitutionally protected. See Levi, *The Parke, Davis-Colgate Doctrine: The Ban on Resale Price Maintenance*, 1960 Sup. CT. Rev. 258, 284 n.143, citing *Grenada Lumber Co. v. Mississippi*, 217 U.S. 433, 440 (1910) ("That any one of the persons engaged in the retail lumber business might have made a fixed rule of conduct not to buy his stock from a producer or wholesaler who should sell to consumers in competition with himself, is plain. No law which would infringe his freedom of contract in that particular would stand.") The force of that decision is strengthened rather than weakened by the fact that it involved a secondary as opposed to primary refusal to deal and hence countenanced injury to an innocent neutral. That legislation (e.g., open-occupancy and dealer franchise statutes) impairing the right may be valid would seem by now to be clear. Significantly, the restriction of the use of trespass statutes to enforce refusals to deal based on racial distinctions took place against a background of collective discrimination, including secondary boycotts. For other authorities suggesting the narrowing scope of the individual right, see, in addition to the antitrust cases discussed in *Parke, Davis*, the following authorities: *Bergen Drug Co. v. Parke, Davis & Co.*, 307 F.2d 725 (3d Cir. 1962) (refusal to deal with treble damage suitor held antitrust violation); *Schnapps Shop, Inc. v. H.W.*

Wright & Co., 377 F. Supp. 570 (D. Md. 1973). See Posner, *Exclusionary Practices and the Antitrust Laws*, 41 U. Chi. L. Rev. 506 (1974). These antitrust decisions are of arguable merit in the light of the fact that section 1 of the Sherman Act purports to reach only contracts, combinations, and conspiracies. 15 U.S.C. § 1 (1970).

205. *FTC v. Beech-Nut Packing Co.*, 257 U.S. 441, 457 (1921) (Holmes, J., dissenting).

206. See *Moog Indus. v. FTC*, 355 U.S. 411 (1958) (indicating the wide discretion left to the FTC).

207. The discretion of trademark proprietors under the fair trade acts was limited by a number of equitable doctrines that did not restrict public agencies. Where uniform enforcement was not shown, courts might refuse or dissolve injunctions or grant them conditionally. In addition, disfavored retailers might sue their competitors under many state acts.

208. 118 U.S. 356 (1886).

209. See, e.g., *State v. LeVien*, 44 N.J. 323, 209 A.2d 97 (1965).

210. E.g., Conant, *Constitutionality of Non-Signer Clauses*, 109 U. Pa. L. Rev. 539 (1961).

211. See cases cited in 4 K. Davis, Administrative Law Trestise § 28.19 (1958) (review); 1 id. § 7.19 (Supp. 1970) (hearing).

212. Cf. *Bi-Metallic Inv. Co. v. State Bd. of Equalization*, 239 U.S. 441 (1915); *Bell Tel. Co. v. FCC*, 503 F.2d 1250, 1266 (3rd Cir. 1974).

213. For a vigorous economic defense of the practice, see P. Andrews & F. Friday, *Fair Trade: Resale Price Maimtenance Re-Examined* (1960). Such works, however, are in a distinct minority. See, e.g., Hudson, *Constitutionality of the Florida Fair Trade Act and Continuing Myths of Resale Price Maintenance*, 24 U. Fla. L. Rev. 641 (1972). The issues are ably defined in A. Neale, T*he Antitrust Laws of the United States of America*, 336-64 (2d ed. 1970). The federal authorizations of state fair trade laws were repealed in 1976.

214. Cf. the justification of the practice in *The Brandeis Guide to the Modern World*, 218 (A. Lief ed., 1941): "The fixing of the price has possibly prevented one retailer from selling the article a little lower than the other, but the fixing of that price has tended not to suppress but to develop competition, because it has made it possible in the distribution of those goods to go to an expense and to open up another sphere of merchandising which would have been absolutely impossible without a fixed price. The whole world can be drawn into the field. Every dealer, every small stationer, every small druggist, every small hardwareman can be made a purveyor of that article by comprehensive advertising and you have stimulated, through the fixed price, the little owner as against the department store."

215. Decisions condemning price maintenance statutes contrasted strangely with the reluctance of many of the same state courts to narrow the range of administrative actions made unreviewable by statute and with the willingness of many courts to justify arbitrary denial of occupational licenses on the basis that "privileges" rather than "rights" are involved. See cases cited in 1 K. Davis, Administrative Law Treatise § 7.19 (Supp. 1970).

216. See, e.g., W. Gellhorn, *Federal Administrative Proceedings*, 116-44 (1941). Delegation problems inherent in student or faculty adjudicatory discipline committees in state colleges and universities are discussed in Hornby, *Delegating Authority to the Community of Scholars*, 1975 Duke L.J. 279.

217. *A.L.A Schechter Poultry Corp. v. United States*, 295 U.S. 495, 552 (1935) (concurring opinion).

218. E. Freund, *Administrative Powers Over Persons and Property* 52 (1928). A few federal bodies had been constituted on the principle of interest representation prior to Freund's work. See generally Chamberlain, *Democratic Control of Administration*, 13 A.B.A.J. 186 (1927). Note in particular Act of May 28, 1924, ch. 202, § 3, 43 Stat. 177, 178; Act of June 7, 1924, ch. 315, § 2, 43 Stat. 599 (District of Columbia Optometry Board, Dental Board); Act of Feb. 28, 1920, ch. 91, § 304, 41 Stat. 456, 470 (Railway Labor Board provision of Esch-Cunmings Act). The Federal Reserve Board open-market committees elected by directors of federal reserve banks pursuant to 12 U.S.C. § 263 (1970) supply one such example. The participation of three members elected by bar associations in the seven-man judicial nominating commissions under the so-called Missouri Plan provide another, less clear example. Delegations to professional bodies, like delegations to public utilities, are frequently deemed unobjectionable by reason of the "duty to serve" assumed to limit such bodies in the exercise of the granted powers or by reason of the job mobility and consequent greater independence of professionals. See De Grazia, *Public and Republic*, 219 (1951).

219. *Fink v. Cole*, 302 N.Y. 216, 97 N.E.2d 873 (1951); *Murtha v. Monaghan*, Misc. 2d 568, 169 N.Y.S.2d 137 (Sup. Ct.), aff'd mem., 5 App. Div. 2d 695, 169 N.Y.S.2d 1010 (195), aff'd mem., 4 N.Y.2d 897, 151 N,.E.2d 83 (1959).

220. *Hetherington v. McHale*, 329 A.2d 250 (Pa. 1974).

221. *Union Trust Co. v. Simmons*, 116 Utah 422, 211 P.2d 190 (1949). See also *Montana-Dakota Util. Co. v. Johanneson*, 153 N.W.2d 414 (N.D. 1967) (invalidating statute requiring consent of a rural electric cooperative as a condition to granting a certificate of convenience to a public utility).

222. *Group Health Ins. v. Howell*, 40 N.J. 436, 447, 193 A.2d 103, 109 (1963). See also *Humane Soc'y of the United States v. New Jersey State Fish & Game Council*, 129 N.J. Super. 239, 322 A.2d 841 (Ch. Div. 1974) (appointment to Fish and Game Council limited to sportsmen, farmers, or commercial fishermen).

223. Group Health Ins. v. Howell, 43 N.J. 104, 202 A.2d 689 (1964).

224. See generally Heuerman, *Dealer Territory Security and "Bootlegging" in the Auto Industry*, 1962 Wis. L. Rev. 486.

225. *Ohio Motor Vehicle Dealers' & Salesmen's Lic. Bd. v. Memphis Auto Sales*, 103 Ohio App. 347, 356, 3 Ohio Op. 2d 377, 382, 142 N.E 2d 268, 274 (1957). The decision also condemned the statute as violative of a constitutional prohibition against "special laws" and on substantive due process grounds.

226. E.g., *Joyner v. Centre Motor Co.*, 192 Va. 627, 66 S.E.2d 469 (1951), which condemned an "anti-bootlegging" statute as a special law, the decision also partly resting on delegation grounds. The constitutionality of a similar South Dakota statute was upheld, in the dissent urging application of the nondelegation doctrine. *In re Hinesley*, 82 S.D. 532, 558, 150 N.W.2d 834, 837 (1967); accord, *Semke v. State ex rel. Oklahoma Motor Vehicle Comm'n*, 465 P.2d 441 (Okla. 1970) (within police power).

227. *Louisiana Motor Vehicle Comm'n v. Wheeling Frenchman*, 235 La. 332, 346Y 103 So. 2d 464, 469 (1958). Cf. Annot., 7 A.L.R 3d 1173, 1192 (1966).

228. 235 La. at 350, 103 So. 2d at 471.

229. *White Motor Co. v. United States*, 372 U.S. 253 (1963). See *Dr. Miles Medical Co. v. John D. Park & Sons Co.*, 220 U.S. 373 (1911).

230. 57 Cal. 2d 228, 368 P.2d 101, 18 Cal. Rptr. 501 (1962). Cf. *D'Amico v. Board of Medical Examiners*, 11 Cal. 3d 1, 520 P.2d 10, 112 Cal. Rptr. 786 (1974). The analogy of many such statutory schemes to the medieval and post medieval guilds is a close one, though this fact ought not be considered dispositive of their validity. See Grant, *The Guild Returns to America*, 4 J. Politics 303, 458 (1942).

231. 57 Cal. 2d at 235, 236, 368 P.2d at 104, 105, 104, 18 Cal. Rptr. at 504, 505, 504 (1962).

232. One might contrast older state bar association reqirements of apprenticeship.

233. Cf. Buttenweiser, *The Young Doctors' Dilemma*, 193 The Nation 429 (1961).

234. See, e.g., *Easton v. Grubbs*, 329 F. 2d 710 (4th Cir. 1964); *Greisman v. Newcomb Hosp.*, 40 N.J. 389. 192 A. 2d 817 (1963), But see *People v. Barksdale*, 8 Cal. 3d 320, 337, 503 P.2d 257, 270, 105 Cal. Rptr. 1, 13 (1972).

235. *Proceedings in Memory of Mr. Justice Brandeis*, 317 U.S ix, xiii-xiv, xv (1942) (remarks of Learned Hand).

236. 330 U.S. 552 (1947). The *Blumenthal* case was extended even further by the decision in *Rosner v. Peninsula Hosp. Dist.*, 224 Cal. App. 2d 115, 36 Cal. Rptr. 332 (1964), which invalidated as a delegation of power to insurance companies a statute requiring doctors in state hospitals to post malpractice insurance. This decision in effect precluded the state from electing to use the market as an appraiser of the qualifications of its doctors (since there was no showing that insurance companies would be motivated by considerations other than profit in deciding whether to insure particular doctors). While most of the delegation decisions thus far considered would be applauded by devotees of a free market, the *Rosner* case well revealed that the doctrine can cut both ways, since invalidation of statutes on this ground will frequently present the state with only two alternatives: no regulation at all or regulation via public ownership or direct admistrative control.

237. McCloskey, Economic Due Process and the Supreme Court: An Exhumation and Reburial, 1962 Sup. Ct. Rev. 34, 46.

238. See Twain's amusing account, *The Pilots' Monopoly*, in *Life on the Mississippi*, ch. 15 (1967). Twain himself seems not to have been adverse to resale price maintenance either. See *Clemens v. Estes*, 22 F. 899 (C.C.D. Mass. 1885).

239. Cf. *McGautha v. California*, 402 U.S. 183, 199-201 (1971); Note, *The Power of Dispensation in Administrative Law*, A Critical Survey, 87 U. Pa. L. Rev. 201 (1938).

240. E. Freund, *Administrative Powers Over Persons and Property*, 48 (1928) (footnotes omitted).

241. Co. 113b, 2 Brown. 255, 77 Eng. Rep. 646 (1610).

242. See generally Plucknett, *Bonham's Case and Judicial Review*, 40 Harv. L. Rev. 30 (1926).

243. 8 Co. at 118a, 77 Eng. Rep. at 652. Cf. *Ward v. Village of Monroeville*, 409 U.S. 57 (1972).

244. See especially *Groenvelt v. Burwell*, I Raym. 213, 252, 454, 91 Eng. Rep. 1038, 1065, 1202 (K.E. 1697-99), which modified several of the holdings in *Bonham's Case*; see also *College of Physicians v. Levett*, I Raym. 472, 91 Eng. Rep. 1214 (K.B. 1699).

245. "And it was well ordained, that the professors of physic should be profound, sad, discreet, &c and not youths, who have no gravity and experience," 77 Eng. Rep. at 651.

246. "[F]ive manner of persons were to be promoted, as appears by the said Act, those who were: 1, profound; 2, sad; 3, discreet; 4, groundly learned; 5, profoundly studied." Id.

247. 77 Eng. Rep. at 657-58. These questions are no more settled now than they were then. See K. Davis, *Administrative Law Treatise* §§ 26.01.07 (Supp. 1970).

248. See, e.g., *Upchurch v. Adelsberger*, 231 Ark. 682, 332 S.W.2d 242 (1960). See generally 10 E. McQuillin, *The Law of Municipal Corporations* § 29.48 (1966), and cases there cited.

249. Two cases invalidating statutes requiring the label of a specific union are *Upchurch v. Adelsberger*, 231 Ark. 682, 332 S.W.2d 242 (1960); *International Printing Pressmen & Assistants Union v. Meier*, 115 N.W.2d 18, 20 (N.D. 1962): "Here we are not concerned with a law which requires union labor or the use of a union label, but we are considering the validity of a statute which requires the use of one particular union label . . . to the detriment of all other union labels. Thus the argument advanced by the appellants that the requirement of a union label guarantees superior work is irrelevant because the Conrad company does have a union label; it merely does not have the right to use the particular label which is required by our law."

250. See notes 166-68 supra.

251. See 65 Am. Jur. 2d Public Works and Contracts § 201 (1972).

252. 15 U.S.C. § 780-3 (1970). See generally *Nassau Sec. Serv. v. SEC*, 348 F.2d 133 (2d Cir. 1965); Rutter, *The National Association of Securities Dealers*, 7 Vill. L. Rev. 611 (1962).

253. *R.H. Johnson & Co. v. SEC*, 198 F.2d 690, 695 (2d Cir.), cert. denied, 344 U.S. 855 (1952). See *United States v. National Ass'n of Sec. Dealers*, 95 S. Ct. 2427 (1975) (by implication). Cf. *United Black Fund, Inc. v. Hampton*, 352 F. Supp. 898, 904 (D.C. Cir. 1972). See generally Jennings, *Self Regulation in the Securities Industry: The Role of the Securities and Exchange Commission*, 29 Law & Contemp. Prob. 663, 679-90 (1964); Hed-Hoffmann, *The Maloney Act Experiment*, 6 B.C. Ind. & Com. L. Rev. 187 (1965); Rediker, *Civil Liability of Broker-Dealers under SEC and NASD Suitability Rules*, 22 Ala. Rev. 15 (1969); Comment, *Implied Civil Liability Arising from Violations ion of the Rules of the National Association of Securities Dealers*, 8 Loy. L.A.L. Rev. 151 (1975).

254. The Securities Act amendment of 1964 retained the automatic stay pending appeal to the SEC but allowed the SEC after notice and brief hearing (upon affidavit and oral argument) to set aside the stay in particular cases. 15 U.S.C. § 780-3(g) (1970); cf. *Harwell v. Growth Programs, Inc.*, 451 F.2d 240 (5th Cir. 1971) (existence of antitrust immunity a question of fact); *Ricci v. Chicago Mercantile Exch.*, 409 U.S. 289 (1973).

255. See *Hogan v. State Bar*, 36 Cal. 2d 807, 228 P.2d 554 (1951). Cf. note 196 supra.

256. 45 U.S.C. §§ 151-63, (1970).

257. See generally Garrison, The National Railroad Adjustment Board: A Unique Administrative Agency, 46 Yale L.J. 567, 584 (1937).

258. *Union Pac. Ry. v. Price*, 360 U.S. 601 (1959).

259. *Gunther v. San Diego & Ariz. E. Ry.*, 382 U.S. 257 (1965); *Ruffin v. Division 3, Nat'l R.R. Adjustment Bd.*, 368 F. Supp. 990, 992-93 (E.D. Pa. 1973).

260. See *Pennsylvania R.R. v. Day*, 360 U.S. 548 (1959), which, however, involved an independent action in the district court, not an effort to seek de novo review of the board's award.

261. *Washington Terminal Co. v. Boswell*, 124 F.2d 235 (D.C. Cir. 1941), aff'd by an equally divided Court, 319 U.S. 732 (1943). Cf. *Barnett v. Pennsylvania Reading Seashore Lines*, 245 F.2d 579 (3d Cir. 1957). The carrier's right of review was narrowly

limited by 45 U.S.C. § 153 (1970) to jurisdictional questions, fraud or corruption, id. § 153(1) (p), and awards "actually and indisputedly without foundation in reason or fact," 1966 U.S. Code Cong. & Ad. News 2287, and a corresponding right of review given to employees. The constitutionality of this limitation of the employers' former right was sustained without reference to the *Washington Terminal* decision in *Brotherhood of R.R. Trainmen v. Denver & Rio Grande W. R.R.*, 370 F.2d 833 (10th Cir. 1966), cert. denied, 386 U.S. 1018 (1967).

262. *Reisman v. Caplin*, 375 U.S. 440 (1964); *Washington Terminal Co. v. Boswell*, 124 F.2d 235 (D.C. Cir. 1941); *Rossi v. Trans World Airlines*, 350 F. Sapp. 1263 (C.D. 1972).

263. See K. Davis, *Administrative Law Treatise* § 28.13 (Supp. 1970).

264. *IAM v. Central Airlines*, 372 U.S. 682 (1963).

265. See P. Bator, P. Mishkin, D. Shapiro & H. Wechsler, *Hart & Wechsler's The Federal Courts and the Federal System* 737-38 (2d ed., 1973).

266. *Pennsylvania R.R. v. Day*, 360 U.S. 548 (1959) (waiver by arm's-length contracts).

267. *National Bank Bldg. v. Goldsmith*, 204 Okla. 45, 226 P.2d 916 (1951).

268. *Moore v. Illinois Cent. R.R.*, 312 U.S. 630 (1941); but cf. *Slocum v. Delaware L. & W.R.R.*, 339 U.S. (1950), involving a subsisting employment relationship. The distinction is sometimes said to rest not on contract notions but on the fact that future relations between the railroad and other employees are less involved in discharge than in grievance cases. Moore was overruled, the constitutional question being expressly reserved in *Andrews v. Louisville & N.R.R.*, 406 U.S. 320 (1972). Justice Douglas dissented on constitutionalgrounds. The prevailing opinion perhaps significantly stresses the absence of preexisting remedies at common law. Id. at 324.

269. A state remedy for wrongful discharge has been held unavailable under the NLRA; see *Republic Steel Corp. v. Maddox*, 379 U.S. 650 (1965), where the alternative was a public administrative remedy. Significantly, in distinguishing *Moore*, the Court referred to "the various distinctive features of the administrative remedies provided by the [Railway Labor] Act . . . e.g. the makeup of the Adjustment Board, the scope of review from monetary, awards and the ability of the Board to give the same remedies as could be obtained by court suit," as possibly justifying provision for an alternative remedy to adjustment board procedures in discharge cases. Id. at 657 n.14.

270. Even the removal of grievance claims from the courts disturbed Justice Black. See id. (Black, dissenting); *Smith v. Evening News Ass'n*, 371 U.S. 195, 204-05 (1962) (Black, dissenting). As to repleving and cognovit notes, compare *Fuentes v. Shevin*, 407 U.S. 67 (1972) (nonwaiver of procedural rights by contract of adhesion), discussed in note 16 supra, with *D.H. Overmyer Co. v. Frick Co.*, 405 U.S. 174 (1972) (waiver by arm's-length contracts).

271. The validity of statutes requiring appointment of boards from industry panels usually arises in a procedural due process rather than nondelegation context. See, e.g., *Floyd v. Thornton*, 220 S.C. 414, 68 S.E.2d 344 (1951); *Fleisher v. Duncan*, 195 Ga. 309, 24 S.E.2d 15 (1943); *Lucas v. State ex rel. Board of Medical Regis. & Exam.*, 229 Ind. 633, 99 N.E. 2d 419 (1951). See also the cases collected in Jaffe at 231 n.78. But see *Kachian v. Optometry Exam. Bd.*, 44 Wis. 2d 1, 170 N.W.2d 743 (1969). Even if the minority view that a public official's oath and his removability are not sufficient guarantees of an absence of bias is taken, one might still suggest that a distinction be drawn between legislative functions such as rate-fixing on the one hand and judicial functions such

as license revocation on the other.

272. See notes 47 & 236 supra & text accompanying. But cf. *Bullock v. Carter*, 405 U.S. 134 (1972).

273. *Board of Supervisors v. State Milk Comm'n*, 191 Va. 1, 60 S.E.2d 35, appeal dismissed, 340 U.S. 881 (1950). See also *Southeast Milk Sales Ass'n v. Swaringgen*, 290 F. Supp. 292, 307 (1968) ("A person aggrieved . . . has a right to appeal and to be heard de novo . . .").

274. *State ex rel. James v. Schoor*, 45 Del. 18, 28, 65 A.2d 810, 814 (1948). Contra *Driscoll v. Sakin*, 121 N.J.L. 225, 1 A.2d 881 (Sup. Ct. 1938). The distinction was vigorously rejected by the dissenting judges in Schoor: "As the important questions is whether the Constitution prohibits the delegation of the legislative power to appoint statutory officers to persons not members of the State government, we are unable to see how any of the cases relied on by the minority of this Court can be distinguished on the ground that the named agents were only required to appoint from a list of names furnished by each of the major political parties. The number that could be named from any one political party was, also, limited." 45 Del. at 40, 65 A.2d at 820 (Harrington, C., dissenting).

275. *Nixon v. Condon*, 286 U.S. 73 (1932), was, to be sure, alluded to by the court in its decision. But cf. *O'Brien v. Brown*, 409 U.S. 1 (1972). See generally Annot., 97 A.L.R.2d 361 (1964).

276. 45 Del. at 37, 65 A.2d at 819 (Harrington, C., dissenting). Cf. *United Citizens Party v. South Carolina State Election Comm'n*, 319 F. Supp. 784 (D.S.C. 1970), invalidating a statute that had the effect of permitting a major party to exclude minor parties from the ballot by altering its primary and convention dates.

277. 11 N.Y.2d 317, 183 N.E. 2d 670, 229 N.Y.S. 2d 380, appeal dismissed, 371 U.S. 74 (1962).

278. Of course, delegation of the power to name judges is somewhat different from delegation of power to name administrators whose decisions are subject to some measure of judicial review. But the delegation contemplated by the typical "Missouri Plan" scheme is a limited one. Usually the governor is required to select judicial appointees from persons recommended by a panel, half of whose members are selected by the governor or legislature and half of whom are elected by the bar. Bar associations serve on nominating committees in the bar elections, though nomination by petition remains possible. See, e.g., K. Llewellyn, *The Common Law Tradition: Deciding Appeals* 33-34 n.24 (1960). Cf. A. De Grazia, *Public and Republic*, 103, 214-19 (1951); 1 M. Farrand, *The Records of the Federal Convention of 1787*, at 119 (1934). Hostility toward delegation of judicial powers to persons not drawn from the community at large or selected by politically responsible officials may account for the demise of the "special jury" in the United States. Cf. *Fay v. New York*, 332 U.S. 261 (1947).

279. See, e.g., M. Friedman, *Capitalism and Freedom* (1962).

280. Cf. A. de Tocqueville, Democracy in America, pt. 4, ch. 7 at 675-76 (G. Lawrence transl., T. Mayer & M. Lerner eds., 1966): "In our day everything threatens to become so much alike that the peculiar features of each individual may soon be entirely lost in the common physiognomy. Our forefathers were always prone to make an improper use of the idea that private rights should be respected, and we are by nature inclined to exaggerate the opposite view, that the interest of the individual should always give way to the interest of the many.

It would seem that sovereigns now only seek to do great things with men. I wish that they would try a little more to make men great, that they should attach less importance to the work and more to the workman, that they should constantly remember that a nation cannot long remain great if each man is individually weak, and that no one has yet devised a form of society or a political combination which can make a people energetic when it is composed of citizens "who are flabby and feeble."

281. *Fox v. Standard Oil Co.*, 294 U.S. 87, 100 (1935) (Cardozo, J.) (upholding Kentucky chain store tax act). Cf. *Louis K. Liggett Co. v. Lee*, 288 U.S. 517, 541 (1933) (Brandeis, J., dissenting); *Louis K. Liggett Co. v. Baldridge*, 278 U.S. 105, 114 (1928) (Holmes, J., dissenting) (invalidating act reqturing majority of shareholders in drugstores to be registered pharmacists). The continuing force of the latter case was questioned in *Daniel v. Family Sec. Life Ins. Co.*, 336 U.S. 220, 225 (1949), and the case was later overruled.

282. See K. Davis, *Administrative Law Treatise* § 12.03 (Supp. 1970).

283. W. Gellhorn, *Individual Freedom and Governmental Restraints* 149-50 (1956) (footnote omitted). Cf. F. Hayek, *The Constitution on Liberty* 227, 492 n.9 (1960).

284. Cf. Jaffe at 234-53.

285. E.g., *H. P. Hood & Sons, Inc. v. United States*, 307 U.S. 588 (1939); *Schwegmann Bros. Giant Super Mkts. v. McCrory*, 237 La. 767, 112 So. 2d 606, appeal dismissed, 361 U.S. 114 (1959); and the cases cited in Jaffe at 241 n.110 (all involving agricultural schemes). Cf. *Walker v. Louisiana Exp'y Auth.*, 274 So. 2d 716, 722 (La. App. 1973).

286. *Sunshine Anthracite Coal Co. v. Adkins*, 310 U.S. 381 (1940) (labor standards); Spiers v. Magnolia Petroleum Co., 206 Okla. 503, 244 P.2d 843 (1951) (oil unitization acts); *Palmer Oil Corp. v. Phillips Petroleum Co.*, 204 Okla. 543, 231 P.2d 997 (1951), appeal dismissed, 343 U.S. 390 (1952).

287. *State v. Allstate Ins. Co.*, 231 Miss. 869, 97 So. 2d 372 (1957) (insurance rates). Cf. Annot., 54 A.L.R.3d 916, 918-22 (1973) (barbershops).

288. *Hollingsworth v. State Bd. of Barber Examiners*, 217 Ind. 373, 28 N.E.2d 64 (1940) (barber's prices and hours); *Opinion of the Justices*, 337 Mass. 796, 151 N.F-2d 631 (1958); *Revne v. Trade Comm'n*, 113 Utah 155, 192 P.2d 563 (1948).

289. See *Booth v. State*, 179 Ind. 405, 100 N.E. 563 (1913), aff'd, 237 U.S. 391 (1915) (installation of washrooms required on petition); P*orter Coal Co. v. Davis*, 231 Ala. 359, 165 So. 93 (1935) (appointment of weighman on petition of miners).

290. 291 U.S. 502 (1934).

291. See the cases cited in notes 271 & 286 supra.

292. 40 Cal. 2d 436, 254 P.2d 29 (1953). The court observed that "legislature attempts to delegate its powers to an administrative board made up of interested members of the industry, that delegation may well be brought into question." Id. at 449, 254 P.2d at 36. An asserted lack of standards was also emphasized. In *State v. Harris*, 216 N.C. 746, 6 S.E.2d 854 (1940), a statute similar to that in the *Thrift-D-Lux* case was invalidated on substantive due process grounds and for want of standards. The court observed that the composition of the board though "[n]ot of itself sufficient to invalidate the statute . . . invites the scrutiny of the Court as to the public nature of the objectives really pursued." Id. at 762, 6 S.E.2d at 864-65. But cf. Union School Dist. v. Commissioner of Labor, 103 N.H. 512, 176 A.2d 332 (1961), upholding a statute giving an industry-dominated board power to set the "prevailing wage rate." See generally Stewart, *The Reformation of American Administrative Law*, 88 Harv. L. Rev. 1667, 1793-1802 (1975).

293. 40 Cal. 2d at 254 P.2d at 36.

294. Id. at 456, 254 P.2d at 40.

295. *Fox v. Mohawk & Hudson River Humane Soc'y*, 165 N.Y. 517, 59 N.E. 353 (1901), is the leading case stressing this distinction.

296. See text accompanying notes 280-283 supra.

297. 25 Cal. App. 3d 1014, 102 Cal. Rptr. 368 (1972).

298. Id. at 1020, 102 Cal. Rptr. at 372.

299. See *Olinger v. People*, 140 Colo. 397, 344 P.2d 689 (1959) (voters of conservancy districts invalidly delegated authority to enact penal ordinances); *People v. Maimud*, 5 Misc. 2d 65, 158 N.Y.S.2d 838 (Spec. Sess.), rev'd on other grounds, 4 App. Div. 2d 86, 164 N.Y.S.2d 204 (1957) (invalid delegation of voice in making penal rules to bondholders of bridge and tunnel authority). For an analysis similar to that in *McGautha v. California*, 402 U.S. 183 (1971), discussed in text accompanying notes 10-11 supra, see *Cokley v. People*, 168 Colo. 280, 450 P.2d 1013 (1969) (jury).

300. *United States v. Grimaud*, 220 U.S. 506 (1911).

301. E.g., *Fuentes v. Shevin*, 407 U.S. 67 (1972). Cf. *Mitchell v. W.T. Grant Co.*, 416 U.S. 600, 619 (1974) ("the process proceeds under judicial supervision and management").

302. See generally P. Woll, *Administration in Law: The Informan Process* (1963).

303. Landis, book review of Friendly, *The Federal Administrative Agencies*, 30 U. Chi. L. Rev. 597, 600 (1963).

304. *People ex rel. Adamowski v. Chicago R.R. Terminal Auth.*, 14 Ill. 2d 230, 151 N.E.2d 311 (1958). See also *People ex rel. Hanrahan v. Caliendo*, 50 Ill. 2d 72, 277 N.E.2d 319 (1971) (Urban Transportation District Act).

305. 14 Ill. 2d at 240, 151 N.E.2d at 317.

306. *Crain v. First Nat'l Bank*, 324 F.2d 532 (9th Cir. 1963).

307. 348 U.S. 26 (1954). Cf. *Salyer Land Co. v. Tulare Lake Basin Water Storage Dist.*, 410 U.S. 719, 729 (1973), holding the principles of the reapportionment cases inapplicable to a water district "not exercis[ing] what might be thought of as normal governmental authority." Contra, *City of Amsterdam v. Helsby*, 79 Misc. 2d 676, 362 N.Y.S.2d 698 (Sup. Ct. 1974), holding in violation of the Equal Protection Clause a state statute requiring compulsory arbitration of public employee labor disputes, since impasse arbitrators wield governmental power but were not chosen in accordance with the one-man, one-vote rule.

308. *Board of County Comm'rs v. White*, 79 Wyo. 420, 445, 335 P.2d 433, 442 (1959).

309. *Rockwood Volunteer Fire Dep't v. Town of Kossuth*, 260 Wis. 331, 50 N.W.2d 913 (1952).

310. *State ex rel. Fire Fighters Local 946, IAFF v. City of Laramie*, 437 P.2d 295 (Wyo. 1968). See generally note 119 supra.

311. Of course, at common law the police had rights little greater than those of private citizens. See Hall, *Legal and Social Aspects of Arrest without a Warrant*, 49 Harv. L. Rev. 566 (1936).

312. See, e.g., *Fagan v. Pittsburgh Terminal Coal Corp.*, 299 Pa. 109, 149 A. 159 (1930). But cf. *Dart Drug, Inc. v. Linthicum*, 300 A.2d 442 (D.C. App. 1973). See generally Annot., 92 A.L.R.2d 15, 51-61 (1963). Cf. Ind. Ann. Stat. §§ 35-3-2-1 to-6 (Code ed. 1975) for authority and immunity for shopkeepers in detaining suspected shoplifters.

313. See Shalloo, *The Private Police of Pennsylvania*, 146 Annals 55 (1929). See generally Comment, *Private Police Forces: Legal Powers and Limitations*, 38 U. Chi. L. Rev. 555 (1971).

314. *Griffin v. Maryland*, 378 U.S. 130 (1964); *United States v. Hoffman*, 498 F.2d 879 (7th Cir. 1974).

315. See *Dennis v. United States*, 341 U.S. 494, 561, 577 (1951) (Jackson, J., concurring).

316. *Hughes v. Superior Ct.*, 339 U.S. 460 (1950); *Milk Wagon Drivers Union v. Meadowmoor Dairies, Inc.*, 312 U.S. 287 (1941).

317. *Milk Wagon Drivers Union v. Meadowmoor Dairies, Inc.*, 312 U.S. 287, 293 (1941).

318. See *King v. Smith*, 392 U.S. 309 (1968).

319. *Lemon v. Kurtzman*, 403 TJ.S. 602 (1971).

320. See M. Friedman, *Capitalism and Freedom* (1962); E. West, *Education and the State: A Study in Political Economy* (2d ed., 1970) Boulding, Book Review [of West, supra.], 33 U. Chi. L. Rev. 615 (1966). See also J.S. Mill, *On Liberty*, in *Utilitarianism, Liberty, and Representative Government* 81, 216-17 (A. Lindsay ed., 1950).

321. Cf. Kurland, *Foreword, Church and State in the United States: A New Era of Good Feelings*, 1966 Wis. L. Rev. 215; Marcus, *The Forum of Conscience: Applying Standards under the Free Exercise Clause*, 1973 Duke L.J. 1217.

322. 403 U.S. 602 (1971).

323. E. Corwin, The Twilight of the Supreme Court (1934).

324. Jaffe, *The Right to Judicial Review* 11, 71 Harv. Rev769 (1958).

325. Reich, *The New Property*, 73 Yale L.J. 733 (1964).

326. Similar tests are of course relevant in determining when administrative agencies should act by rule. Cf. A. Pekelis, *Law and Social Action* 90 (1950).

327. *Horace Mann League of the United States v. Board of Pub. Works*, 242 Md. 645, 220 A.2d 51 (1966).

328. *Murray v. Comptroller of the Treasury*, 241 Md. 383. 216 A.2d 897, cert. denied, 385 U.S. 816 (1966); see also *Walz v. Tax Comm'n*, 397 U.S. 664 (1970).

329. 241 Md. at 399, 216 A.2d at 906.

330. See *Norwood v. Harrison*, 413 U.S. 455, 464 (1973); *Cochran v. Louisiana State Bd. of Educ.*, 281 U.S. 370 (1930). Cf. Kurland, *Of Church and State and the Supreme Court*, 29 U. Chi. L. Rev 1, 14 (1961).

331. It may be well to allude here to the less fashionable portions of President Eisenhower's farewell speech, including the reference to government-financed research contracts as virtually a substitute for intellectual curiosity. *Farewell Radio and Television Address to the American People*, Jan. 17, 1961, in 1960-61 Public Papers of the Presidents of the United States: Dwight D. Eisenhower, at 1035, 1038 (1961).

332. J. Gray, *The Nature and Sources of the Law* 2 (1921).

333. Some, even, would restrict private rights to the constitutional minimum. See Henkin, *Some Reflections on Current Constitutional Controversy*, 109 U. Pa. L. Rev. 637 (1961).

334. A. Pekelis, *Private Governments and the Federal Constitution*, in *Law and Social Action* 91, 124-26 (1950).

335. See *Reynolds v. Sims*, 377 U.S. 533 (196-4); *Linkletter v. Walker*, 381 U.S. 618 (1965); cf. Mishkin, *Foreword To The High Court, The Great Writ, and the Due Process of Time and Law*, 79 Harv. L. Rev. 56 (1965).

336. *Shaughnessy v. United States ex rel. Mezei*, 345 U.S. 206, 224 (1953) (Jackson, J., dissenting).

337. J. Hurst, *Law and Social Process in United States History* 142 (1900).

338. 42 U.S.C. §§ 4321, 4331-33, 4341-47 (1970).

339. A. Whitehead, Symbolism: Its Meaning and Effect 88 (1927).

340. O.W. Holmes, *Law and the Court*, in *Collected Legal Papers* 291, 295 (1920).

Part II

RESTORING JUDICIAL MODESTY

4

The Core of the First Amendment

Thirty years ago the present writer participated in one of the most entertaining of law school classes, Professor Harry Kalven's picturesquely entitled course on "Redress of Certain Harms," perhaps better described as "Torts minus Auto Accidents." The course was rendered memorable by the interaction of the instructor's quicksilver mind with a body of widely selected and frequently hilarious materials. Professor Kalven went on from his case book on torts to write a work on the First Amendment and the civil rights revolution—the central political event of the 1960s. Subsequently, in the early 1970s he undertook what he hoped to make a definitive work on the First Amendment. The first two portions of that work dealing with regulation of content and regulation of association were published fifteen years after his death, in consequence of the devoted efforts of his son, assisted by Professor Owen Fiss of Yale. According to the editor, "A projected third section on non content regulation remains unwritten," although as is later noted, much of what would have appeared in this can be gleaned from Professor Kalven's "The Negro and the First Amendment" and from his numerous and widely scattered articles.

Because Professor Kalven is the most influential of the modern commentators on the First Amendment, any assessment of what is sound and what is unsound in contemporary doctrine must begin with his work.

Perhaps because the last section was omitted, Kalven's last book is redolent of the political and constitutional controversies of the McCarthy period. As an actor as well as an academic, Professor Kalven entertained a bias familiar at the University of Chicago but less known elsewhere in favor of a measure of laissez-faire in all things. Professor Kalven's writings on progressive taxation and on the tort system exhibited a skepticism about the conventional liberal agenda, while his writings on First Amendment issues rendered him a frequent ally of, if not hero to, the far left. In all contexts, however, Professor Kalven was never what

Cardozo referred to as a lazy judge who swept his opponents' cards from the table.

His writings on both economic and constitutional matters were consistently informed by clear perception and statement of the other side of issues. It is this as much as the particular conclusions asserted that renders his posthumously published work on the First Amendment a volume of enduring value, perhaps the most important book on free speech issues since the works of Alexander Meikeljohn and Zechariah Chafee.[1]

A Worthy Tradition, unlike Professor Kalven's torts case book is not wide ranging in its sources but is focused upon legal doctrine as declared by the Supreme Court. Although this chronicle reflects what Professor Kalven regarded as progress in doctrine, the quotations from past opinions make it clear that if good prose and clear statement are essential to the survival of political liberty, the contemporary dangers to the "worthy tradition" are greater than Professor Kalven admits.[2] Plainly the days of Black and Jackson, let alone Holmes and Hand, are no more.

UNTOUCHABLE CONTENT

Blasphemy and Sacrilege

The work begins with a chapter on forms of speech that the Supreme Court has always considered untouchable by the law. First among these is blasphemy. Its position at the core of the First Amendment appears unappreciated by some writers in England and even in this country, whose response to the Rushdie affair has been to proclaim their tolerance for the intolerant Nonetheless, there seems little reason to doubt the continuing force of Justice Frankfurter's reminder in *Burstyn v. Wilson* "the crime of blasphemy in seventeenth century England was the crime of dissenting from whatever was the current religious dogma."

As with blasphemy, so with sacrilege which can only be given legal force only in its narrow meaning of "physical damage to religious personnel or symbols."

False Doctrine

Government is likewise prohibited in all contexts from penalizing false doctrine and from prohibiting speech only because it conflicts with particular religious symbols or values. On this basis, Kalven finds a common thread between *Epperson v. Arkansas*, striking a statute prohibiting the teaching of the doctrine of evolution and *Kingsley v. Regents*, rejecting the concept of thematic obscenity.

Public Sensibilities

Finally, Kalven urges, the court has frowned upon the suppression of speech purely in the interest of public taste or sensibilities. For this proposition he relies on *Winters v. New York*, striking an effort to prohibit "massed stories of bloodshed and lust likely to incite to crimes of violence," and *Cohen v. California*, involving the wearing of a jacket on which the slogan "Fuck the Draft" was clearly visible.

The chief limitation on this principle is that supplied by *Chaplinsky v. New Hampshire*, the "fighting words" case which declared that "there are . . . narrowly limited classes of speech the punishment of which has never been thought to raise any constitutional problem. These include the lewd and obscene, the profane, the libelous and the insulting or fighting words—those which by their very utterance inflict injury or tend to incite an immediate breach of the peace." Kalven regarded the *Cohen* case as inconsistent with the prohibition of profanity, and undoubtedly he is right. However, *Cohen* and several of its progeny were five to four decisions resting, as Justice Harlan notes, on the proposition that words may be chosen for their emotive as well as cognitive force. Those who found the basis for First Amendment protection in a preference for discussion over force and who find the roots of freedom of speech in the Enlightenment may be less inclined to protect expressions that are "emotive" rather than "cognitive" or which in Justice Murphy's phrase "by their very utterance inflict injury." This, as noted later, is a large question and one not as definitively resolved as Kalven would suggest by the series of closely divided opinions following upon the Cohen case. The only sensible justification for throwing a cloak of protection over mindless abuse is the desire to enfranchise the inarticulate, though the link between gutter language and gutter politics makes this a high price to pay.

Whatever may be said of the systematic use of profanity or of words designed to assail rather than convince, it is clear that ridicule, satire, and hyperbole have been added by Chief Justice Rehnquist's recent opinion in the *Hustler v. Falwell* case to "the consensus on untouchable content."

"THE MINOR JURISDICTIONS OF CENSORSHIP"

From a discussion of areas enjoying total immunity from government regulation, Kalven proceeds to what he describes as the "minor jurisdictions of censorship": contempt by publication, obscenity, the protection of child audiences, and what is left of the law of libel. Although he credits the court with leaving "only the husks of censorship" he suggests that tactically this may not be enough; "free speech policy may in the end turn on the strategy of over-protecting speech in order to protect the speech that matters." But the reverse is also arguable; casting the First Amendment as the enemy of common morals, enhancing the arrogance of the institutional press, and making the victims of defamation and privacy invasions objects of public sympathy may not be the best ways to enhance public support of the court's central role in protecting political speech.

Contempt

In his discussion of contempt by publication, Kalven notes, as did the Reardon Commission some years ago, that orders precluding publication only during duration of a trial result in "censorship [which] is only temporary . . . public opinion is irrelevant; no one wants such matters determined by majority vote." The strongest case for prohibition is presented by disclosure of suppressed evidence to an unsequestered jury. Professor Kalven correctly notes that the court has sedulously avoided this problem; "the court is determined to postpone as long as possible the confrontation with the press." The price of its so doing, however, is frequently a diminution of defendants' rights to a representative and competent jury. The problems involving publicly compelled evidence in the *North* and *Poindexter* cases should remind us that where pretrial publicity is left unfettered, a defendant in any case of prominence is accorded only a right to a trial by persons who are idiots (private persons) in the classical sense. The Court's success in avoiding confrontation in this area has been greatly aided by a factor not mentioned by Kalven: the exclusion of contempts by publication from the 1831 federal contempt statute; it is no accident that the few test cases have come up from state courts.

Obscenity

The discussion of obscenity proceeds on the premise that courts have excluded obscenity from constitutional protection not because it may lead to antisocial sexual action, offense to sensibilities, or the propagation of doctrine with bad effects but solely where its function is confined to physical arousal; the protection of emotive as well as cognitive speech apparently has this limit. Kalven acknowledges, however, that the *Paris Theatre* case, whatever its formal doctrine, which does little to facilitate obscenity prosecutions, adopts a rationale that accords legitimacy not only to the prevention of physical reactions but also to the interest of the public in the quality of life . . . family life, community welfare and the development of human personality." Kalven is critical of the emphasis of the *Guinzburg* case on the intent of the publisher, yet *Guinzburg* seems merely an application to the sphere of obscenity of the stress on proscribed intent of many of the early opinions involving political speech. Kalven notes that the effect of the most recent decisions is to provide that the "pruriency and patency wings of the test—though, significantly, not the "social value" wing—are to be judged by local rather than national standards. He notes that "in a society so pervaded by mass communication it will be difficult to isolate the local community." It is also difficult to separate local mores of tolerance from tolerance resulting from compulsion by prior judicial opinions. In consequence the practical effect of the movement away from the *Memoirs* test has manifested itself only gradually.

If, however, political speech is the core of First Amendment protection, the court has probably acted properly in reserving to itself andapplying national standards to the issue "whether the work, taken as a whole lacks serious literary, artistic, political, or scientific value." Since this is the core of the matter one must wonder whether anything would be lost if Chief Justice Warren's early suggestion were accepted and the court renounced factual review of the pruriency and patent offensiveness issues. It is certainly doubtful that the court will or should embrace Kalven's favored conclusion that "even the narrowest concession to censorship cannot be justified in the case of consenting adults, in view of the costs of regulation and the absence of any compelling state interest in policing the sexual fantasies of adults." The court majority has acted on the premise that in the words of Professor Joseph Tussman," The community may insist on a special public language, special reticence, a veiled obscurity . . . it senses—confusedly but doggedly—that irreverence at this point is deeply destructive. Sex, for example is not a trivial matter and a society may be very sensitive about it." Not out of fear, or stupidity, or neurosis, but out of a healthy respect for a basic human passion."[3] Not only is obscenity, as the early Alexander Meiklejohn and Professor George Anastaplo have recognized, some distance from political speech, but its protection involves the protection of words (or, more usually, pictures) used for their emotive and not cognitive force, an issue that also raises itself in other contexts. As a critic of Kalven's views has noted, "the governing of the forum should not be indifferent to the decay of reason or unconcerned about the effects of its institutional arrangements on the mind. The hope is that the forum can become the sustainer of the mode of communication that is more than a form of conflict."[4]

Child Audiences

For similar reasons, Kalven's discussion of the problem of child audiences as a "minor exception" to the rule against censorship fails to fully satisfy. Kalven states the case for such restriction at its strongest in the language of Mill: "liberty as a principle has no application to any state of things anterior to the time when mankind have become capable of being improved by free and equal discussion; despotism is a legitimate mode of government in dealing with barbarians, provided the end be their improvement and the means justified by actually affecting that end." Kalven expresses concern that recognizing a restriction for minors upon such grounds can provide an argument against free speech on the ground that the general public is not ready for it. In the leading case of *Ginsberg v. New York*, Justice Stewart, echoing Mill, noted that "the first amendment rights of children are different and in a sense less than those of adults [since they] are not possessed of that full capacity for individual choice which is the preconception of the first amendment guarantee." Kalven points to the concern that free speech can become a prerogative of only a limited class determined to be "enlightened" and the correlative danger that incentives may arise to keep those outside the charmed circle in ignorance: "it was impermissible to teach a slave to read." But it seems inescapable that the need for paternalism is rooted in the nature of man. It would seem a sufficent guarantee of liberty to draw the line at the age of majority or emancipation rather than to adopt principles of freedom that assure that all are equal in that none is disciplined or adequately educated. The *Ginsberg* case may be a "solemn ratification in constitutional terms of the 'generation gap,'" but it is not necessarily to be deplored on that account.

Libel

The fourth "special jurisdiction" discussed by Kalven is libel, his discussion of which is informed by insights gained from his role as a torts professor. The central insight of Kalven's book, as of the work on free speech of professors Meiklejohn and Anastaplo, is here succinctly stated: "In my view the presence or absence in the law of the concept of seditious libel defines the society. A society may or may not treat obscenity or contempt by publication as legal offenses without altering its basic nature. If, however it makes seditious libel an offense it is not a free society, no matter what its other characteristics." Seditious libel is succinctly described: "criticism of government is viewed as defamation and punished as a crime." Kalven conclusively demonstrates how the doctrine of *New York Times v. Sullivan* with the apparent immunities it provides to irresponsible and careless false statements, is derivative from the problems created by common law of defamation doctrines by which the burden of demonstrating the truth of a defamatory statement was placed upon a defendant, general damages were allowed without the necessity for proof of specific loss and the presumption of malice negated any requirement of intention or negligence. The truth defense was further circumscribed at common law by being inapplicable to matters of opinion. With these rules accepted as a given, the holding of *New York Times v. Sullivan,* that "neither factual error nor defamatory content suffices to remove the constitutional shield from criticism of official conduct" is not surprising, though the opinion for an unanimous court may have been overexubcrant in declaring that "debate on public issues should be uninhibited, robust, and wide open."

In the subsequent case of *Rosenblatt v. Baer*, Justice Stewart, who had joined in *Sullivan,* indicated that he would confine its rule to the circumstances giving it birth; the "rule should not be applied except where a state's law of defamation has been unconstitutionally converted into a law of seditious libel . . . [we] have not stripped private citizens of all means of redress for injuries inflicted upon them by careless liars . . . surely if the 1950's taught us anything they taught us that the poisonous atmosphere of the easy lie can infect and degrade a whole society." What the New York Times rule ultimately protects is defamatory falsehood." The strategy implicit in these observations by Justice Stewart—limiting the *New York Times* rule by recasting the common law of defamation doctrines which gave rise to the need for it—has been limited thus far to libel of private persons.[5] Kalven notes that an approach urged by Justice Marshall with respect to private individuals who have become involuntarily newsworthy would "allow the State to apply whatever standard it thought appropriate, but would restrict the damages awarded the plaintiff to 'actual losses', that is, he would not allow punitive or presumed damages . . . such an approach would eliminate the most significant factor producing self censorship—the threat of huge damage judgments—while affording individual reputation a greater degree of protection than is provided by the 'reckless disregard' standard."[6] It is clear, however, that thus far the Court has not significantly retreated from the *New York Time*s doctrine as applied to public officials.

In *St. Amant v. Thompson*, a decision that Kalven does not discuss, the Court rejected an effort by Justice Fortas in dissent to apply more exacting rules to the institutional press in determining compliance with the "reckless disregard" standard. Indeed, but for the resolve of Senator Goldwater in subjecting his private life to intensive discovery in order to prevail in the extreme case of *Goldwater v. Guinzberg*, it is not unreasonable to state that there would be no effective limits applicable to libel of public officers. It may be however, that the approach taken in the celebrated *Sharon* case of permitting juries to render special verdicts on the different elements of defamation has begun to supply a partial answer to press arrogance—the allowance to victims of carelessness of what amounts to a declaratory judgment in the guise of a special verdict on each of the separate legal issues in the case. Few plaintiffs, however, are likely to be determined or well-heeled enough to pursue results which will be appreciated only by connoisseurs of defamation doctrine. It does not impugn the central insight of *New York Times v. Sullivan* to predict its ultimate modification to curb abuse by the institutional press lest "new presbyter be but old priest writ large."

If the burden of proof on the issue of falsehood was shifted to plaintiffs, statements of opinion remained nonactionable, malice was not presumed but made dependent upon a finding of gross departure from normal journalistic standards of care, and general damages were eliminated in favor of a declaratory judgment, nominal damages, fee shifting, or actual damages conservatively defined, it would be difficult to urge that allowing libel actions by public officers would create a cause of action akin to seditious libel. Kalven would prefer overprotecting speech in order to protect "the speech that matters." History, however, records notable example of the corrosive effect of systematically propagated falsehoods about public officers.[7] Absolute rights or rights that are perceived as being virtually absolute do not induce humility in their possessors. As Learned Hand declared, "The hand that rules the press . . . rules the country . . . every year adds to its potency and to the finality of itsjudgments."[8] It is this that militates against Justice Black's "unconditional right to say what one pleases about public affairs"; while the press may be victimized by "high emotions and deep prejudices which frequently pervade local communities where libel suits are tried," propagation of falsehood can also fan "high emotions and deep prejudices." The particular form limitations take is probably less important than that they are perceived to exist.

Political Advocacy

From the discussion of the 'minor jurisdictions' of censorship, Kalven proceeds to regulation of political speech as such, beginning with the problems created by the heckler's veto or the hostile audience. On these issues, Kalven makes note of Justice Jackson's notable postwar opinions informed by his experience at Nuremberg. Against the unfairness of suppressing a speaker because of the acts of his audience must be set appreciation of the frequent tactic of deliberate provocation of audience violence, In his dissenting opinions in the *Terminello* and *Kunz* cases, both involving street corner speeches, Justice Jackson would have allowed the suppression of forms of group defamation, words that he defines as "always and in any context insults which do not spring from reason and can be answered by none." This fear of the irrational, of mob psychology, of emotive rather than cognitive speech, informs Justice Jackson's opinion: "Unity of purpose, passion, and hatred which moulds the many minds of a crowd into the mindlessness of a mob almost invariably is supplied by speeches. It is naive or worse to teach that oratory with this object or effect is a service to liberty. No mob has ever protected any liberty, even its own, but if not put down it always winds up in an orgy of lawlessness which respects no liberties." Though sympathetic to limitations on group defamation in the context of public speech, Justice Jackson dissented in the *Beauharnais* case, the only Supreme Court decision upholding the group defamation concept on the basis that such prohibitions addressed to leaflets do not have the justification of prevention of "disorder in the street." He would apply the then-fashionable "clear and present danger" test to "considering whether a leaflet is as emotionally exciting to an immediate action as the spoken word, especially the incendrious street or public speech." Kalven does not fully share Justice Jackson's fears, observing, without discrimination between speech and press, that "public forums should be protected not out of nostalgic regard for bygone days when leaflets and soapbox orators were important, but because it may again be central to the dynamics of dissent among free men." Elsewhere he notes the interplay between public demonstrations and the coverage by media of mass communication. He concludes, as did Justice Black in the prevailing opinion in the *Feiner* case, "assuming that in the name of preserving order [the police] ever can interfere with a lawful public speaker they must first make all reasonable efforts to protect him." He further urges "the court should not underestimate its symbolic and educative role. It can affect the attitude and training of the police and it can influence the popular attitude which in turn will affect the police." That these observations accurately describe the present law cannot be denied. Whether the rule of *Feiner* is viable in less quiet times may be more open to question. Perhaps the approach espoused by Justice Jackson and validated in *Beauharnais* in what he rightly deemed an inappropriate context has something to be said for it; the narrowly drawn statute directed solely at "insults which do not spring from reasoning and can be answered by none" and applied only to speeches in public and not private halls made with a purpose of provocation. Kalven observes that "such a statute has not been forthcoming. I suspect the difficulties of drafting reveal a point of principle—the worthless offending speech cannot be safely disentangled." Since virtually all the nations of continental Europe most affected by the abuses of which Justice Jackson wrote have legislation in this sphere, the difficulties may not be as great as suggested, at least where the proscribed speech is designed to provoke and inflame an audience against the speaker's views rather than to persuade it to them.

In *Cohen v. California*, in an opinion strikingly protective of extreme political speech, Justice Harlan distinguished *Feiner* by declaring, "We do not have here an instance of the exercise of the state's police power to prevent a speaker from intentionally provoking a given group to hostile reaction" Kalven in this context again observes, "We may have a gap between realism and what practically can be isolated by legal drafts and safely entrusted to juries to pass on." Against this must again be set the disadvantages that arise when rights are declared to their extreme.

Kalven in his discussion of the civil rights cases notes that the courts have consistently refused to permit violation of a police order to disperse to be an independent source of illegality. "Lawmaking is not entrusted to the moment to moment judgment of the policeman on his beat . . . to let a policeman's command become equivalent to a criminal statute comes dangerously near making our government one of men rather than of laws." Criticism of discretion, however, is coupled by willingness to accept legislative limitations: "as Justice Black has made clear on several earlier occasions, he does not like public issue picketing and demonstrations. He sees in them the seed of mob violence. . . . He makes it abundantly clear that the state could stringently regulate this type of protest, especially when it invades the privacy of the home, by means of a carefully drafted narrow statute." This insight has recently borne fruit. In being more generous than Justice Black to demonstrations that go beyond speech, Kalven observes, "The sophistication of modern communication technology enhances rather than diminishes the impact of street corner speech. The old-fashioned forms of protest and the mass media collaborate; the former supply the colorful newsworthy episodes; the latter supply the national and global coverage." This is no doubt accurate, but normative evaluation seems lacking. Is government by "visual" what the First Amendment is all about? Is it in fact correct, as Justice Harlan assumed in *Cohen v. California*, that the states may not regulate "in order to maintain what they regard as a suitable level of discourse within the body politic," because proscribing the profane would have the effect of "limiting the participation in public discourse of those for whom such language is an accepted vernacular . . . words are often chosen as much for their emotive as well as their cognitive force." In speaking of the residential picketing in a hostile neighborhood involved in *Gregory v. Chicago*, Kalven with characteristic honesty notes, "Certainly this act of communication, given its notoriety in coverage by the news media, conveys—and is meant to convey—a complex and highly charged message that goes beyond the flat assertion that the superintendent of schools must be changed." In fact the message is one of physical force, of menace, of coercion, of words chosen for their emotive as well as their cognitive force. To what extent can society afford to encourage and reward these forms of discourse? The answer was clearer to Kalven in 1974 than it would have been in 1939.[9] The *Cohen* case on its facts was trivial and the court may have been right in declining to suppress a political utterance because of the injury to sensibilities later described by Justice Powell: "The shock, sense of affront and sometimes the injury to mind and spirit can be as great from words as from some physical attacks." But the more general issue raised by *Cohen*, whether protection of political speech can be confined to discourse that is at least arguably persuasive, is not trivial and is one that troubled justices Black and Jackson also.

Subversive Advocacy

Kalven then outlines what he describes as "subversive advocacy; the core issue" in the series of cases ending in *Brandenberg v. Ohio*. He begins with a striking insight, which is unfortunately not pursued further: "In part the concession to the censor in this area [subversive advocacy] has rested on an analogy to ordinary crimes, such as theft, arson and murder. The common law has long accepted the concept of incitement and solicitation to such crimes. A moment of reflection, however, makes it apparent that the matter is not so simple. Surely there is a profound difference between inciting to arson by the use of words and inciting to revolution by the use of words."

The distinction, one would think, is between inciting to an end—revolution—which in some times or places may be desirable and inciting to means—theft, arson, and murder—that are condemned by the ordinary law of all societies and that the law cannot protect whether engaged in for political or other ends. Surely Learned Hand was right in saying, "Words are not only the keys of persuasion but the triggers of action, and those which have no purport but to counsel the violation of law cannot by any latitude of interpretation be a part of that public opinion which is the final source of government in a democratic state." So was Lord Acton in writing of "the injunction against murder" as at the core of his political philosophy. Society has a clear interest in the prevention of political change by terror or by the action of armed minorities, but it has a less clear interest in combating exhortations reducing the legitimacy of the existing order since, in many of history's beneficient political changes, "power was left lying in the street" through just such a process. The danger of subversive advocacy may be assumed to be limited where unaccompanied by terror and where defenders of the existing state of things have an opportunity to espouse their views on their merits.

Kalven's work devotes several hundred pages to discussion of the progress of the law of subversive advocacy, from Judge Learned Hand's opinion in the *Masses* case to the per curiam opinion in *Brandenberg vs Ohio.* There is, however, a gaping hole in this discussion: There is no discussion except that already quoted of solicitation statutes properly so called, or of the principle enunciated by Judge Hand in the Masses case; "There has always been a recognized limit to such expressions, incident indeed to the existence of any compulsive power of the state itself. One may not counsel or advise others to violate the law as it stands."

Justice Brandeis, in later writing of the allied inchoate crime of conspiracy, went somewhat less far in recognizing solicitation offenses but still far enough to reach solicitation of most serious political violence:

> Prohibition of free speech and assembly is a measure so stringent that it would be inappropriate as the means of averting a relatively trivial harm to society . . . it is hardly conceivable that this Court would hold constitutional a statute which punished as a felony the mere voluntary assembly with a society formed to teach that pedestrians have the moral right to cross unenclosed, unposted, waste lands and to advocate their doing so, even if there was imminent danger that advocacy would lead to a trespass. The fact that speech is likely to result in some violence or in destruction of property is not enough to justify its suppression. There must be the probability of serious injury to the state.

Surely, however, whatever may be said of Justice Brandeis' anticipation of the sit-in demonstrations, solicitation of the more serious felonies would constitute under this formula the probability of serious injury to the state.[10] The issue of solicitation to trespass anticipated by Brandeis in *Whitney* was never decided by the Supreme Court in the context of the sit-in demonstrations of the 1960s, the court successfully avoiding the question in *Shuttlesworth v. Birmingham* and *Cox v. Louisiana*, of which Kalven in another work remarks, "The issue raised by this advocacy of sit-in demonstrations dropped out of the case, however, thus eliminating a difficult free speech issue. On what would the legality of advocating sit-ins depend? Clear and present dangers of sit-ins? Legality of the sit-ins?" The failure to discuss the permissible scope and nature of solicitation statutes is a gap at the heart of this work as of most articles on free speech doctrine. It is difficult to justify solicitation of particular violent acts on the basis of the apologia for solicitation of violent revolution suggested. But "where the man is seriously enough at odds with the society to advocate violent overthrow, his speech has utility not because advocating violence is useful but because the premises underlying his call to action should be heard." Although Kalven does not say so loudly, however, it is plain that he would prefer a rule that permits prosecution of solicitation of crime even without a clear and present danger limitation but that would otherwise protect political speech to a rule which would require that any prohibited speech present a clear and present danger of substantive evil. He describes the *Masses* decision as "vastly superior to Holmes' effort." Under the Holmes approach, speech that contained no concrete advocacy of action might be reached if the danger were great enough. By contrast, the Hand approach might fail to reach speech that was imminently dangerous but cleverly worded, and it might also fail to protect speech that was militantly worded but not in fact dangerous. My own feeling is that the Hand approach serves to interpose a weightier barrier against the state's impulse in times of tension to intercept serious radical criticism. It is true, as Kalven recognizes, that where solicitation statutes are the only restraints on political speech, "a general militant program which argues for the use of violence as a necessary means to a desired social change may generate over time a climate in which the use of specific violent means becomes possible." But where suggestion of specific means is avoided, it is unlikely, to borrow Brandeis's phrase in *Whitney* that "the incident of the evil apprehended is so imminent that it may fall before there is opportunity for full discussion." Viewed in this light, it is not clear that statutes proscribing advocacy of overthrow serve any useful purpose at all. Even a requirement of clear and present danger or imminence may concede too much to censorship where the statute is sweeping and general and directed at criticism of a form of government.

It is hard to see how a program of overthrow could ultimately be carried out without at some point soliciting specific felonies. Prosecutions for soliciting felonies as distinct from soliciting overthrow also have practical advantages: They call to their aid the unambiguous public abhorrencefor common law crimes rather than appearing in the guise of persecution of a political minority.

In *Herndon v. Lowery*, this insight informs Justice Roberts's opinion, which condemns "a law general in its description of the mischief to be remedied" and points out; "the act does not prohibit incitement to violent interference with any given activity or operation of the state" or "with a willful attempt to obstruct a described defined activity of the government." *Taylor v. Mississippi*, a neglected decision directly addressing a solicitation statute, "struck a statute prohibiting communications discouraging saluting of the flag, relying on the Barnette decision." Kalven notes "Justice Roberts in *Taylor* comes close to asserting that whenever the state leaves the individual free to decide for himself whether or not to do certain acts, it must be open to others to urge advocate or incite him either to act or not act. This idea could be far reaching; it could yield the premise that the state can enlist the criminal law against speech only as an adjunct to its enforcement of the criminal law itself." In such a formulation the only permissible regulation of political speech would be solicitation statutes.

Kalven continues to trace what he regards as the progress of the law away from the clear and present danger doctrine and toward the requirement of specificity alluded to by Judge Hand in the *Masses* case and expressed in the language of the *Yates* case: "Those to whom the advocacy is addressed must be urged to do something now or in the future." The series of cases culminates in *Brandenberg v. Ohio*, which revives clear and present danger as a requirement additional to specific advocacy. In discussing the limitations upon *Brandenberg*, Kalven does not allude to the possibility that the clear and present danger or imminence requirement does not exist in cases involving solicitations of specific felonies, but he does refer to another possible limiting principle, that *Brandenberg* may apply only to individual speech rather than group advocacy: "This question cannot be said to be settled by Brandenberg and still must await further clarification."

Since *Brandenberg* did not purport to overrule *Dennis*: "The court [in *Yates*] and Justice Harlan are not willing to go that far . . . they set the lines for group speech as incitement to future action." Kalven concludes: "Twenty years after Dennis the law still awaits an answer to the question: What is the constitutionally appropriate counter move if any against an organization with the power, purpose, and teachings which Justice Jackson ascribed to the Communist party in 1951? Jackson may well not have been right on the facts, but whether he was right or not, he put a question we need a rule of law to answer." The present principle is that of the *Scales* case.

Kalven proceeds to a discussion of the compulsory disclosure cases, referring initially to *Talley v. California*, in which Justice Black for the majority in invalidating a statute requiring the author and publisher of handbills to be identified on them emphasized "that anonymity has sometimes been assumed for the most constructive purposes." The dissenters took the view that "the ordinance makes for the responsibility in writing that is present in public utterance." This controversy recurs in the journalist's privilege cases, which Kalven did not live to address in his work.

The *Talley* decision is contrasted with *New York ex rel Bryant v. Zimmerman* in which an early New York statute requiring disclosure of the membership of the Ku Klux Klan was upheld. Kalven points out, "The chilling impact of the disclosure is justified not as a necessary byproduct of some other proper state purpose but as the very point of the statute."

The *Bryant* case was limited by later decisions relating to efforts of southern states to require disclosure of membership in the NAACP. Here the court applies an explicit balancing test to limit the *Bryant* principle: "where there is a significant encroachment upon personal liberty the state may prevail only upon showing a subordinating interest which is compelling," which was found to be lacking. The balance, however, was struck differently in *Communist Party v. Subversive Activities Control Board.* This decision Kalven regards as "the precedent which carries the greatest threat to political freedoms in the future." It is not the compulsory disclosure aspects of the case that upset Kalven: "perhaps the sanction of official stigmatism should be available to government under special circumstances," but rather use of "parallelism"—comparison between the Party's position and that of a foreign power—as evidence. "This line of proof can never be worth what the legal system must pay for it in First Amendment values." In seeking the central principle of the case, Kalven rejects Justice Frankfurter's effort to limit the case to groups dominated by foreign powers: "organizations are subject to it only when shown, after administrative hearings subject to judicial review, to be dominated by the foreign power or its organs and to operate to advance its purposes." Kalven observes, "Surely the court is not holding that the use of such sanctions against a group is justified only when the group is foreign controlled and dominated." But this is not an absurd distinction. In light of the powers available to modern governments, it is often said to be a truism that few armed insurgencies succeed in the absence of overwhelming public support without the assistance of a foreign government.

Kalven concludes his discussion of the case by noting the subsequent difficulties in applying it in light of the privilege against self-incrimination. "When the rationale for disclosure is substantial, it is likely that criminal laws will bear upon the subject and hence that the disclosure requirement will run afoul of the Fifth Amendment." Once again it is seen that sedition laws add little or nothing to the effectiveness of the ordinary criminal law dealing with problems of political insurrection.

Partial Sanctions

Kalven proceeds to a discussion of cases involving the so-called attorney general's list and other efforts to stigmatize groups as such. He rejects the position of Justice Reed: "This designation does not prohibit any business of the organizations, subject them to any punishment or deprive them of liberty of speech or other freedom . . . they are in the position of any proponent of unpopular views. Heresy induces strong expressions of opposition." Kalven shares the view of Justice Frankfurter's concurrence that "official stigmatization is a sanction subject to judicial review under the Constitution." It is doubtful, however, that the *Joint Anti-Fascist* case with its multiple opinions goes this far. Read together with the later case of *Greene v. McElroy*, it can be read as holding that the stigmatization requires judicial review when it triggers additionalsanctions imposed by government. This reconciles the *Joint Anti-Fascist* case with the otherwise irreconcilable cases involving publicity activities by government agencies and indeed those involving compelled public invocation of the Fifth Amendment privilege itself.

"The judicial process in the partial sanction case can be viewed as a form of balancing," Kalven observes. "All partial sanction cases have a twin aspect. A law providing that you cannot be a Y if you are a member of X may be viewed either as an abridgement of the freedom to be a Y or as an abridgement of the freedom to belong to X." He praises the opinion of Chief Justice Vinson in the *Douds* case as a holding that "In partial sanction cases the constitutionality of the sanction must be tested by viewing it in each of its twin aspects." Kalven might have noted that a similar analysis was applied under the rubric of "unconstitutional conditions" in cases involving efforts to extend federal regulation of economic activity. Many of the same issues arise today in connection with conditional exercises of the federal spending power. It is an understatement to say that the Supreme Court's treatment of these matters has not always partaken of the sensitivity displayed in the *Douds* case.

In his discussion of *Douds*, Kalven notes in passing the holding of *United States v. Brown* extending the prohibition of bills of attainder to efforts to impose partial sanctions on named persons or members of named groups. In both the prior *Lovett* case and numerous other cases Justice Frankfurter would have applied not the attainder clause or other specific guarantees but principles of procedural due process so as to define the separation of powers between legislative and judicial branches. Kalven is certainly correct in saying that "the prohibition against attainders embodies values similar to those set forth in the great generic amendments as the First and the Fifth."

Kalven commences his discussion of "partial sanctions" with a quotation from Justice Black's opinion in the *S.A.C.B.* case on their cumulative effect: "Having thus made it mandatory that Communist organizations and individual Communists make a full disclosure of their identities and activities, the Act then proceeds to heap burden after burden upon those so exposed . . . and thus makes it extremely difficult for a member of the Communist party to live in this country and at the same time makes it a crime for him to try to get a passport to get out." Earlier in the *Douds* case, Black observed: "Restrictions imposed on proscribed groups are seldom static, even though the rate of expansion may not move in geometric progression from discrimination to arm-band to ghetto or worse. . . . Thus I cannot regard the Court's holding as one which merely bars Communists from holding union office and nothing more. . . . For its reasoning would apply just as forcibly to statutes barring Communists and their suspected sympathizers from election to political office, mere membership in unions, and in fact from getting or holding any jobs whereby they could earn a living." That these fears are not chimerical is illustrated by the use of such comprehensive sanctions in Czechoslovakia to relegate to menial employment members of the short-lived 1968 government, and by the casual proposals that have sometimes been made in the United States for the broad use of employment disqualifications ancillary to criminal convictions.

Test Oaths

Kalven discusses at length the frequent use of test oaths as employment disqualifications. His discussion here might have referred, but does not, to the post-Civil War experience. He notes that the court in *Douds* and in the later *Gerende* case upheld the use of negative oaths, largely by analogy to the positive oaths required of public officers by the Constitution and by summary rejection of the premise that use of an oath constitutes a religious test for public office forbidden by Article VI of the Constitution. In his discussion of the *Douds* case he notes the partial dissents of Justices Frankfurter and Jackson, who would have invalidated the negative oath there challenged because it required a declaration as to matters of "belief." Justice Jackson there observed, "It is time enough for the law to lay hold of the citizen when he acts illegally, or in some rare circumstance when his thoughts are given illegal utterance. I think we must let his mind alone." Kalven observes,

> The question is whether any meaningful additional protection is afforded to liberty beyond that given by freedom of speech by holding that beliefs are inviolate. When a belief is translated into words, it loses any distinctive immunity as belief; when belief is silent, it would seem protected not by law but by the sheer impracticality of policing it. This suggests that the one occasion when talk of inviolate beliefs makes sense is when we deal with religion. And as Justice Black argues from history, the chief if not the only way the law can reach such inner activities is by way of the oath, by compelling affirmance of that which the true believer cannot affirm.

Kalven finds in the cases strictly reading negative oath requirements (and in the *Baggett* case positive oath requirements as well) a tendency to apply the *Scales* principle not only in the context of the criminal law but in that of the "partial sanction" of denial of public employment. "What is at stake is whether the risk calculus of the prudent employer is not in a radical sense at war with the normal regard we have for First Amendment freedoms. . . . The actuary always imputes guilt by association. But respect for the air of freedom in the United States requires that the government as employer live dangerously." The later opinions of justices Warren and Brennan in the *Robel* case seem to suggest that a balancing test may be applied to validate oaths going beyond the criminal law *Scales* standard with respect to sensitive positions in defense plants: "Perhaps 'the keeper of the arsenal' may still be disqualified for mere membership in the Communist Party." The *Keyhesian* case, however, is said to bar going beyond the *Scales* standards in denying employment to teachers, as to which considerations of academic freedom have been relied upon to justify a strict standard.

Foreign Affairs

Professor Kalven goes on to discuss another partial sanction, denial of a passport. He is unconvinced by Justice Goldberg's effort to rest his decision in the *Aptheker* case on the notion that travel enjoys a preferred position akin to speech and association. Rather he would analyse the case as a freedom of association case; if so viewed, there existed "the awkward fact that Flynn and Aptheker because of the active nature of their membership, could be said to satisfy the Scales standards." At a more extreme level than denial of a passport, he finds some merit in preferred treatment of the right to travel, quoting Justice Douglas's opinion in *Aptheker*: "The ticketing of people and the use of identification papers are routine matters under totalitarian regimes . . . once the right to travel is curtailed, all other rights suffer, just as when curfew or home detention is placed upon a person." This use of extreme restrictions on travel and telephone communication as a device to suppress political speech and association was dramatically in evidence in connection with the Polish declaration of martial law. But the appropriate analysis, for Kalven, is still one focusing not on the interference with travel but the interference with association, at least where the travel restrictions are not imposed on society at large. Where they are, as in the case of restrictions on dissemination of mail, the court in *Lamont v. Postmaster General* effectively adopted the view of Justice Holmes' dissenting opinion in the *Burleson* case: "the use of the mails is almost as much a part of free speech as the right to use our tongues," or, as Justice Brennan put it, "it would be a barren marketplace of ideas that had only sellers and no buyers."

Kalven proceeds to a discussion of sanctions "out from under the Constitution"—deportation, denaturalization, exclusion, and the regulation of passports. The *Scales* standards are inapplicable to deportation of resident aliens. In the Bridges case, statutory construction was employed to hold that the "affiliation" with communism required was more than parallism with the party's lawful aims, and limiting constructions have been given the "meaningful association" limitation in the statute. The principal limitation imposed on denaturalization is that of *Baumgartner v. United States*: "Utterances made in years subsequent to the oath are not readily to be charged against the state of mind existing when the oath was administered." The passing of the McCarthy era has not reduced litigation in this sphere, which has continued in consequence of the activities of the Justice Department's Office of Special Investigations relating to alleged Nazi war criminals.

The exclusion cases likewise relate to what is still, by reason of recent immigration from Haiti, Southeast Asia, and Central America, a live issue. The cases as of 1974 still stood for the proposition that "the entrant alien stopped at the border, the resident alien faced with a deportation order, and even the naturalized citizen threatened with denaturalization though they may stand on American soil are excluded from the domain of the First Amendment." In the *Mandel* case, Justice Blackmun acknowledged that "First Amendment rights are implicated" but concluded that making an argument against exclusion based on them would prove too much since some Americans could be found who would claim an interest in interacting with any person. Kalven found the seeds of possible future growth in the *Mandel* opinion and in the dissenting opinion of Justice Jackson in the *Mezei* case with its proposition that "when indefinite confinement becomes the means of enforcement . . . due process requires that the alien be informed of its grounds and have a fair chance to overcome them."

With respect to the regulation of passports, Kalven notes the Supreme Court's policy of narrow construction of restrictions, manifested in *Kent v. Dulles*, and then refers to Justice Goldberg's unsatisfying opinion in the *Aptheker* case, with its apparent recognition of a right of international travel. In *Zemel v. Rusk* a restriction on travel to Cuba was upheld on the basis that it was imposed not because of any characteristic peculiar to appellant, but rather because of foreign policy considerations affecting all citizens. The court declared, "The right to speak and publish does not carry with it the unrestrained right to gather information." Later years have seen further elaboration of the so-called right to gather information, as Kalven forecast, with his reference to "novel and refreshing First Amendment challenges about the danger of decreased data flow."

Legislative Investigations

Kalven turns to a discussion of First Amendment restrictions on legislative investigation. He alludes to the enthusiastic defense of investigatory powers by liberals inquiring into business practices in the 1930s, and acknowledges, "The Senate Watergate Committee seemed to many of us who had been bitterly critical of HUAC two decades earlier an example in a time of need of one of democracy's better institutions. The vast publicity focussed upon individual witnesses was seen as performing the indispensable function of influencing public opinion; the theatrical posturing of the Senators was perceived as the orderly process of law—at last." Kalven distinguishes Watergate from earlier congressional inquiries on the not altogether convincing ground that "the Watergate investigation was an investigation of government itself and not of private individuals. It is true too the individual witnesses in 1973 were persons who were or had been men of power and status, with friends in the White House itself so that the contest was at a little more on parity. Also the procedures and etiquette of the investigators had improved markedly and counsel for the witness was allowed some role in the proceedings." Kalven notes that the grievance against compelled testimony by investigative committees derives from their characteristic as a "trial" of the individual, "a perfectly wretched trial, a trial which transgresses almost all norms of procedural decency." Such inquiries also "where the legislative inquiry touches the opinions of the witnesses or membership in various organizations . . . impose sanctions—the unpleasantness of the proceedings themselves and the private reactions such as loss of employment that appearance before a committee may trigger." Kalven wrote before the era of use immunity and the resulting phenomenon of compelled public testimony followed by a criminal trial before a jury of persons who are idiots in the classical sense. It is not difficult to imagine what he would have thought of it.

Kalven begins his discussion of legislative inquiry by noting the principle of *Kilbourn v. Thompson*, decided in 1881, that Congress lacks any general power of making inquiry into the private affairs of the citizen. He notes that the principle was nominally reaffirmed in the *McGrain* case, but negated by the principle that the court will not go behind declarations that the compulsory inquiry is in aid of legislation. Kalven would revive *Kilbourn*: "The unexamined step is the assumption that facts about individuals who are unwilling to disclose them voluntarily are the kind of information that on any theory of legislation informs the lawmaking judgment. It is surely absurd to assume, as we solemnly have done for years, that the best route to legislative insight is to inventory the

Communists in the United States, one at a time." The difficulty with this argument and with Kalven's efforts to revive *Kilbourn* is that it disregards facts of human nature and political life. Kalven elsewhere recognized that "the motivating force behind much congressional investigation today is the need for Congress to match the President as a focal point of news. . . . Congressional inquiries, if they are little else, are newsworthy." Persons, activities, and practices may be illustrative of the evils campaigned against. This was true of Charles Evans Hughes's inquiries into the insurance and gas trusts that formed the background of modern state public utility regulation; it was true of the Pecora committee inquiries giving rise to securities legislation, of Senator Black's lobbying investigation prior to enactment of the Public Utility Holding Company Act, and of the Kefauver investigations of organized crime. Whatever one may think of either the technique or the legislation, impairment of congressional investigatory power would readjust the powers of the branches of government to the detriment of Congress.

The dissents that would have curbed investigatory power during the McCarthy period stressed the sanctions imposed by private opinion. Judge Edgerton in the *Barsky* case declared, "The investigation restricts freedom of speech by uncovering and stigmatizing expressions of unpopular views. . . . there has been some suggestion that it restrains only timid people. . . . I think it nearer the truth to say that among the more articulate it affects in one degree or another all but the very courageous, the very orthodox and the very secure." While this may be true, one must call to mind Justice Brandeis's observation that "courage is the secret of freedom."

Kalven notes the reluctance of the courts to interfere on substantive grounds and observes, "There is a strong argument to be made . . . that democratic civilized values are most essentially protected by norms of procedural due process rather than by First Amendment norms."

In his discussion of procedural restrictions, Kalven makes note of the effort of justices Jackson, Black, and Frankfurter to disqualify government employees as jurors in all cases the government prosecutes. Justice Frankfurter asserted the view that "if a particular group no matter what its beliefs is under pressure of popular hostility, excluding jurors particularly susceptible to such pressure is not an expression of regard for political opinions but recognition by law of the facts of life." This declaration, joined in by the three greatest justices of their time, has contemporary resonance in view of the abuses attendant upon compelled public testimony and the habit of the government of bringing political prosecutions before juries in the District of Columbia composed largely of government employees, a practice that makes nonsense of the purposes sought to be served by the vicinage clauses of the Constitution.

Kalven recalls that the course followed by the Court as stated by Justice Jackson in the *Eisler* case leaves the responsibility for the behavior of its committees squarely on the shoulders of Congrees'. In the *Christoffel* case, conviction for contempt was reversed because of the absence of a quorum that "moderates somewhat the excesses of one man committees." In the *Rumely* case, the lack of authorization of the committee was held decisive; in the *Bart* case it was held that a committee must explicitly direct a witness to answer; while in the *Watkins* case the nub of the decision despite broad rhetoric was that the particular question was not pertinent to the authorizing resolution.

Kalven also notes the decision in the *Quinn* case that a witness could not be compelled to answer a question about communist affiliation because of the danger of prosecution under the Smith Act, another illustration of the frequently counterproductive nature of sedition legislation. This made possible the phenomenon of the "Fifth Amendment Communist" since "in the legislative investigation context the privilege to refuse to answer on self-incrimination grounds tends to boomerang." With the advent of use immunity the predicament of the public congressional witness worsens further. He is no longer required or entitled to condemn himself publicly by invoking the privilege; instead his public compelled testimony infects any future trial by requiring the exclusion of the more literate or truthful jurors.

In *Sweezy v. New Hampshire* the breadth of a delegation to a state attorney general was held to invalidate the statute, but direct limitation of investigatory power was avoided, although justices Frankfurter and Harlan would have done so. "An inquiry into what was being taught in a university and an inquiry into a witness' affiliations with a conventional political party" are prohibited. Kalven speculates that a majority was not found because justices Warren, Black, Douglas, and Brennan wanted to extend this protection to inquiries into Communist affiliations. In consequence, Justice Frankfurter's eloquent words about the position of universities remain dicta, although they have continuing pertinence to not merely congressional investigations but the later activities of the civil rights enforcement agencies. Quoting a remonstrance of South African scholars, he referred to "the four essential freedoms of a university—to determine for itself, on academic grounds, who may teach, what may be taught, how it shall be taught, and who may be admitted to study."

In the *Barenblatt* case the court expressly declined to impose a First Amendment limitation on inquiries about communism, subjecting the considerations adduced in *Sweezy* to balancing against "the long and widely accepted view that the tenets of the communist party include [ultimate violent overthrow], a view which has been given formal expression by Congress." Thus the sedition legislation despite its ineffectiveness in other contexts validated legislative inquiries that might otherwise be proscribed. The court's final conclusion was that "the strict requirements of a prosecution under the Smith Act are not the measure of the permissible scope of a congressional investigation for of necessity the investigatory power must proceed step by step." In *Uphaus*, immunities assumed in *Sweezy* to be available to universities and legitimate political parties were held unavailable to other associations. The later *Deutsch* and *Russell* cases enforced pertinency requirements, while the *Gibson* case found that the investigating committee failed to show a sufficient nexus with the subject of its investigation. The subsequent *Gellen* case involves an issue that the advent of use immunity may cause to recur. It held that a committee must comply with its own rule permitting executive session testimony, over the objection of dissenters that "public revelation of the truth . . . does not fall within the area of unjust injury to reputation." The subsequent *Gojack* case invalidated a contempt citation on the basis of an insufficient legislative delegation to a subcommittee. It is doubtful that the *Barenblatt* holding, with which Kalven disagreed, justifies his conclusion that "the law has failed to work itself pure." The procedural cases, as he acknowledges, constitute movement toward insistence upon "political responsibility for the course charted by legislative inquiry." That, rather than the effort to impose substantive limitations on sanctions which in the end are imposed not by government but by public opinion appears the course demanded by the separation of powers. A different rule, of course, may apply where the government itself through future criminal prosecution or by collateral government- imposed sanctions seeks to use the compelled testimony adversely to the witness.

Affidavit Requirements

From congressional inquiry, Kalven turned to a discussion of affidavit requirements for public privileges. In *Speiser v. Randall*, the court declared, "the state bears the burden of persuasion to show the appellants engaged in criminal speech . . . the possibility of mistaken fact finding inherent in all litigation will create the danger that the legitimate utterance may be penalized." In *Speiser*, the statute was condemned because the oath, though cast in a form permissible under *Yates*, was not accepted as conclusive. "The burden was placed upon the taxpayer of showing his innocence of prohibited advocacy."

Although the bar admission cases resemble the loyalty oath cases, the Court, led by Justice Harlan, vigorously asserted the state's right to go beyond the *Scales* target questions "to supplement that evidence and to test the applicant's credibility." More recent cases decline to accept the argument that "there inheres in such a system so consistent a threat to applicants that constitutional deprivations will be inevitable. The implication of this argument is that no screening will be constitutionally permissible beyond academic examination and extremely minimal checking for serious concrete character deficiencies." This is Kalven's preference. He expresses the fear that "the relatively moribund inquiry into character . . . provides in times of political stress a ready-made loyalty program. It is tempting therefore to suggest breaking the easy linkage from inquiry into moral character to inquiry into political reliability. But this surely throws out the baby with the bathwater."

Kalven adduces as an example of what is to be feared Justice Blackmun's expressed concern about "courtroom spectacles brought about by attorneys . . . who give indications of ignoring their responsibilities to the judicial process." Kalven observes, "If Arizona had more directly pursued this interest in not having trials politicized, it would have posed a difficult but genuine issue of constitutional policy in which one could argue both about the desirability of the ends and the suitability of the means." In his discussion of the Chicago contempt trials, he elaborated further on his views as to the behavior of lawyers in political cases.

TIME, PLACE, AND MANNER RESTRICTIONS

This summary of Kalven's work brings us to the chapters not written, which would have dealt with non-content regulation. We know from other writings,however,something of what Kalven would have said here. As to public demonstrations, Kalven was credited by both his allies and his critics with popularizing "the concept of the public forum." His essays so doing were inspired by the civil rights movement with its "structured ceremonials of protest; they are not riots."

Kalven notes that *Edwards v. South Carolina* invalidated breach of the peace convictions because of the generality of the offenses charged. The subsequent case of *Cox v. Louisiana* deliberately left muddied the question whether a conviction could stand for a demonstration that obstructed a public passageway, the court instead treating the statute as an informal permit or licensing arrangement. The court however was explicit in upholding a courthouse picketing statute. Kalven asserted the proposition "that in an open democratic society the streets, the parks, and other public places are an important facility for public discussion and political process . . . a public forum that the citizen can commandeer; the generosity and empathy with which such facilities are made available is an index of freedom."[11] But Kalven went further, asserting that "only confusion can result from distingushing sharply between 'speech pure' and 'speech plus'. . . . What is required is a Robert's Rules of order for the new uses of the public forum."

Kalven alluded to Justice Roberts's dictum in *Hague v. C.I.O.* that streets and parks have "time out of mind been used for purposes of assembly, communicating thoughts between citizens and discussing public questions." This dictum, joined by at most two other justices, was followed by Justice Black's declaration in *Jamison v. Texas* suggesting that distributors of literature rightfully on a street enjoyed "the constitutional right to express . . . views in an orderly fashion." Finally, in *Niemotko*, Justice Frankfurter, summarizing the cases, said that they proscribed only totally arbitrary control of public places.

In *Schneider* the court, anticipating *Jamison*, held that concern about littering did not take precedence over First Amendment rights, though "a person could not exercise this liberty by taking his stand in the middle of a crowded street contrary to traffic regulations and maintain his position to the stoppage of all traffic." Three subsequent cases involving leaflet distribution reaffirmed that littering was not enough. In the *Talley* case the court said that speech on public throughfares may not be unduly burdened or proscribed.

"There are," Kalven observes, with what some may regard as gross understatement, "Some differences between a lone distributor of leaflets on a city street and two thousand pickets at a courthouse." *Cox v. Louisiana* distinguished between "patrolling, marching, and picketing" and leafleting, the latter alone being regarded as "pure speech." Kalven regarded this distinction as untenable, since it would impugn the conduct in *Edwards* (the decision in which, however, rested on the vagueness of the statute). He urged that "all speech is 'speechplus.' If it is oral, it is noise . . . if it is written, it may be litter." Surely this argument goes too far. Even the recent flag-burning case rejects it.

Kalven concedes, as a substitute limiting principle, that "speech has always depended on some commitment to order and etiquette." He approvingly quotes Alexander Meiklejohn: "No one may, without consent of nurse or doctor, rise up in a sickroom to argue for his principles or his candidate. . . . Anyone who would thus irresponsibly interrupt the activities of a lecture, a hospital, a concert hall, a church . . . a classroom, a football field or a home does not thereby exhibit his freedom. Rather he shows himself to be a boor, a public nuisance who must be abated, by force if necessary."

Prior Restraint

Cox v. New Hampshire upheld a parade permit ordinance aimed at giving authorities notice to permit proper policing, and allowing adjustments in time, place, and manner as would avoid disturbance but "did not tell whether certain congested areas or . . . times of the day might . . . always be held unavailable . . . nor whether the size of some crowds might always be too large."

Kalven notes the role of licensing schemes in this area, where "detailed legislative regulation is a clumsy inflexible device." "There is little, if anything, left today of the idea that prior licensing is bad per se, regardless of the criteria used . . . the historical reaction was against general licensing with unlimited or unspecified grounds for exercise of discretion." Kalven noted that *Times Film* had upheld a prior restraint, although *Freedman v. Maryland* spoke of the "heavy presumption" against prior restraints and the later *Pentagon Papers* case and *Carroll v. Princess Anne* carried the presumption further.

Kalven fairly notes "the parade, the picket, the leaflet, the sound truck have been the media of communication exploited by those with little access to the more genteel means of communication." Although critical of *Cox v. Louisiana*, he notes that in it "the court had the benefit of the counsel of a deliberate, specific and relevant legislative judgment." But he is clearly too casual in dismissing the concern that mass demonstrations interfering with the normal activities of others frequently turn into tests not of ideological but of physical strength. Plazas and parks may indeed be public fora; it is less clear that obstructed streets should be, Kalven's criticism of *Cox* notwithstanding, "Symbolic speech" in the streets or elsewhere may cause problems of public order that "speech pure" does not, precisely because of its emotive and simplistic nature. There is little basis save a revived group defamation to distinguish between a burnt flag and a burnt cross or scrawled swastika.

Picketing, Kalven grudgingly concedes, "carries an ambiguous hint of coercion and economic pressure." Its limitation in labor cases was founded on the insight, expressed in the *Meadowmoor* case[12] that "It must never be forgotten . . . that the Bill of Rights was the child of the enlightenment. Back of the guarantee of free speech lay faith in the power of an appeal to reason by all the peaceful means for gaining access to the mind. It was in order to avert force and explosions due to restrictions upon rational modes of communication that the guarantee of free speech was given a generous scope. But utterance in a context of violence can lose its significance as an appeal to reason and become part of an instrument of force."

Privacy

Kalven's writing on privacy issues as they impact free speech was also extensive. He describes *Public Utilities v. Pollak*, the famous District of Columbia bus music case, as "the captive audience issue, standing alone." He approvingly quotes Justice Douglas's criticism of "a form of coercion to make people listen." He notes that this freedom, if made absolute "makes the closed mind a principal feature of the open society and is inconsistent with compulsory education," undervaluing here the special position of minors in free speech doctrine. He is not averse to the temporary conscription of unwilling audiences by symbolic speech, door-to-door calling, or public demonstrations, and his point here seems well taken.

He is critical of *Time Inc. v. Hill*,[13] which "extended constitutional scrutiny of tort law to whatever is newsworthy . . . this giant step without being forced to an explicit justification for it." He approves of Justice Harlan's opinion stressing the lack of any assumption of risk by the Hills and the lack of an effective ability to reply and favors a qualified privilege for the press defeasible by negligence similar to that which Justice Fortas in *St. Amant v. Thompson* urged for libel of public figures. "Other professional activity of great social value is carried on under a duty of reasonable care and there is no reason to suspect the press would be less able to do so." He is unimpressed with most of the discussion of a right to privacy.[14] "We are left as the core concerns with the computer, the subliminal stimulus, the polygraph, and the personality test. . . . I am not fully persuaded that these core problems are serious problems and I am less persuaded that they concern privacy."

Mass Communications

Kalven did not live to comment on *Buckley v. Valeo* and the strikingly counterproductive post-Watergate campaign finance legislation. He was sceptical of the fairness doctrine: "It is most unlikely that public discussion will have muscle tone if each publisher must worry about being fair to both sides." He was hopeful that the progress of technology would eliminate concerns about concentration of control over broadcasting: "What would be left of the case for governmental control over broadcasting if licenses were allocated to the highest bidder and if there was widespread pay TV."[15] At an early age, at least, he felt with Learned Hand that "application of the antitrust laws will help and Mr. Ernst suggests certain minor controls—graduated postage subsidies, incentive taxes, etc."[16] These hopes have not been realized. He cautioned that "Minow should watch his step in the wasteland."[17] And yet, with characteristic realism, he was alarmed by the influence of television on the young, which "may argue for a revision of the holding in *Butler v. Michigan* . . . since television is so much the child's medium of entertainment today it is not altogether easy to decide how far if at all general television programming might be regulated on their behalf." Presumably he would regard with some sympathy the practice of some European countries of beginning their broadcast day at 6:00 in the evening.

Commercial Speech

Kalven's chapter on commercial speech, though apparently complete, was deleted by his editors[18] in the least defensible of their editorial judgments. The stated ground is that his account, which apparently supported the rule of the *Valentine* and *Breard* cases, was rendered obsolete by the later law and that his probable attitude toward the legalization of professional advertising, effectively a revival of economic due process, was unclear. This would justify relegation of the chapter to an appendix, but not its deletion from the work. Equally regrettable is the failure to reproduce the comprehensive bibliography of Kalven's writings that appears at 43 *University of Chicago Law Review* 15 (1975).

The recent decision of the Supreme Court upholding a Florida regulation prohibiting lawyers from soliciting personal injury claimants within thirty days of the occurrences giving rise to their claims has prompted not one but two bemused columns by Linda Greenhouse. A public educated by Philip Howard's *Death of Common Sense* and Mary Ann Glendon's *A Nation Under Lawyers* must share her puzzlement. It must seem fortunate that homes in Florida are accompanied by hurricane cellars, in which the survivors of accidents may take refuge from plaintiffs' lawyers on the thirty-first day following their injuries. For under current doctrine, a lawyer who solicits clients immediately following an accident is potentially a criminal but is transformed after thirty days into a possessor of constitutional immunities. Bankruptcy and divorce lawyers are not yet subject to the new principle; they may descend without delay on judgment debtors and participants in domestic disputes, since their activities have not yet been found to comparably offend against good taste or impair the reputation of the bar, the controlling considerations in this latest twist to "commercial speech" doctrine. "The Supreme Court," Chief Justice Hughes once observed, "is forever building new mansions of constitutional law, which collapse when too many stories are added." The demise of what remains of "commercial speech" doctrine is long overdue. The notion that the First Amendment, conceived as a protection of political speech and the public's right to self-government, extended also to commercial advertising and solicitation was a novelty invented by Mr. Justice Blackmun in 1975 to protect the right of a District of Columbia abortionist to advertise in Virginia. This result required the repudiation of a case upholding state regulation of interstate advertisement by optometrists that had been decided by a unanimous court less than ten years previously, and of two earlier similarly unanimous decisions joined in by, among others, Justices Black, Douglas, Frankfurter, and Jackson, none of whom were noted enemies of the First Amendment. From this inauspicious beginning, roundly. criticized by most legal commentators at the time, has sprung an almost uniquely confused body of doctrine. State regulations of legal and medical advertising have been condemned by opinions that seemingly restrict state power to the prevention of common law fraud, notwithstanding the inequality of knowledge as between clients and professionals. Solicitation by lawyers has been similarly allowed, and restrictions on self-laudation dispensed with, as observers of the Simpson trial may have noticed. On the other hand, advertising by casinos in Puerto Rico may be restricted, since neighboring citizens, as distinct from tourists, may be corrupted thereby. Tupperware parties on college campuses, which potentially affect the offspring of lawyers and judges, may properly be prohibited. Commercial speech, we are told, is constitutionally protected, but not as much as political speech; the Supreme Court, and before it the lower courts, will tell us when it is and when it is not.

A field day of litigation has ensued. Egged on by our contemporary Jacobin clubs, the civil liberties unions, a rich harvest of local regulations has fallen under the judicial scythe. Regulations of liquor billboards in slums, of street beggary in declining central cities, of real estate blockbusting in troubled neighborhoods, of boardwalk displays in decaying resort communities have been condemned or subjected to prolonged and expensive challenges. Defenders of such local efforts are informed by the "civil libertarians," who generally live elsewhere, that they are addressing symptoms, not causes, and that "larger solutions," must be found to social ills, presumably from a more socialist government at Washington. Professional regulations have met with a similar fate: The notion that professional relationships are sounder when initiated by the client rather than the professional has gone by the board, as has the view that professionals are transmitters of values, not merely sellers of indulgences. The excesses in lawyers' television advertisements have often been remarked; the medical profession, less versed in its legal rights, has been slower off the mark, but some of its excesses—widespread advertising of potentially dangerous eye operations and the growing direct promotion of prescription drugs—have been even more appalling. Yet the professions and their regulators have been held disentitled to prefer competition in quality of services to competition in advertising budgets. Lawyers who once sought public notice through political, civic, and scholarly activities now are free to hire public relations men; medical specialists who once would have attracted few patients without the approbation of their peers now can directly appeal to a credulous public. Nor are the litigation excesses those of the left only; nullifying standards of behavior is a game that any number can play, and there is a mounting industry assault on regulations of the liquor, tobacco, and gambling traffic and indeed on the securities laws.

The doctrine has received acquiescence in surprising quarters. Judge Robert Bork in a recent article in *Commentary* criticizing almost all aspects of current free speech doctrine had not a word to say on commercial speech.

Yet there remain those who are as repelled by compulsory Thatcherism as by compulsory Jacobinism. They recall the neglected words of Mr. Justice Cardozo: "A motive to build up through legislation the quality of men may be as creditable in the minds of some as a motive to multiply the quantity of trade. Courts put this matter aside as beyond their lawful competence." The "commercial speech" doctrine effectively disenfranchises those who doubt that all problems are susceptible of market solutions on the one hand or national government solutions on the other and who suspect that our present social difficulties are in no small measure due to the undermining of civic spirit and the authority and self-confidence of local and professional institutions. Virtually all human activity involves verbal communication; to allow the courts a roving commission to invalidate all "speech regulations" is to convert them into a third house of the legislature in respect to all social and economic regulation. The constitutional convention of 1787 three times rejected proposals for a judicial Council of Revision for federal legislation as inconsistent with self-government. This judgment has not been respected by the courts. The vague and constantly shifting doctrines they have generated are equivalent to no rules at all, but merely labels applied to the naked exercise of judicial discretion. Regulations that the courts find tasteful are upheld; those that judges find displeasing are invalidated. The recent case renders this principle explicit. The First Amendment—a shield of rights of political self-government, is perverted when used as a sword for destruction of social and economic legislation of which ACLU officers or their brethren in the right-wing think tanks disapprove.

The Supreme Court has generally rendered itself an object of ridicule when it has extended the speech and press clauses beyond political speech properly so-called, as witness the law of obscenity and the dubiously reconcilable decisions involving "symbolic speech," in the form of the burning of flags, crosses, and draft cards. Judges who proclaim that they know prohibited activity when they see it are engaging in a function inconsistent with constitutional democracy and one that endangers the vital protections accorded political speech. One need not be too hard on Justice O'Connor's efforts at whittling away a doctrine which she at least has wisely never accepted. But the best comment on the present state of affairs in regard to "commercial speech" is that of Justice Jackson in another context: "the more you explain it, the more I don't understand it."

LESSON OF A LIFE

Kalven was concerned through all his work with values and doctrine, but doctrine conditioned by immersion in fact. At an early age, he observed, "It is because social scientists have been too quick to raise a superstructure of theory without painstaking observation that the social sciences lag." Kalven was not typical of "the modern student of society who has less and less ordinary contact with society." His life also was consistent with another self-directed admonition, written at the age of thirty-one, the motive force of a more than academic career: "If it is imperative that a free market place be available, it is also imperative that it be used. It is here that the university and the bar have their traditional and special responsibility. The men who have the truth and who have the ability to present it are perhaps charged with a public interest too."

NOTES

1. Because this discussion tracks the order of Kalven's book and references are identified there, they are omitted here.

2. "Liberty, he argues, is connected with prose, and bureaucrats who want to destroy liberty tend to write and speak badly and to use pompous or wooly or portmanteau prose in which their true meaning or any meaning disappears. If we write and speak clearly, we are likelier to think clearly and to remain comparatively free." E. M. Forster, *George Orwell*, in *Two Cheers for Democracy* (1951), at 3.

3. Tussman, *Government and the Mind* (1977), 91.

4. Clor, *Obscenity and Public Morality* (1969).

5. *Gertz v. Robert Welch*, infra, note 6.

6. See *Gertz v. Robert Welch*, 418 U.S. 323 (1974), ably discussed in Freeman, *Justice Powell's Constitutional Opinions*, 45 Washington and Lee L.Rev. 411, 417-22 (1988).

7. Kalven, though referring to the "famous conspiracy of silence by the press in reporting libel actions against fellow newspapers," was skeptical that good men would be deterred by free libel from seeking public office. Cf. the letter of Jacob Burckhardt to Von Preen, 19 February 1881, in Dru (ed.), *The Letters of Jacob Burckhardt* (1955), at 201: "Among us the irresponsible malice of a few miserable guttersnipes disgusts decent people, the ones who are ready to make sacrifices in office, or secretly leads them not to take office, so that they limit their activity to charity and that kind of thing. 0, there is a lot to say on that score."

8. Hand, Mr. Justice Brandeis, in Dilliard (ed.), *The Spirit of Liberty* (3d ed., 1960), at 172. "Unlike administrative acts, which rest on considerations of convenience and expediency, judicial decisions rest on law, that is on right and wrong, and they always enjoy the limelight of publicity. Law is perhaps the most pernicious of all weapons in political struggles, precisely because of the halo that surrounds the concepts of right and justice. 'Right,' Hocking has said, 'is psychologically a claim whose infringement is met with a resentment deeper than the injury would justify, a resentment that may amount to passion for which men will risk life and property as they would never do for an expediency.' When it becomes 'political,' justice breeds hatred and despair among those it singles out for attack. Those whom it favors, on the other hand, develop a profound contempt for the very value of justice; they know that it can be purchased by the powerful. As a device for strengthening one political group at the expense of others, for eliminating enemies and assisting political allies, law then threatens the fundamental convictions upon which the tradition of our civilization rests." Neumann, *Behomoth: The Structure and Practice Of National Socialism* (1944), at 20-21; see also Kircheimer, *Political Justice* (1961).

9. Cf. Neumann, op. cit. supra note 6, at 23: "The [Weimar] courts were only too willing to forget the fundamental maxim of any democracy and of every state, that the coercive power must be a monopoly of the state through its army and police, that not even under the pretext of serving the state may a private group or individual take arms in its defense unless summoned to do so by the sovereign power or unless actual civil war has broken out."

10. "[T]he criterion he advanced is the importance in the judge's eyes of the law whose violation is urged." Bork, *Neutral Principlesand Some FirstAmendment Problems*, 47 Ind. L. J. 1 (1971).

11. Waskow, *From Race Riot to Sit-In* (Anchor ed., 1966) carries this reasoning a step further: "Just as the disorderly pamphleteering press focussed the energies of the urban middle class and the disorderly labor movement focussed the energies of working men, so the new forms of disorder have already indicated they have the power to create a politically alive citizenry out of . . . Negro Americans." Waskow urged "the protection of creative disorder used by either side in the racial conflict" by "some form of federal police force [which] must be created" but which "would have to be carefully restricted from itself defending one view or the other of racial justice." Some, mindful of both seventeenth-century England and contemporary Latin America, will think this a high price to pay for legitimizing "creative disorder."

12. 312 U.S. at 287. See Gregory, *Labor and the Law* (2d ed. 1961), ch. 11.

13. *The Reasonable Man and the First Amendment: Hill, Butts, and Walker*, 1967 Sup. Ct. Rev. 267.

14. *The Right of Privacy in Tort Law*, 31 Law and Contemp. Problems 66 (1966).

15. *Broadcasting, Public Policy and the First Amendment*, 10 J. Law and Economics 16, 47 (1967).

16. Review of M. Ernst, *The Best Is Yet*, 13 U. Chi. L. Rev. 114 (1945).

17. 66 Fortune Magazine, October 1962, at 116.

18. *A Worthy Tradition*, at 606-08.

5

Lawyers and the Poor

The rhetoric utilized in support of the federal legal services program since 1964 seems by now to have been cast in amber. We are told that the rich have lawyers and thus the poor must too. We are told that corporate lawyers are aided by tax deductions and therefore the lawyers for the poor must be fully federally financed. The sympathy that all must feel for the individual who is injured or evicted is harnessed to the different cause of federally financed class actions in federal courts. The various forms of federally financed legal controversy are represented as being the only thing that saves us from violence in the streets. As one who finds almost equally offensive the rhetoric of defenders of the program and that of its critics in Washington, I would invite examination in more particularized terms of what the program does, in what ways criticisms of it may be justified, and what the future should bring. The fact is that the federally sponsored Legal Services Program does not one thing but several different things.

CASES INVOLVING PERSONAL LIBERTY

A relatively minor but totally necessary portion of its activities directly involve liberty of persons from confinement. That Legal Services lawyers have shed light on some of the dark corners of the systems for commitment of the mentally ill, of juveniles, and of persons addicted to the use of alcohol and drugs stands heavily to the program's credit in Washington. Its representation of the hitherto unrepresented in matters of personal liberty has been a service to American law that should be continued in some form.

SMALL CLAIMS AND EVICTIONS

Personal injuries, insofar as they are compensated through the courts or workmen's compensation systems, are purposefully excluded from the Legal Services Program and processed through the contingent fee system of the private bar. Thus, the second large class of cases we must consider is made up not of injuries cases but of those involving the civil affairs of the poor in lower courts—primarily landlord-tenant disputes and collection small claims cases. The Legal Services Program undoubtedly plays a useful role here, but its existence has distracted its political constituency and the bar from the question whether this purpose might not be as well served through elimination or at least restriction of the bar's monopoly of representation in these cases. Monetarily small matters generally involve recurring fact situations that should not require the services of more or less highly compensated people with three years of postgraduate education. Some state courts such as the District Court of Maryland have long permitted the prosecution of certain types of civil action by agents on behalf of landlords and by officers of corporations. It is hard to believe that there are not other classes of people—social workers, paralegals, and persons who have undergone specified courses of training—who would not be equally or better qualified to deliver legal services characteristically delivered in the civil branch of the lowest courts to the extent that these are significantly shunned by the private bar. Certainly the poor, the confused, and the uneducated should have advocates in these forums. It is not clear that these advocates must be lawyers, let alone federally funded lawyers. Indeed, few activities seem to be more appropriately the functions of state government than the administration of civil justice in the state courts.

ADMINISTRATIVE LAW

A third large class of cases is those involving a confrontation of individuals with bureaucratic regulations of state and federal agencies and the administration of social welfare programs. Here too the Legal Services Program as it now exists might be recast. Some services are done better by other professionals and appropriately trained laymen, including citizen volunteers. There is much that can be learned here from the British Citizens' Advice Bureaux discussed elsewhere in this work. Such programs make available advisers who are mature and from a variety of occupations, not those who characteristically are just starting their careers. In addition, there is no reason save habit and the vested interests of lawyers, not least those of the lawyers of the Legal Services Program, for these matters to be as "legalized" in their administration as they are,as the late Judge Henry Friendly pointed out in his article "Some Sort of Hearing." The relaxation of the bar's monopoly of representation before administrative agencies can do much to reduce both the costs and the scope of any program of legal services that may continue to be provided. Similarly, reliance on internal administrative remedies as means of control rather than exclusive reliance on judicial review can do much to correct patterns of abuses, as in Continental systems.

DIVORCE AND BANKRUPTCY

A fourth category of cases is the "consumer goods" of the legal services industry—divorces and individual bankruptcies. It is clearer to defenders of the Legal Services Program than it is to the present writer that the immediate gratification of the desires of the less well off to rid themselves of social obligations is a benefit to those concerned or to society at large. Here the easy availability of bankruptcy and the prevalence of abuse in both the grant and use of credit cards badly serves both debtors and creditors. It is hard to believe that it is wrong for poorer persons to bear at least part of the costs of those legal proceedings that result in the dissolution of important personal obligations.

CLASS ACTIONS AND CONSTITUTIONAL LITIGATION

Finally, we come to the last category of cases, those at the root of the legal services controversy: class actions directed at vindicating rights of the poor or Legal Services lawyers' conceptions of what the rights of the poor should be. There are a number of things to be said about this. The first is that the lawyers of the program--creatures of the welfare state themselves—have generally been quite selective about the programs they attack. Thus, one finds in the chronicle of thousands of cases brought and decided in the course of the thity-year history of the program few, if any, challenges directed at the bewildering array of conflicting and overlapping wage and hour laws, child labor regulations, requirements of working papers for those beyond the compulsory education age, regressive payroll and unemployment taxes, burdensome educational restrictions, and requirements of tax withholding almost inevitably resulting in refunds for those who bother to claim them, which heavily burden and reduce the employment of the young, particularly the minority young. This is so not only because those who need help are not those most likely to seek it but also because of the ideology permeating the program. The agenda for reform pursued by Legal Services lawyers is a highly selective agenda. It is only in part a reflection of their clients' interests. It is directed chiefly at attempting to broaden the scope of social welfare programs, which cannot be universalized except at high costs; realization of its agenda has been foredoomed by general acceptance of the proposition succinctly stated in this context by Professor Geoffrey Hazard that "taxation without representation is tyranny."

It is true that of late, in the language of one defender of the program "Courts—which decide almost every issue of public concern, from bussing and abortion to prison overcrowding and prayers in schools—have as much to do with governing this country as do Presidents, Governors, and Legislators." This present characteristic of our political system, however, is in important ways, the product of a self-fulfilling prophecy: our courts are overimportant because the government subsidizes and facilitates litigation. Certainly the rationality of American political controversy has not improved since the creation of the program in 1964: Almost all political discussion is now cast in terms of claims of absolute right. Examples of judicial intervention commonly given are not among the great success stories of modern American government. The busing decisions (I refer not to the disestablishment of separate schools worked by *Brown* but to the judicial management of school systems in the later cases) have resulted in little discernible improvement either in the quality of education or in the state of race relations in the communities subject to them. The abortion decisions have nurtured religious animosities while doing nothing to stem the rising tide of illegitimate births, and the prison overcrowding cases have done as much to embarrass efforts at prison reform as to nurture them, while the cases involving school prayer rarely eliminated any sort of real religious oppression and were frequently rooted in at least as much intolerance as the practices that they attacked.

Abandonment of the habit of recourse to the courts for every grievance will not cause the poor to be "ready to abandon rational discourse and to settle . . . mounting grievances in the streets." It is at least as likely that grievances will be more effectively voiced in the political process.

The curtailment of the Legal Services Program will not eliminate constitutional controversy over the rights of the indigent: The history of the labor and civil rights movements, which vindicated their legal claims through highly competent counsel without benefit of federal subsidy, adequately demonstrates that. But there is some curtailment of both the volume and vehemence of litigation which results when the parties to it, be they corporations, foundations, or voluntary associations, must bear a portion of its costs. The need to raise money to bear some costs assures that constitutional litigators are at least somewhat responsive to the preferences and priorities of their clients and that they represent real constituencies and are not engaged in socially destructive frolics of their own.

The reduced volume of litigation that this change may bring thus may be welcome on a variety of grounds. It may focus domestic political controversy upon the wise design of tax and welfare systems and not merely upon the destruction of those present rules that are most conveniently subject to judicial attack. It may enhance a recognition that those who would change present practices are under an obligation to suggest what should be put in their place and, more particularly, how it should be paid for. Professor Ernst Freund, one of the great American students of administrative law, observed early in this century, "the common law is long on justice and short on policy."

Many lawyers will not agree that with respect to social and economic issues "the truth or its closest approximation is most likely to emerge from the clash of competing courtroom forces" or that the system of constitutional litigation nurtured by federal subsidy "resembles familiar economic models in its assumption that competitors each acting in its own self interest will produce the most socially desirable result," as asserted by one overenthusiastic defender of the program. Courts cannot create, design, or administer social security systems, food stamp programs, or school systems. There is little reason to believe that their part-time tinkering with them does much to improve their functioning, necessary though it sometimes may be to curb the worst outrages. Judicial process in its application to great social and economic issues does not produce a more refined version of truth. Even as to narrower controversies it is a necessarily blunt and imperfect instrument. It is not for nothing that Judge Learned Hand observed that he would fear a lawsuit as much as sickness and death.

There is a distinction, as Senator Moynihan has pointed out, between government under law and government by lawyers. Too often, in recent years, the latter has meant the process described by the late Justice Walter Schaefer of Illinois: "The use of words and phrases with independent lives." As Dean Francis Allen observed: "The courts are well adapted to weigh litigants; but they are poorly equipped to resolve broad issues of policy involving, for example, the reallocation of resources among large social groups or classes. Law-making in the latter area is confronted by a dual peril; it may ignore considerations relevant to intelligent policy formulation, or, in taking them into account, it may inspire doubts about the integrity of the judicial process." When those urging new claims are themselves members of a group segregated by age, by political convictions, and by education, these dangers are enhanced. Although legal services offices are not as yet the legal employers of last resort, the program also has not been immune to the usual life cycle of government agencies. It is tempting for members of a party or faction in opposition to defend to the utmost the continuing existence of this source of resistance. Even so, one observer may be pardoned his doubt that this governmentally funded kept opposition possesses full legitimacy. In a period of rising public concern not confined to any economic class or classes with the deterioration of the educational system, the erosion of family relations, the declining effectiveness of the criminal law, and the stagnation of the economy, many of its adherents pursue an agenda at best irrelevant and at worst in conflict with these public concerns, while the bar too often feels itself excused by the existence of the program from interest in the normal forms of political organization.

In the end, the legal profession cannot enforce upon society a political agenda of its own. The cautionary words of Judge Learned Hand addressed to the conservative lawyers of the 1930s remain worthy of consideration by their liberal counterparts now:

> With . . . piety must go a taste for courageous experiment, by which alone the law has been built as we have it, an indubitable structure, organic and living. It is in this aspect that the profession of the law is in danger of failing in times like our own when deep changes are taking place in the convictions of men. It is not as the priest of a completed revelation that the living successors of past lawmakers can most truly show their reverence or continue the traditions which they affect to regard. . . . [T]he profession of the law has its fate in its own hands; it may continue to represent a larger more varied social will by a broader more comprehensive interpretation. The change must come from within; the profession must satisfy its community by becoming itself satisfied with the community.

It must assimilate society before society will assimilate it; it must become organic to remain a living organism. No political mechanism designed to accomplish this by fear will succeed, if the inward disloyalty of purpose remain. A lawyer must learn to live more capaciously or be content to find himself continuously less trusted, more circumscribed, till he becomes hardly more important than a minor administrator, confined to a monotonous round of record and routine, without dignity, inspiration, or respect.

6

The Federal Injunction and the Federal Criminal Law: A Dangerous Explosion

The widespread editorial criticism of the recent Supreme Court decision in the *Lopez* case limiting federal criminal jurisdiction was misplaced. The decision is not a repudiation of the constitutional revolution that accompanied the New Deal but is fully consonant with the views of its authors. Mr. Justice Jackson, the author of the decision extending the Commerce Clause to grain consumed on a farmer's own farm that is usually held up as the furthest extension of the commerce power, was resolute in declaring that Congress's power over local crime was limited. Following his examination at Nuremburg of Hitler's seizure of power, he cautioned that decisions rendered in the context of national regulation of business enterprise should not have compelling force over the different questions involving allocation of police powers and civil liberties.[1] It is no accident that he was the author of the leading decisions limiting the use of the federal tax code to reach local crime[2] and that he joined in the leading decision curbing the scope of the federal criminal civil rights statutes.[3] In the latter case it was observed, in words that have special resonance now: "Evil men are rarely given power; they take it over from better men to whom it had been entrusted." The opinions and writings of Justices Frankfurter and Black likewise advert to limitations on centralized law enforcement power; both were mindful that the Bill of Rights and the military and militia clauses of the Constitution were in large measure inspired by a desire to prevent the re-creation on American soil of the dictatorship of the Earl of Stafford. Attempts to assert plenary federal criminal jurisdiction began with the Great Society, not the New Deal. Indeed, no small part of Roosevelt's initial platform was his pledge to repeal national prohibition so as to end the abuses by federal policing agencies disclosed by the Wickersham Report in 1932. There will be no cause to complain of the Court's new decision unless and until it is applied in a civil or regulatory context, and not as a curb on the development of federal policing agencies of uncontrollable size and scope.

Congress in recent years has been careless in its expansion of federal criminal jurisdiction, though it has wisely resisted Senator D'Amato's proposals to federalize all firearms offenses and the sweeping proposals to expand federal jurisdiction and authorize federal injunctions against crime put forward by the National Commission on Reform of Federal Criminal Laws in the early 1970s and since promoted by Senator Kennedy. Recently, however, Congress has enacted two statutes authorizing such injunctions, racketeering legislation, subsequently broadly applied in a case involving abortion clinics, and a federal statute authorizing injunctions against obstruction of clinic entrances.

The present writer shares the view of the Brown Commission's consultant on jurisdiction, Professor Norman Abrams, that "ultimately, the question of what the federal role ought to be in this area goes to the heart of our federal system and the respective parts to be played by the federal and state governments." Statutory draftsmen should proceed on the premise that jurisdiction once conferred is apt eventually to be exercised. The prestige and power of the federal government should not be involved actually or potentially in every controversial criminal occurrence that takes place within the frontiers of this country. So to approach questions of federal jurisdiction will lend a desperate intensity even beyond that existing at present to political contests for the control of the national government.

Use of federal equity power is not something to be casually authorized since it has implications for federalism, the separation of powers, procedural due process, the right of jury trial, and the orderly administration of systems of federal regulation. The effect of any provision for injunctions is to significantly curtail the right of jury trial. It is for this reason that one finds recognition in our law of the precept that equity will not enjoin a crime. Thus Professor James William Moore observed:

> Is there not limit to government by injunction? Or, stated differently: do not the Sixth and Seventh Amendments, with thir guarantee of jury trial in criminal and civil cases at law, raise a barrier at some point beyond which injunctions may not run? The National Prohibition Act raised these questions in acute form. . . . The clash of "criminal equity" with the Sixth and Seventh Amendments has never received the full dress and considered treatment by the Supreme Court that the subject deserves. It is probably too late in the day and the effectiveness of the injunction too appealing to challenge the power of a federal court to grant the prerogative injunction in times of national emergency, and to issue the statutory injunction in the economic area (using this term broadly) and in the abatement of public nuisances where specific property is involved. And government by injunction may advance some further and undefined distance.[4]

Certainly the extension of such provisions to incitement to riot and to simple drug possession would seem questionable, however much one may oppose riots or the possession of drugs. Once an injunction has been entered or a temporary restraining order, which can be ex parte, has been entered, the defendant can be tried for contempt and sentenced to six months' imprisonment without a jury. At his trial he may not contest the validity of the underlying order, and his defenses are limited to showing that he did not breach the injunction, however valid or invalid the injunction may be. The effect in any situation in which time is of the essence is to deprive the defendant of the opportunity to litigate fully the issue of his right to engage in the proscribed conduct before any tribunal, judge or jury, by reason of the availability of restraining orders and temporary injunctions. The effect also is to deprive the defendant of the right to jury trial in the contempt proceedings.

It is no answer to this to say that if the underlying offense were defined as a petty offense, the defendant might have been tried, convicted, and sentenced to less than six months' imprisonment without a jury. For in the latter situation, the defendant would at least have had the opportunity to effectively litigate his right to engage in his conduct.

Specific federal regulatory statutes such as the Food and Drug Act, the Securities Exchange Act, and the Federal Trade Commission Act expressly confer limited authority on various federal agencies to seek injunctions against fraudulent practices, and in many instances (under the Federal Trade Commission Act, for example) this authority has not traditionally been held to extend to the grant of temporary restraining orders.

The occasional federal injunctions entered in civil rights cases against private mass violence by the Justice Department had as their justification the assumed unwillingness of state policing authorities to protect narrowly defined federal civil rights or to enforce injunctions. If injunctions against demonstrations become commonplace, the federal government will be under pressure, invoked by private litigants, to intervene in connection with every threatened campus or political demonstration or mass assemblage of any kind. The use of substantial amounts of federal law enforcement power becomes a necessity. Indeed, the *Debs* case, frequently cited as precedent for federal intervention, necessitated the use of the military.

Equally significant is the fact that federal law enforcement manpower is being used not for what is presently its paramount purpose, the detection and investigation of already-committed crimes, but instead for preventative and police functions. Wide provisions allowing injunctions are sufficient to guarantee either the repeated and habitual use of the army in domestic disturbances or the creation of a federal agency of a size and with functions that will render it indistinguishable from a national police force, with an accompanying increase in preparatory federal investigatory and intelligence activities.

Hitherto, federal injunctions have been limited by the provisions of 18 U.S.C. § 3691, part of the Clayton Act, providing for jury trial of charges of contempt against privately obtained injunctions and the provisions of Rule 65(d) of the Federal Rules of Civil Procedure enacted as part of the Norris-La Guardia Act, prohibiting so-called "John Doe" injunctions against persons not served with complaints.

Little can be added to what was said half a century ago by Professor

Zechariah Chafee in the context of the labor injunction:

> Instead of setting ourselves diligently to reorganize the administration of criminal justice, we shrink from the difficult task and try to make the injunction do the same job of stamping out harmful enterprises and maintaining order in industrial disputes. Sooner or later, we shall pay the price. In a jury trial, the responsibility is distributed. In a court of equity, there is nothing to take up the slack. The judiciary, the most delicate part of our political machinery, is subjected to a terrific strain when it is made to do unaided, and in highly controversial cases, work fitted for the rougher mechanism of the criminal law. The use of the injunction to put men in prison without a jury trial for reasons that seem insufficient to a considerable body of their fellow citizens is liable to produce a resentment that may eventually sweep away some judicial powers that had better be preserved, along with what can be spared. . . . An equity judge ought not be turned into a super-policeman.[5]

Any large change in the permitted scope of federal injunctions against crime can only result in the aggrandizement of the size and scope of federal policing and law enforcement activities and of eventual impairment of that "freedom from fear" upon which all of our other political freedoms ultimately depend. We would do well to recall the words of Learned Hand eulogizing Brandeis: "Haphazard as they might be in origin and devoid of much present significance, the states were the only breakwater against the ever-pounding surf which threatened to submerge the individual and destroy the only kind of society in which personality could survive."

NOTES

1. Statement to the Columbia Oral History Project, quoted in Kurland, *Robert H. Jackson* in 4 *The Justices of the Supreme Court 1789-1969* (L. Friedman and F. Israel eds., 1970) at 2543, 2565.

2. *United States v. Kahriger*, 345 U.S.22 (1953); see also *United States v. Denmark*, 346 U.S. 441, 447 (1953).

3. *Screws v. United States*, 325 U.S. 91 (1945).

4. 5 Moore, *Federal Practice* § 38.24[31].

5. Chafee, *Freedom of Speech in the United States* (1941), 341-42.

7

The Abortion Distortion

Whether or not the Supreme Court's recent opinion in the Webster abortion case is a way-station toward the overruling of *Roe v. Wade*, the unformed and confusing separate opinions have insights and merits of their own, though not always those intended by their authors.

The most discussed opinion, that of Justice O'Connor, declares her view that the court's post-*Roe* opinions (with the exception of the *Akron* opinion, from which she dissented) declared "with fair consistency that a regulation is not unconstitutional unless it unduly burdens the right to seek an abortion." This "undue burden" test, unsuccessfully urged on the court by former Solicitor General Rex Lee in *Akron* to the accompaniment of abusive heckling from Justice Blackmun, had been expressly applied by the court in *Harris v. McRae* and by Justice O'Connor in her *Akron* dissent, where "undue burden' was variously defined as "an absolute obstacle" and "a heavy and unnecessary burden." It seems to follow that regulations that do not doom in advance a particular woman's quest for an abortion, but that impose requirements of delay, counseling with parents, spouses, and disinterested physicians, or justification of the requested procedure do not offend the test; outright bans might do so.

The least discussed and most arresting opinion, that of Justice Stevens, arrives at a not dissimilar position. For him, the vice of a prohibitory statute is that it is an "official endorsement of [a] theological tenet" as to when life begins. However, regulations with secular justifications, such as parental notification requirements and requirements of "other appropriate counsel" are not subject to this fault, nor would a prohibitory statute with a pronatalist justification at "times in history when military and economic interests would have been served." At the start of the opinion is a suggestion, not taken to its logical conclusion, that there is scientific as distinct from theological support for the proposition that protectable life begins no sooner than implantation of the fertilized ovum in the uterine wall, since only 50 percent of fertilized ova ultimately become implanted.

Finally, the dissenting opinion of Justice Blackmun notes that a portion of the Missouri statute could be invalidated under the equal protection clause without reference to *Roe*, as "an arbitrary imposition of discomfort, risk, and expense, furthering no discernible interest except to make the procurement of an abortion as arduous and expensive as possible."

At the Bork hearings, former Attorney General Levi observed of *Roe*: "It is a part of the fabric of our law, to some extent, but there is something wrong with it. It is misshapen. It doesn't fit . . . privacy is a construct that hasn't been worked out. No one knows its limitations, and the language itself is not helpful. And since . . . there isn't agreement as to what part of the Constitution to point to in terms of helping to define it—it needs more work. it needs more lawyer's work."

The opinions described do not fully rise to this challenge, but they at least mark a partial return to conventional modes of constitutional reasoning. Neither contending faction now has reason to feel disenfranchised. The proponents of liberal legislation will have to take some heed of the views of the minority who consider abortion as the taking of life and the probable majority who consider that it at least cheapens it. Attention may be paid to the fact that about 15 percent of women obtaining abortions have had two or more prior abortions, a percentage that has increased fivefold since 1975.

Those favoring more restrictive laws for their part must now support them before legislatures on the basis of secular justifications. One of these rests on paradox and thus has played little role in the debate thus far: the discouragement of illegitimate births. In *Roe*, the court gave short shrift to the proposition that the public interest in sexual responsibility justified abortion laws: "Texas does not advance this justification, and it appears that no court or commentator has taken the argument seriously." Justice Stevens, in *Webster*, made the customary assumption that "If the secular analysis were based on a strict balancing of fiscal costs and benefits, the economic costs of unlimited childbearing would outweigh those of abortion.

However, the hope of the proponents of freer abortion that *Roe* would reduce the number of illegitimate births has not been realized, by reason of the greater number of women placed at risk by the new mores. For it is indeed true, as Justice Blackmun declared, that "millions of women have ordered their lives around the right to reproductive choice" and have assumed that any absence or failure of precaution can be remedied by abortion. Yet, when unwanted pregnancies do occur, they find themselves unable to avail themselves of the much-vaunted constitutional right. In part this is due to ignorance, cost, family pressure, or the survival of religious feeling. In greater part, one may suspect, it is due to a factor that the feminist agenda cannot alter. As Allan Bloom has put it: "Man can walk away from a sexual encounter and never give it another thought. But a woman may have a child, and, in fact, as becomes ever clearer, may want to have a child. Sex can be an indifferent thing for man, but it really cannot quite be so for women [who] have an instinctive attachment to children that cannot be explained as self-interest or calculation." This premise may explain the appalling development since 1973: an explosion of births out of wedlock.

It is not unreasonable to think that the type of law most likely to alter these statistics favorably is one that, while leaving abortion quite freely available in the early stages, sends the unmistakable message that it is not a private transaction, another form of birth control, but a last resort, available only after an unpleasant and uncertain process. Here there is the German and French example: requirements of counselling with persons not financially involved in the operation and parental and/or spousal notification, to which might be added prohibition of frequently repeated abortion and of abortion for prohibited purposes such as sex selection or monetary extortion.

There is a second secular justification for some restrictions: regulation of medical ethics as such. The pre-1973 law, as Justice Blackmun recognized, found its root in the rise of the medical profession from the era of laissez faire and quackery: The prohibitory laws were applied not to women but to their doctors. The Burger Court's other social innovation, unlimited professional advertising, has done much to restore the earlier standards, but the speed of this development appears to have startled the court. Justice Stewart in an early post-*Roe* opinion and Justice O'Connor have been bemused by the phenomenon of the American commercial abortion clinic, the latter sardonically observing in *Akron*, "It is certainly difficult to understand how the court believes that the physician-patient relationship is able to accommodate any interest that the state has in maternal physical and mental well-being in light of the fact that the record in this case shows that the relationship is nonexistent." The French have been concerned to separate abortion counseling from profit; in an age of required second opinions for routine surgery, it is hard to believe this concern is misplaced. As a noted law professor once observed in a different context, "able men object to participating in the operations of an abattoir."

Yet even when *Roe* is discarded, as the opinions suggest it someday may be, constitutional protections against extreme legislation will remain. Three in particular are worth noting. The equal protection clause, pace Justice Blackmun, does have something to say about regulations which have no purpose but to burden. It also seems inconsistent with procedural due process to allow private persons to impose on rape victims, young minors, and mental defectives lacking the capacity to consent to intercourse the burden of bearing a child; and a standardless and unreviewable veto in husbands or parents may raise similar problems. Finally, if anything of the *Griswold* privacy doctrine survives, the court may distinguish abortion from contraception at the point suggested by Justice Stevens and by the German law, which declares, "Acts the effects of which occur before implantation of the fertilized egg in the uterus, are deemed not to be interruptions of pregnancy." This would preserve the viability of the "morning-after" pill.

Justice Blackmun in defining the crux of his position availed himself of a dictum of former Solicitor General Fried written during his days as a law professor, referring to the "moral fact that a person belongs to himself and not others nor to society as a whole." For some, this may seem reminiscent of Dante's description of the innermost circle of Hell; others may prefer Learned Hand's more judicious formulation: "It may be idle to seek the Soul of Man outside Society; it is certainly idle to seek Society outside the Soul of Man." Certainly the *Roe* doctrine, and the ideology that has come to surround it rest on the consecration of selfishness—on an extreme laissez-faire in the social realm which, as Professor Mary Ann Glendon of Harvard has demonstrated, has been consciously rejected on the Continent. It is no coincidence that the ascendancy of *Roe* coincided with a period of indifference to the economic position of low-income families and ever-higher levels of regressive payroll taxation. That the demise of *Roe* coincides with renewed interest in earned-income allowances and the like is a heartening thing. Some may hear echoes of Roosevelt's first inaugural address: "We have always known that heedless self-interest was bad morals; we know now that it is bad economics."

For there is a secular case for abortion restrictions. Judge Learned Hand, the premier modern critic of judicial activism, once urged that its temptations be resisted since sweeping change by judges would generate "frictions undreamed of by those who avail themselves of this facile opportunity to enforce their will." The twenty years of sound and fury detonated by *Roe v. Wade* amply vindicate this prophecy. The court has now by fits and starts retreated toward the position of substantially all the western European countries, where efforts substantively to limit abortions in the early months of pregnancy have been abandoned and procedural restrictions designed to discourage sexual irresponsibility have been retained, as have regulations designed to maintain medical ethics. Given the liberalization of the law that had taken place in California, New York, and other major states without great controversy prior to 1973, as well as the ability of liberal states to erode restrictions in conservative ones, exemplified by the law of divorce, there is no reason to think that the same development would not have taken place here.

The judicial "short cut" to this result, however, has produced significant collateral consequences. These include the resentment of religious fundamentalists at being politically disenfranchised; the development of equally shrill opposing movements, fueled by the notion that votes are worthless and liberal rules can only be the product of courts; and the adoption by contending factions of ever more extreme and absurd positions, which have caused national elections to assume the character of religious wars and which at least as to judicial appointments and confirmations have made a nullity of the Constitution's proscription of religious tests for public office.

These competing excesses can be readily identified. The fundamentalists, who once sat quite still for the repeal of the remaining restrictions on sale and distribution of contraceptives, now strenuously resist introduction of the French abortion pill, which in its functioning is indistinguishable from IUD devices in that it operates to prevent the implantation in the womb of an already fertilized ovum. The use of fetal tissue in medical research is now a subject of controversy. The failure to prohibit abortion is sought to be redressed by encumbering federally financed family-planning programs with requirements of verbal hocus-pocus that bring discredit to the law. Differing rules are sought to be imposed on populations most vulnerable to federal legislative restrictions--medicaid recipients, users of military hospitals and the like, without regard to principles of either fairness or federalism. Demands for a "human life" amendment to disenfranchise the "liberals" are persisted in on the principle that turnabout is fair play, even though no one thinks that such an amendment could be ratified, or, if ratified, enforced.

The "liberals" for their part seek to cloak with claims of absolute immunity medical practices of commercial abortion mills of a type unknown and not tolerated in the rest of the western world and seek to preserve what amounts to abortion on demand even for the 1 percent or less of cases in the last third of pregnancy. Counseling requirements, waiting periods, and notification requirements are opposed on the basis that occasional tragedies among the already pregnant may result; the effect of knowledge of restrictions on the behavior of the not-yet-pregnant is ignored. Techniques of character assassination not seen since the decline of the Weimar republic are practiced at judicial confirmation hearings. Government by injunction is sought to be revived, and federal marshals and military are deployed at the instance of private suitors to suppress symbolic and sporadic protests in a fashion not seen since the days of Henry Clay Frick. Scare propaganda about the overruling of *Roe* is resorted to, even though that development would give rise to severe substantive restrictions, for a time, in only a handful of small states with few extant abortion clinics.

While all this has been going on, few have sought to evaluate abortion on demand as a secular public policy. The premise of justices Stevens and Blackmun has been that the only possible secular justification for abortion restrictions is a pronatalist policy. Yet adoption of *Roe's* rule, here and in large measure in England, has brought no slackening of births out of wedlock; rather, the contrary. When situation ethics is proclaimed as a rule of constitutional law, restraint and caution in sexual relationships are casualties. High school principals realize what journalists do not, that the last twenty years have seen an explosion in births out of wedlock among teenagers. What was once a negligible phenomenon, at least among the nonblack population, is now a major one:

Births to Unmarried Women, in 1000s, and as a Percentage of All Births

	1970	1975	1980	1985	1988
White	175.1(5.7%)	186.4(7.3%)	320.1(11.0%)	433.0(14.5%)	539.7(17.7%)
Black	215.1(37.6%)	249.6(48.8%)	325.7(55.2%)	365.5(60.1%)	426.7(63.5%)

One can agree that "the cat is out of the bag" and that there is no prospect of curtailing the basic right of choice in early pregnancy. But the rules vociferously defended by some educated and professional women for their own benefit also apply to uneducated and confused teenagers, and abortion legislation affects the behavior of not only women who are pregnant but also those who have not yet become so. The perception that there is no accountability for abortion, to parents, to counselors, to society, or even to oneself through encounter with the facts of fetal development leads to both carelessness and license. Many who become pregnant in reliance on society's indulgence then find that because of residual religious feeling, indecisiveness, or a previously unrecognized maternal instinct, they do not want or cannot obtain abortions. "There are many unwanted pregnancies and few unwanted children." Hence the explosion of illegitimate births. Notification and counseling requirements and waiting periods are not fig leaves; they are measures that send a message, influencing the behavior of the nonpregnant, that abortion will be unpleasant and that it will result in some need to account to parents, counselors, and ultimately oneself. This message is more powerful and unambiguous than any that can be transmitted through the distribution of free leaflets and condoms. An earlier generation used maternity homes, some of which survive, to reinforce this message and foster parenting skills; their revival seems no part of the agenda either of those interested only in the next world or of those supporting untrammeled license in this one.

Those who continue to maintain extreme positions as political recruiting devices have much to answer for. This applies both to the wilfully archaic Republican platform of 1992 and to the mendacious pandering of the Clintons to the "choice" lobby, symbolized by the denial of speaking rights to the politically incorrect Governor Casey and by Mrs. Clinton's inflammatory award to Anita Hill in San Francisco.

The costs of this are threefold: the corruption of the law and of public respect for it; the perpetuation in national politics of an issue that does not belong there, a danger to our basic Constitution, as General De Gaulle, among others, would have reminded us;[1] the continuing neglect of the interests of immature women and of what Justice Holmes referred to in a not irrelevant context as "the product of ruined lives."

NOTE

1. "Other(s) advocated the so-called 'presidential system' on the American pattern. Executive and legislative would thus go through the whole duration of their respective mandates without either of them ever being able to coerce the other. . . . [The United States] is a federation of states each of which, with its governor, its representatives, its judges, and its officials—all, elected—takes upon itself responsibility for a large part of the immediate business of politics, administration, justice, public order, economy, health, education, etc. while the central government and Congress normally confine themselves to larger matters: foreign policy, civic rights and duties, defense, currency, overall taxes and tariffs. For these reasons the system has succeeded in functioning up to now in the north of the New World. But where would it lead France . . . a country the demands of whose unity coupled with the perpetual threats from outside have induced to centralize its administration to the utmost, thus making it ipso facto the target of every grievance. . . . The inevitable result would be either the submission of the President to the deputies or else a pronounciamento." De Gaulle, *Memoirs of Hope: Renewal and Endeavor* (1971), 323-24.

Part III

REVIVING CIVIL SOCIETY

8

Community and Law Enforcement: Back to the Future

One who is neither an academic student of the criminal law nor a law enforcement professional must proceed with hesitation in writing on such subjects. Thus, even though war is too important to be left to the generals, the purpose of an essay such as this must be to provoke rather than to prescribe. Today, it is generally held, we face a crisis in law enforcement, particularly in our large cities. Those who seek to address it offer two competing sets of prescriptions. The police and criminal justice community broadly seeks more resources and powers: more and better paid police, more and better prisons, and the relaxation of restraints on criminal procedure. Those who resist these approaches, for fear of their liberties, advert in general terms to the social causes of crime and seek more funds for drug treatment programs, social work among families, and the educational and welfare systems. Given limited resources and sharply competing values, progress is slow.

The premise of this discussion is that there is a third approach, not alternative but complementary to the two familiar agendas, which has been neglected but which offers at least as much promise as either of them. That approach involves the recreation in modern form, parallel to the existing law enforcement system, of the institutions which provided the basis of English and American law enforcement for six hundred years, from the Statute of Winchester (1285)[1] until the statute of 1856 requiring all English counties to maintain professional police forces. The institutions provided for by the Statute of Winchester were four: the local constable, appointed in England, elected from small precincts in the United States; the neighborhood hue and cry; the night watch, later supplemented by a day watch, on which in theory all adult males were bound to periodically serve; and the *posse comitatus*, consisting of all males over the age of fifteen, a variant of the citizen militia established by the Assize of Arms (1181),[2] the antecedent of the "well-regulated militia" of the Second Amendment. As functioning civic institutions, all four of these have fallen into desuetude. Their replacement by the professional police, initially created by Sir Robert Peel's police act for London in 1829[3] has recently been ably recounted.[4] These institutions were each and all institutions of direct democracy, nonbureaucratic in nature, and these were the law enforcement institutions taken for granted at the time of the enactment of the American Constitution and the Bill of Rights. The then best-known alternative to them was the "thorough" dictatorship of the Earl of Stafford, with its standing army quartered on the people; the Constitution and the Bill of Rights constituted as much as anything else a series of prohibitions against creation of such an institution on American soil, hence the restrictions on duration of military appropriations and suspension of habeas corpus in the Constitution, the militia clauses of the Constitution and the Bill of Rights, and the reservation of powers (including law enforcement powers) to the states in the Tenth Amendment.[5]

The development of fast means of transportation and communication, the massive migration from rural areas into large cities, and large-scale immigration rendered the old system inadequate, both in the United States and in England. The older institutions had as their premise private prosecution; the protections they afforded thus varied sharply with the means of the victim. Hence the rise of the professional police, who we take for granted as instruments of law enforcement, notwithstanding that they were "the kind of hireling body considered dangerous by conventional political theory." There was a felt need for what James Bryce referred to as "a force strong enough to suppress tumults in their first stage," having regard to the fact that "democracy does not secure the good behavior of its worse and newest citizens."[6]

Recent years, however, have seen not merely the dominance of the professional police but early signs of the spontaneous recreation of the earlier institutions. Today nearly 30 percent of the American population lives in residential community associations with elected officers, a large percentage of which have assumed some security functions.[7] The systematic publicizing of crimes and wanted persons, once confined to the halfhearted posting of wanted posters in post offices, now extends to popular television programs, the sides of shopping bags, and the regular publication of police blotters in neighborhood and metropolitan newspapers. "Neighborhood watch" groups have appeared in many communities. The ever-more widespread private ownership of firearms for purposes of individual self-defense revives a militia, albeit not a "well regulated" one. Law enforcement might benefit, without peril to liberty, from a more self-conscious organization and exploitation of these tendencies. The four institutions will be discussed in turn:

THE CONSTABLE

The English constable was an appointed feudal remnant whose archetype in literature is Shakespeare's Constable Dogberry.[8] In his American manifestation, he was an elected official, generally selected from a very small district akin to an election precinct. With the rise of professional police he and his county equivalent, the elected sheriff, have increasingly either been abolished or had their functions restricted to service of civil process. Jefferson's vision of ward government in which an elected constable would be the principal agent of law enforcement in an area of six square miles with a population of five hundred has never been realized.

The constable, in his original setting, had his virtues. These were extolled by the English opponents of the legislation of 1829 and 1856 establishing and generalizing the police. Professionals, it was said, make "no appeal to the sympathies of neighborhoods." They "introduce brute force where moral persuasion ought to prevail. A box on the ear or a stroke or two with an ash plant might be as good as punishment for shaking an apple tree as a regular justicing under Peel's act."[9] In their inception, at least in the United States,the ward police departments were quite decentralized, adjuncts of the ward organization.[10] The recent interest in community policing may belie the prediction of Eric Monkkoren in 1977 that there is "little chance that the authorities will reopen the old precincts and restore their former boundaries." These proposals, however, contemplate decentralization of the police bureaucracy rather than recourse to popular institutions. However, the increasing involvement in security matters of the hundreds of thousands of residential community associations created by the developers of residential subdivisions since the early 1960s has given rise to a new sort of constable; the neighborhood watch or security committee chairman.[11] He too is elected by a local community and is not part of a police bureaucracy. The function of these new institutions is generally preventative in nature; the surveying of street lighting, locks, bars and alarms; the reporting of crimes to the police and to neighbors; and the mounting of watches whose purpose is to deter rather than to apprehend.[12] The instinctive reaction of many to these new developments is to reproach them as a new vigilantism or a recrudesence to the medieval walled town [13]or to express fear that the result will be a withdrawal of support from existing police institutions. It is fair to suggest, on the contrary, that the appropriate reaction should involve an effort to extend these new institutions to established blocks, streets, and housing projects where crime problems are greater by enactment of state laws authorizing and assisting small street and block associations, giving them powers to assess limited dues and imposts to support their activities.[14] These activities may include street regulation, as with the *woonerf* street associations of the Netherlands and the private street associations of St. Louis and cooperation in law enforcement.[15]

THE WATCH

The night watch as originally conceived was an uncompensated body drawn by lot from among all adult males. Its desuetude began when the hiring of substitutes was permitted, leading it to be described in its American setting as "a decrepit force of unemployables." With the rise of professional police, any effort to enlist or enforce public participation in law enforcement was abandoned. An "enlightened" *Yale Law Journal* article in 1992 reproached the ten or twelve states that continue to maintain statutes allowing police officers to commandeer the assistance of bystanders.[16] Yet the inevitability of this decline is far from obvious. "Until well into the nineteenth century volunteer watchmen, not policemen, patrolled their communities to keep order. . . . Their presence deterred disorder or alerted the community to disorder that could not be deterred."[17] The volunteer fire department continues to survive as a social instrumentality in many parts of the country, and its decline in large cities was initially due not to the present need for special training but to the desire for political patronage and the interest of insurance companies (many of which started as fire companies) in being relieved of the costs of upkeep of the volunteer forces. The recent decline in the perceived effectiveness of law enforcement has given rise to the organization of "neighborhood watch" activities by many of the mostly suburban residential community associations. Proposals have been made to strengthen such activities through better definition of the power of citizen's arrest and statutory expansion of immunities from suit.[18] To these familiar suggestions one may add others: 1) that contributions or dues to neighborhood associations performing such functions be accorded the same tax deductibility as taxes paid to public bodies; 2) that organization of block and street associations in established neighborhoods and housing projects be facilitated; 3) that individuals participating in such watch functions receive, as did nineteenth century and some contemporary volunteer firemen, recognition for their service in the form of exemption from other public obligations, such as jury duty[19]; and 4) that functions such as parking enforcement and the provision of school crossing guards be transferred to such bodies where appropriate.

The utility of these "watch" organizations is primarily deterrent in nature, derived from improved security measures and reporting of crimes and crime suspects, particularly in metropolitan areas where the police are an alien force.[20] The increased emphasis on the social organization of housing projects, on concierge systems and concepts of "defensible space"[21] indicates that the relevance of this concept is not confined to the twelfth century. [22]

THE HUE AND CRY

In its initial form, the hue and cry had as its object the organization of what Jane Austen called "a neighborhood of voluntary spies"[23] and involved shouting, the blowing of horns, and the ringing of church bells. With the advent of the press, these primitive mechanisms for organizing the general chase of an offender were replaced by printed warning and reward notices and directories of wanted criminals of the type outlined in Sir John Fielding's General Prevention Plan of 1772-73. The best-known publications were John Fielding's own broadsheet, the *Hue and Cry* and Henry Fielding's *Covent Garden Journal*. Lord Mansfield declared in 1783: "How are felons in general taken up? From descriptions of them circulated in handbills."[24]

One of the critics of Peel's police bill observed in 1829, in terms that have continuing resonance: "complete and speedy publicity of all acts of delinquency would effect far more good without a police than a police could effect without publicity."[25] It has been observed that "during the second half of the nineteenth century, the circulation of information about criminal offenders and offences increasingly became internalized within the police—narrowcasting to an audience of officials. Professional bureaucratic policing as it developed in England was not reconciled with a continuation of the kind of public participation that had underpinned the success of the eighteenth-century crime advertisement. The willingness of victims of property offenses to rely upon the new police and the tendency of the new police themselves to monopolize law enforcement played important roles here. So too perhaps did technological developments like the telegraph, which was more suited to channeling criminal information through a police bureaucracy than to public broadcasting."

A great deal has changed since Tocqueville's observation that "the criminal police of the United States cannot be compared with those of France; the magistrates and public agents are not numerous. Yet . . . in no country does crime more rarely elude punishment. The reason is that everyone conceives himself to be interested in furnishing evidence of the crime and in seizing the delinquent . . . in America he is looked upon as an enemy of the human race, and the whole of mankind is against him."[26]

The advent of new means of information transmission such as the television set and the fax machine has not given rise to significant expansion of use of wanted posters and publications by the police. Yet the public hunger for this sort of information is attested by the fact that virtually all neighborhood newspapers now publish discouragingly long lists of offenses, unaccompanied by any information that would assist in solving them. The publication on shopping bags of pictures of missing children and the advent of television programs depicting wanted criminals is entirely a product of private enterprise.

It is hard to escape the conclusion that a revival of Fielding's Hue and Cry would be a useful and beneficial contribution to law enforcement, particularly in the inner-city areas where clearance rates are lowest, the crime problem is greatest, and policing cannot succeed without public participation. Indeed, the mere existence of such a newspaper-type collection of wanted notices might have a significant deterrent effect.[27]

THE WELL-ORDERED MILITIA

Unlike that of the other institutions mentioned, the history of the militia and the origins and scope of the Second Amendment to the Constitution have not been neglected subjects in recent years. The controversy over gun control however has generated considerably more heat than light. It is clear, however, that private firearms ownership is now so widespread that any legislation curtailing it, if enforced by means consistent with the Fourth and Fifth amendments, would have only limited significance in the short term. The fact is that private firearms ownership stems from a loss of confidence in public law enforcement, and that its suppression or curtailment would therefore be difficult.

There would also seem little basis to doubt that in some circumstances the public possession of arms may have political significance. It has been alleged that this was so with respect to the defense by the antifederalists of Jefferson's first election victory, and it may be that similar situations could arise under modern conditions. In the language of Madison in the *Federalist*, no. 46: "Besides the advantage of being armed, which the Americans possess over the people of almost every other nation, the existence of subordinate governments, to which the people are attached, and by which the militia officers are appointed, forms a barrier against the enterprises of ambition, more insurmountable than any which a simple government of any form can admit of."

The evils that flow from widespread gun ownership are twofold; the possession and use of guns by those bent on crime and numerous accidental homicides or deaths in the course of family quarrels. These sordid events seem far removed from the original political concerns; however, the widespread ownership of firearms undoubtedly operates as a deterrent to nighttime burglaries, store robberies and other property crimes.

The original American militia law [28] required all males of military age to possess a rifle or musket (or pistol or sword if a member of a cavalry or artillery unit).[29] The concept of a "well-regulated militia" embodied in the Bill of Rights in 1791 reflected George Washington's view that "a free people ought not only to be armed but disciplined."[30] The conception here resembled that of the Swiss militia system, in which the universal ownership of military firearms has been found to be not inconsistent with a low homicide rate. [31]By the time of Story's *Commentaries on the Constitution*, there was a "growing indifference to any system of militia discipline."[32] Hamilton in the *Federalist* no. 29 observed: "little more can reasonably be aimed at, with respect to the people at large, then to have them properly armed and equipped, and in order to see that this not be neglected, it will be necessary to assemble them once or twice in the course of a year." Even if an expansive view is taken of the Second Amendment, the validity of state regulation of gun owners, if not of gun ownership, would seem unassailable.

Licensing of gun owners is both politically controversial and constitutionally assailable, at least as applied to rifles, except with respect to felons and others not possessing civil rights. It is possible, however, to conceive of milder measures, which would deny the right of ownership to those not subjecting themselves to a training course, with periodic refreshments, in firearms safety, in self-defense (including alternatives to firearms use,[33] and in first aid and emergency response. This would be consonant with the original purpose of the Second Amendment and consistent with both its political and self-defense objects. Under this scheme, the acquisition, possession or use of a firearm by a person who had not completed such a course would be subject to penalties; those who had completed it would be deemed part of the organized militia, subject to being called to respond to public emergencies. This would recall the ideal of Jefferson's Second Inaugural with its description of a society "where every man at the call of the law, would fly to the standard of the law and would meet invasions of the public order as his own personal concern." Some experimentation along these lines has been undertaken, in which the incentive to participation was not criminal sanctions but the award to participants of decals and certificates, the display of which was found to operate as a deterrent to crime.[34] Mention may also be made of the unarmed auxiliary police of New York and other jurisdictions[35]and the Special Constables now called to the aid of the police by the British 1964 Police Act.[36] It is of course imperative that "auxiliary policemen should be screened carefully and trained, and the powers permitted them, particularly in the use of weapons, should be limited."[37] A still milder approach, not resembling licensing, would enact a presumption of lack of due care with respect to any suit or prosecution where injury results from firearms use by a person not participating in the training program. While this program would not enlist the participation of the existing criminal element, it almost certainly would reduce the incidence of accidental and intrafamily homicides resulting from firearms, as well as fostering social solidarity in high-crime neighborhoods and intelligent cooperation with the police. Given the political and legal constraints on firearms regulation, such an effort to discipline, discourage, and partially co-opt those claiming the right to possess firearms has greater promise than the present cosmetic restraints on ownership and sale, may yield a political consensus, and may in time alter the culture surrounding individual ownership of firearms.

CONCLUSION

The present political dialogue on law enforcement postulates its problems as involving a balancing of the rights and needs of the isolated individual and the commands and requirements of society, conceived as a bureaucratic state. This article suggests the need for reference to a third tradition, one that recognizes that there is "no security except in association and no freedom that did not recognize the obligation of a corporate life"[38] and which calls for continued rediscovery of "the contribution an actively participating public can make to the detection and prevention of criminal offenses."[39] It is appropriate for the law enforcement community to continue to consider these and other suggestions for revival of the institutions of public participation and to thus provide a Statute of Winchester for our time.

NOTES

1. 13 Edw. I, stat 2 (1285). In pertinent part, the statute read: "in every city, six men shall keep at every gate, in every borough 12 men, every town 6 or 4 according to the number of inhabitants of the town, and shall watch the town continually all night . . . and if they will not obey the arrest they shall levy the hue and cry upon them and such as keep the town shall follow with hue and cry with all the town, and hue and cry shall be made from town to town . . . in every hundred or franchise two constables shall be chosen to make the view of armor . . . view of armor shall be made every year two times . . . every man between 15 years of age and 60 years shall be assessed and sworn to armor according to the quantity of their lands and goods . . . they shall follow the cry with the country . . . the defaults shall be presented by the constables to the justices assigned."

2. 27 Hen. II (1185).

3. 10 Geo. IV, 449 (1829).

4. Douglas Hay and Francis Snyder (eds.) *Policing and Prosecution in England, 1750-1850* (1989). See also Martin A. Greenberg, *Auxiliary Police: The Citizen's Approach to Public Safety* (Greenwood, 1984), ch. l.

5. See the *Federalist* no. 45.

6. Handlin, *Preface* to Lane, *Policing the City* (1967). See 2 Bryce, *American Commonwealth* 569-70.

7. See U.S. Advisory Commission on Intergovernmental Relations, *Residential Community Associations* (1989), the best survey of the incidence and function of such associations.

8. Much Ado about Nothing, Act. IV, Scene 2. On early American constables, see Herbert Baxter Adams, *Norman Constables in America* (1883).

9. Jefferson, to Joseph Cabell, February 2, 1816, in Autobiographical Writings, vol. 14, 419.

10. Robert D. Storch, *Policing Rural England before the Police*, in Hay and Snyder, supra, note 4 at 212.

11. On Japanese neighborhood association chairmen serving similar functions for groups of about thirty homes (Bohan Kyokai), see Thornton, supra, 61-62; C.R. Fenwick, *Law Enforcement, Public Participationand Crime Control in Japan*, 1983 Am. J.of Police 83-109.

12. Robert Fogelson, *Big City Police* (1977) 305. On the koban system of the Japanese police, said to have been borrowed from German practice during the Meiji restoration, see Robert Thornton, *PreventingCrime in America and Japan* (1992), 43-45; Walter L. Ames, (1981), ch. l. See also L. R. Lambert, *Police Mini-stations in Toronto*, 50 R.C.M.P.Gazette 6 (1988).

13. *Economist*, July 25, 1992, at 25.

14. For a survey of association activities, see Liebmann, *Devolution of Power to Neighborhood and Block Associations*, 25 Urban Lawyer 335 (1993).

15. E. Monkkonen, *Police in Urban America*, 1860-1920 (1981). See also Samuel Walker, *Popular Justice: A History of American Criminal Justice* (1980), 18-24.

16. Blue, *High Noon Revisited*, 101 Yale L. J. 1475 (1992). Contrast the reference to the *posse comitatus* in the Federalist no. 29 (Hamilton): "It would be . . . absurd to doubt that a right to pass all laws necessary and proper to execute declared powers would include that of requiring the assistance of the citizens to the officers who may be entrusted

with the execution of those laws."

17. J. Q. Wilson, *Thinking about Crime* (Vintage ed., 1985), 87. McChesney, *Government Prohibition of Volunteer Firefighting in Nineteenth Century America*, 15 Journal of Legal Studies 69 (1976).

18. See, e.g. Richard Neely [Chief Justice of West Virginia], *Take Back Your Neighborhood* (1990). On neighborhood watch programs, see T. Hope and M. Shaw, *Communities and Crime Reduction* (1990); Trevor Bennett, *Evaluating Neighborhood Watch*(1990); S. Mukherjee and P. Wilson, *Neighborhood Watch* in P. Wilson, *Trends and Issues in Crime and Criminal Justice*(1990); and K. Whitehead, *Wonder Scheme or White Elephant*, Police Review (1989), all dealing with the English experience; and see Wesley Skogan, *Disorder and Decline* (1991); Dan A. Lewis, et al., *Social Construction and Reform: Crime Prevention and Community Organizations* (1988).

19. See McChesney, supra (exemption from jury service, militia duty, and road taxes).

20. See Norval Morris and Gordon Hawkins, *Letter to the President on Crime Control* (1971), at 30.

21. See Oscar Newman, *Community of Interest*(1972); Shaftoe et al., *Crime, Design and Management*, in *Proceedings of the International Association for Housing Sciences* (1992),692-703.

22. Summerson, *The Structure of Law Enforcement in Thirteenth Century England*, 23 Am. J. Legal History 313 (1979).

23. Jane Austen, Northanger Abbey, ch. 24.

24. Jerome Hall, *Legal and Social Aspects of Arrest without a Warrant*, 49 Harv. L. Rev. 571 (1936).

25. Edwin Chadwick, *Preventive Police*, 1 London Review 285 (1829), quoted in J. Styles, *Print and Policing*, in Hay and Snyder, supra, note 4 at 56. See P. Pringle, *Hue and Cry* (1969).

26. Id. at 94-95. See 2 Tocqueville, *Democracy in America* (Vintage ed., 1955), 99.

27. See Dennis Rosenbaum, Evaluating Community Crime Prevention(1986), ch. 13, on present-day anticrime newsletters; and see K. Carrierre, *The Organization of Community: Prime-Time Television*, 58 F.B.I. Law Enforcement Bulletin 8 (1989) and T. Baxter, *Video Time to Stop Crime*, 35 Law and Order 9 (1987), on the use of television for criminal apprehension, more common in Europe than in the United States.

28. 1 Stat. 271 (1792).

29. See the present 10 U.S.C. § 311: "The militia of the United States consists of all able-bodied males at least 17 years of age and . . . under 45 years of age."

30. 1 *Annals of Congress* 933 (1790).

31. See M. Clinard, *Cities with Little Crime: The Case of Switzerland*(1978), 114-15.

32. 3 Story, *Commentaries on the Constitution* (1833), 746-77.

33. James Jacobs, *Exceptions to a General Prohibition*, 49 Law and Contemporary Problems 5, 34 (1986).

34. Don Kates, *Value of Civilian Arms Possession*, 18 Am. J. Crim. Law 113 (1991), describing such an effort in Florida. For a survey of gun control studies, see J. Wright, *Under the Gun* (1990), at 259, referring to a Dade County, Florida, scheme conditioning a purchase permit on compeletion of a handgun safety and firearms law course. See also G. Kleck and K. McElrath, *Effect of Weaponry on Violence* 69-3 Social Forces 669-92 (1991); 1991 F.B.I. Law Enforcement Bulletin 60-68. C. Bakal, *The Right to Bear Arms*, ch. 13, notes that Connecticut, New York, and Rhode Island conditioned grant of hunting licenses to adults on completion of a firearms safety course, and that the rate of accidental

gun deaths in these jurisdictions was about one-third the national rate. Ten additional states require such courses for minor licensees.

35. See Greenberg, supra note 4, ch. 16, describing auxiliary police programs providing 52 to 381 hours of training in several cities, including use of uniforms, handcuffs, nightsticks, and two-way radios.

36. Police Act, 1964 (Laws, 1964, c. 48, §§ 16,34, 1965 S.I. 536, 1992 S.I. 526. See M.L.Gill and R.I. Mawby, *A Special Constable: A Study of the Police Reserve* (Gower, Aldershot,1990); C.Leon, *The Special Constabulary*, Policing 514 (1989). For proposals for security courses for the public, see Greenberg, *Volunteer Crime Prevention Programs*, 44 Police Chief 60-61 (1977), see generally J. Duncan, *Citizen Crime Prevention Tactics: A Literature Review and Selected Bibligraphy* (1980).

37. George Berkley, *The Democratic Policeman* (Beacon Press,1969), 175-78, describes the 43,000-strong British special constabulary, one-third as numerous as the regular force, who receive 24 hours of training, and the 6,000 strong Berlin auxiliary police, who receive 52 hours of instruction, as well as the Baden-Wurtemmburg auxiliary police, who serve for 6 hours per month after receiving 92 hours of training and who carry pistols on shift.

38. Jack Weber, *The King's Peace*, 10 Am. J. Legal History 135 (1989), quoting Lewis Mumford, *The Culture of Cities*, at 29.

39. Styles, supra, note 26, at 94-95.

9

Reviving Social Work: A Prophet Remembered

The beginning of hearings on the Clinton administration's welfare bill and its competitors initiated another period of political posturing on welfare issues. The president wished to be seen as the prophet of welfare reform. Enactment of a bill—any bill—was essential to this object, hence he produced a proposal that simultaneously paid obeisance both to reform and to Democratic interest groups such as feminists, legal services attorneys, and the anticlericals of the civil liberties unions. Thus, a section of the bill that purported to launch an attack on incentives to illegitimacy was confined to a provision giving states the option of denying small increments in benefits to mothers having children while on welfare, the existing system of individual cash entitlements being otherwise preserved inviolate. Appropriations were provided for propaganda directed at adolescents, but a bizarre provision operated to effectively exclude religious groups—such as the black churches—from any role in the program. The core of the bill was a scheme, similar to many fostered since the Nixon administration, to drive a small percentage of welfare mothers into the workforce and their children into publicly supported day care centers, for which several billion dollars were sought to be approprated—essentially a feminist agenda rather than a welfare reform one. The bill, to its credit, reinforced child support enforcement, denied direct cash benefits to the very youngest mothers (but not to parents with whom they and their children reside, who are not infrequently themselves welfare mothers), and sought to provide casework—a lost art—to recipients under the age of twenty. No effort was made to revive the use of maternity homes, or significantly to enlist churches and private charities in addressing these problems.

A faction of the Republican opposition, for its part, while properly and successfully insisting on a more effective attack on entitlement incentives to unwed motherhood and greater involvement of the voluntary sector by replacing individual entitlements with bloc grants to the states, has engaged in careless talk about an end to all benefits, the revival of orphanages, and the use of welfare as a "wedge issue" to embarrass a Democratic administration.

Each of the contending factions had its favored sociologists and historians. Two frequently cited works are, for the left, Michael B. Katz's *In the Shadow of the Poorhouse* (1986) and, for its opponents, Marvin Olasky's *The Tragedy of American Compassion* (1992). These works unite, however, in their passing attention to one of the greatest of Baltimoreans, the pioneer American social worker Mary Ellen Richmond (1861-1928).

Mr. Katz refers to Miss Richmond twice. After noting the opposition of the charity organization societies, of which Miss Richmond was a leader, to the mothers' pension laws, the state-level precursors of AFDC, on the prescient basis that they would pension "crimes against society," he quotes, not without an air of triumph, from her meticulous 1913 study of case histories of 985 widows, a study which, Mr. Katz says, "proved how useful mothers' pensions could be." This related that a widow:

> applied to the city and received $2 worth of groceries a week and a quarter of a ton of coal. Her application to the C.O.S. was made a little later. The Society replaced the city aid by a regular allowance of $2 a week (later increased to $3) with extra relief in emergencies; the church gave $1 a week besides. Mrs. A took as lodgers her brother and cousin; this,with sewing at home, brought her total weekly income up to $6 or $7, exclusive of relief. When the children got older and went to school, she went out cleaning for part of the day. . . . The regular allowance was first decreased, then discontinued altogether in 1908, although occasional help in emergencies has sometimes been needed since.

It was this sort of case history, so unlike that of today's AFDC recipient, that led Miss Richmond to oppose mothers' pension laws on the basis that: "the claim is made that it is only more income which is needed; that personal service, supervision, continuous oversight and care are not only superfluous but even impertinent. If individualized care is not necessary at this point, if "casework" has no place; then we are confronted here with the solitary exception in the whole range of social endeavor . . . the public schools are finding this out, in connection with their truancy work, their home and school visiting, their vocational guidance, and other activities."

Mr. Katz goes on to note:

> In *Social Diagnosis* (1917) Mary Richmond developed the first major theoretical statement of social work's new direction. Casework, she wrote, consisted of "those processes which develop personality through adjustments consciously effected, individual by individual, between men and their social environment." In the 1920s, Freudian psychology moved casework away from Richmond's concern with environment and toward a focus on personality. . . . Social work never reestablished its claim to

professional standing. One reason is that it chose the wrong alternative. As social workers rejected urban mediation and abandoned social reform, they became second-class therapists, inferior in standing, if not in competence, to psychiatrists.

Mr. Olasky for his part also refers to Miss Richmond: "Charity workers began by interviewing applicants and checking backgrounds in order to answer one question: 'Who is bound to help in this case?' Charity workers then tried to call in relatives, neighbors, or former coworkers and coworshippers. "Relief given without reference to friends and neighbors is accompanied by moral loss, Mary Richmond . . . noted. 'Poor neighborhoods are doomed to grow poorer and more sordid, whenever the natural ties of neighborliness are weakened by our well-meant but unintelligent interference.'"

Philip Klein, in his *Philanthropy and Social Welfare* (1968) notes that *Social Diagnosis* "became the bible of caseworkers. It retained that status for at least three decades, until it was gradually crowded aside by literature inspired by appearance of the psychoanalytic school of thought. *Social Diagnosis* was a major work,, compounding wide reading with experience—unremittinglytesting and being tested."

The rather striking freshness of Miss Richmond's prose as well as her practical sense was the product of an unusual background. She was born in 1861, raised in post-Civil War Baltimore and orphaned while still young. The relatives who raised her did not send her to school until she was eleven. She was, however, taught to read, out of Dickens's Pickwick Papers. When at the age of nine she learned of Dickens' death, she wept for hours and would not be comforted. She spoke with gratitude of a friend of her aunt who lent her books but insisted she be given a summary of them before lending another volume. She attended Eastern High School in Baltimore, there falling under the influence of an inspired English teacher. When she graduated at the age of sixteen, her formal education ended. She went to New York to join her aunt. There they lived in a cheap furnished room and worked in a publishing house. Later, after her aunt suffered a physical breakdown, Miss Richmond returned to Baltimore. During this period she appeared to have suffered successively from tuberculosis and malaria. From 1881 or 1882, she worked in a stationery store in Baltimore, until 1888, when she became employed as a bookkeeper and office assistant in a small Baltimore hotel. There she found boredom and frustration, since teaching was the only intellectual career open to women and in order to enter it "you had to have an education or a political pull—and I had neither." The biographical notes accompanying her posthumously published *The Long View* relate that "While in this rebellious state of mind, she responded to an advertisement that looked interesting and within her scope—the Charity Organization Society of Baltimore wanted an assistant treasurer. She knew literally nothing about the society or what it was for, but she went one rainy night at the age of 28 for an interview with Charles J. Bonaparte, chairman of the Board of Managers, who said in recalling the incident years afterward: "She looked pathetically young and she spoke like the Ancient of Days!'"

Within two years she was hired by Daniel Coit Gilman to succeed two Johns Hopkins men as the society's general secretary; thereafter she was called to similar positions in Philadelphia (1900) and New York (1909). As early as 1897, she called for a training school for case workers, and the summer school of applied philanthropy that she helped organize in the following year is the direct antecedent of the Columbia School of Social Work. Her 1899 text on *Friendly Visiting* and her Social Diagnosis, published in 1917, were the leading casework texts of their time, and she may be deemed the founder of her profession. There follow some samples of her writings:

On beggary (1891): In England begging has been an organized profession for six hundred years, and we find attempts to repress it by legal enactment as far back as 1349 and in Ribton Turner's monumental work on the subject I counted no less than 371 laws since made with the same object. . . . Yet with all this legislating, the beggar still flourishes, and it is evident that punishment alone will never exterminate him. What punishment failed to do, the indulgence of the early church did not succeed in doing; by encouraging able-bodied beggars to lead lives of idleness and profligacy upon the charitable bounty of the religious houses. The point of view which holds that the giver is not responsible for the use made of his gift, that what he gives is laid up to his credit in heaven just the same, belongs to the church of the middle ages. It is distinctly medieval and is just as much of an anachronism now as a Queen Elizabeth ruff and farthingale would be. Yet the modern church gets this out, dusts it, and proudly wears it every once and a while . . . crying that, "The poor ye always have with you"; as if that had anything to do with it. Truly, as Professor Ely says, the perverters of scripture we always have with us too. So, even up to modern times, the beggar, like a wayward child between two unwise parents, petted and coddled by mother Church and punished by father State, has gone on having his own way, for it has never occurred to these parents to combine and reform him. . . . The war against evil and wrong is our inheritance. . . . Some, prudent souls, when drafted into the army, prefer to send a substitute in the shape of a check, until at last there are only a few good soldiers left, and that's why the world, although it moves, moves slowly . . . we must never allow ourselves to give alms to people we don't know all about.

(1908): We do any man, rich or poor, a great wrong when we help to make it possible for him to live without human ties and without occupation. Upon the provision of work immediately, and upon the restoration of home ties whenever possible, all effective aid for the man on the street must be founded. . . . The wayfarers' lodges or municipal lodging-houses . . . are most useful in dealing with an appeal for help and serve only as a first step in effective relief. Every householder and every business house should be provided with free tickets to these shelters, and no such place should be used unless there is a work-test of some sort attached to it. . . .

On nonsupport (1897): On the side of prevention, it seems to me that all the alms wasted on sham families might be better expense in making more adequate provision for the disorganized period between the time when our boys and girls in large cities leave school and the time when they settle down in life. This critical period is quite unprovided for, and in it habits of idleness and irresponsibility are formed. The breaking down of the apprenticeship system, and our failure to develop the technical school as a substitute; the lack, so far, of any adequate number of boys' clubs; the absence of varied and absorbing occupations and amusements of a healthy sort—these conditions are more responsible for the married vagabond than the state of the labor market, or even the saloon.

(1908): To approach any relief question from the point of view of the child's welfare only and to consider nothing else, is a natural enough mistake to make, but its effect upon the child's life is disastrous. . . . We may hold the most approved views about family life, and still be actively engaged in breaking it up, when we fail to treat all questions of income and relief as the affair first of the head of the family, of the mother only secondarily, and of the children not at all.

On dole queues (1896): All public distributions—the giving out of supplies to people who are expected to stand in line and so advertise their needs--are open to this same objection, that charity hurts when it fails to shun publicity. We talk much about "helping people to help themselves"; but how can they help themselves effectively if, through our carelessness, they are robbed of their self-respect and proper pride?

On ideology (1906): One . . . cannot but feel that those who write and lecture with such enthusiasm about socialism, individualism and anarchism would all be benefitted by a good stiff dose of case work. In many of their disquisitions one feels the lack of contact with social classes other than the group to which the writer belongs.

On community chests and "United Ways" (1901): Charity seems to me a thing that goes only a little way along the lines of business and then goes a much longer way along the lines of education . . . the seeker after truth must be unhampered; he must be free. . . . She preferred to see social work more poorly supported, if by that means it might maintain this intimacy of contact among social worker, client, and community . . . if the community chest did not develop some method to protect this value, it would kill social work.

On cash relief (1911): [R]elief has no moral and no immoral qualities. . . . It can never occupy the front row . . . and can never be agitated for or against except as a part, a secondary part, of some plan of curative treatment . . . the sole advantage of large doles over small is that,being more expensive,they are likely to be administered to fewer people. The terms "adequate" and "inadequate relief" are as question-begging in their character as the terms "worthy" and "unworthy." We flung those on the scrap-heap long ago and I should be glad to see these follow. "Inadequate" to what purpose, "adequate" for what end? The emphasis on relief brings a support subject to the law of diminishing returns, while the emphasis on cure assures us a public increasingly willing to go the whole distance. Relief, in other words, is a very good servant, but a bad master.

On the Equal Rights Amendment (1923): What constitutes true equality for women? . . . To treat unequal things unequally or to treat them equally? Surely the former. But a certain type of feminist "sees red" whenever it is suggested that there are some inherent differences between the sexes, and that no question of superior or inferior enters into a frank recognition of these differences. When we ask the state to pass a law that will affect millions of women, should we not try to legislate with reference to the circumstances of the largest possible number? . . . It is easy for a wife who can earn twice as much as her husband and is without children, moreover, to announce with an air of conviction that she does not "approve" of [alimony]; but what about the wife who must support several small children after having spent the best years of her life in bearing and rearing them? . . . A serious objection to blanket legislation of any kind is that it throws upon the courts the task of law making.

On health care (1903): The term "almoner" describes but imperfectly to American ears the duties of one who must interview the applicants of an outpatient department, must visit their homes, and must know and use all charitable agencies that could "render the treatment of the medical staff more effective"; and yet these and no less are the duties of almoners as defined by three London hospitals. . . . And one thinks hopelessly and sadly of the waste, misuse and abuse of the out-patient and casual department . . . where there is no one to see these are used to the best advantage.

As noted, Miss Richmond's vision of the future of social work did not prevail. In 1935, Congress enacted a national program of mothers' pensions (AFDC) as part of the Social Security Act, acting at the behest of the Children's Bureau of the Department of Labor. Secretary Frances Perkins later confessed that she had not appreciated the scope of the legislation:

She felt the Children's Bureau let her down on the provision of aid to mothers with dependent children. She maintained that she always thought that a "dependent mother" was a widow with small children or one whose husband had been disabled in an industrial accident or one who married a ne'er do-well who had deserted her or hit the bottle. She said it never occurred to her, in view of the fact that she'd been active in drives for homes that took care of mothers with illegitimate children, that these mothers would be called "dependent" in the new legislation. She blamed the huge illegitimacy rates among blacks on aid to mothers with dependent children. [1]

The enthusiasts for AFDC in 1935 likewise assumed that its administration would be closely linked with social work. Thus Grace Abbott, according to her biographer, "wanted aid to dependent children given to the Children's Bureau where it could be integrated into a program of social services. . . . She feared that placing the aid to dependent children program in a large new administrative structure . . . would result in loss of standards."

Beginning in the early 1960's, ironically as a result of the "War on Poverty," state "suitable home" requirements as a condition of welfare benefits were invalidated, and the power and discretion of social workers were thereby impaired. The denial of benefits was then subjected to overelaborate hearing requirements notwithstanding a rare protest against these as "mak[ing] government unworkable," by the nation's then most distinguished federal judge, Henry J. Friendly, who proposed instead use of ombudsmen on the premise that "much of the welfare litigation . . . arises from misguided acts of lowly and overpressed officials which their superiors would gladly correct—if only they knew of them." A "declaration" system for the award of welfare benefits dispensing with the need for social investigation was adopted virtually everywhere to avoid a flood of welfare appeals, and the delivery of social services and "income maintainence" were separated in most state welfare departments. Professor Geoffrey Hazard, Jr. in an article originally published in 1968, observed, "Notions of client involvement and rehabilitation--indeed, the notion of "client" itself—are alien to such a system.

The end result, noted by Professor William H. Simon of Stanford, was that, "The (welfare] system is now staffed by people who lack both the power and the aspiration to assist claimants . . . the old ideal of frontline administration by professional social workers has been discarded and the small but influential number of social workers in the system at the time of Goldberg have been expelled."

As Professor Mary Ann Glendon of Harvard has noted, "The American dialect of rights talk disserves public deliberation not only through affirmatively promoting an image of the rights bearer as a radically autonomous individual, but through its corresponding neglect of the social dimensions of human personhood . . . groups or associations that stand between the individual and the state all too often meet with judicial incomprehension.

George F. Kennan, with characteristic incisiveness, has similarly recently observed, "One of the unique features of American government is, in comparison with other modern systems, its neglect of intelligent and discriminating administration . . ." He declares "an aversion to the American tradition of the treatment of social and political problems by great, all-inclusive categories (that is, by abstract and rigid legal definitions with theoretically wide-ranging applicability) and a longing for intelligent discrimination in the treatment of both persons and situations, even where this requires that a single public servant be authorized to decide something on his own responsibility." The great sociologist Karl Mannheim similarly observed in 1954:, "The social worker gives not merely material help but spiritual healing. He adds a touch of emotion and vitality to ordinary intercourse . . . official bureaucracy must be tempered by the charity of the primary groups."

What Miss Richmond would have had to say about all this is summarized in the three now controversial propositions with which she concluded her *What is Social Case Work?* (1922):

> 1. Human beings are interdependent. . . . We achieve personality through right relations to society and in no other way.
>
> 2. Human beings are different . . . A genuinely democratic social program equalizes opportunity by intelligent mass action, and provides at the same time for an administrative policy which does different things for and with different people.
>
> 3. Human beings are not dependent and domestic animals. This fact of man's difference from other animals establishes the need for his participation in making and carrying out plans for his welfare. Individuals have wills and purposes of their own and are not fitted to play a passive part in the world; they deteriorate when they do.

In the face of an exaggerated individualism in both morals and economics, society now seems to find itself increasingly helpless, even in the face of major epidemics. But perhaps we are really in the darkness that precedes the dawn. Former Secretary Joseph Califano has pointed out that society's failure (under the influence of our civil liberties unions) to deal with resolve with the AIDS and drug crises has succeeded in reviving tuberculosis as a major public health problem. This raises the hopeful, but unfortunately remote, possibility that we will again be led from the wilderness—by another tubercular hotel clerk from Baltimore. The recent welfare reform legislation at least raises no obstacles to renewed attention to Miss Richmond's teachings.

NOTE

1. In K. Loucheim (ed.), *The Making of the New Deal: The Insiders Speak* (1983).

10

Neighborhood Zoning

This discussion is an appeal for incremental change in an institution that most Americans take for granted: the protection of the single-family suburb against small accessory apartments in single-family homes and small retail and commercial uses. One who proposes changes in a great and durable social and legal institution is under a duty to candidly recognize its appeal and values. Zoning, though constituting in its typical applications a greater intrusion on property than the usual "petty larceny of the police power," enjoys the support of the most conservative elements of the community.

Defenders of the free market who criticicize this institution, with an abundance of data and in terms of measured reason,[1] are transformed by their subject matter into politically isolated radicals, as are the activist judges and advocacy groups who assail the excesses of zoning from the left, with foredoomed efforts to generate by judicial decree economically and socially mixed communities.[2]

Any effort to alter zoning structures must appeal to the values that sustain the institution. What are these values? Ernst Freund, one of the first and the wisest students of the institution, referred to "the national temperament which at present combines the lowest degree of local attachment with the highest degree of sensitiveness as to neighborhood associations. There is a subtle psychology about this sensitiveness; I think it is connected with our democratic institutions; where you haven't got natural class distinctions you make them artificially."[3] "When we speak of amenity, we have in mind residential preference . . . controlled by physical and by social conditions, the latter being the more powerful."

Freund expressed the hope, as yet unrealized, that the class distinctions fostered and recognized by zoning would in time be replaced by pride in community. "If zoning can produce the standard of stability that is characteristic of cities in older countries, it will render a valuable service." As to the suburbs, the fungibility of zoned communities has defeated this hope. The description by the conservative Judge Westenhaver of the social results of zoning in the *Euclid* case has not been improved upon by his liberal successors: "In the last analysis, the result to be accomplished is to classify the population and segregate them according to their income and situation in life. The true reason why some persons live in a mansion and others in a shack, why some live in a single-family dwelling and others in an apartment or why some live in a well-kept apartment and others in a tenement is primarily economic. It is a matter of income and wealth, plus the labor and difficulty of procuring adequate domestic service."[4]

The recognition and popularity of zoning thus reflect the American attachment to economic incentives and distinctions. "The ownership of real property bred a self-interest which was utterly lacking where ownership was lacking. And it was a national trait."[5] Nor are these attachments illegitimate: as the Supreme Court has recently reminded us, "The Constitution expressly protects against confiscation of private property or the income therefrom."[6]

The vested interests represented by home ownership are deserving of the highest possible respect. For most persons, and particularly those of modest means, the family home represents the largest single investment and one that is not easily disposed of.[7] "One does not trade a house as easily as one might trade a car or switch breakfast cereals."[8] Its location and surroundings importantly influence the upbringing of the family's young, surely an interest deserving of respect. Zoning stands and, whatever its ostensible rationale, is intended to stand as a barrier against change in social surroundings. Where persons have striven all their lives to improve their family's situation and opportunities, minimal respect for the system of economic incentives that we rely on to drive society demands that they not be suddenly or summarily deprived of the environment that is the fruit of their labors. Judicial decisions disregarding this obvious premise may bring momentary fame to their authors but, in the long run, will do little to change the face of society as long as free expression and free elections remain vital principles.

It is, however, the thesis of this chapter, that in two seemingly minor but important respects the traditional structures of Euclidean zoning must be relaxed if its real purposes are to continue to be served in contemporary social conditions. Despite its dramatic overture, this discussion resolves itself into an appeal for some broadening of the permitted scope of two exceptions already recognized by most enacted ordinances defining residential districts: those in favor of accessory uses and those in favor of home occupations.[9] Failure to make such changes may well vindicate the somber prophecy of Jane Jacobs, as to our postwar suburbs, that "Thirty years from now we shall have accumulated new problems of blight and decay over acreages so immense that in comparison the present problems of the great cities and their grey belts will look piddling."[10] Further, the changes proposed, by reason of their consistency with values of private property and with pressing economic needs, may do more to foster, in a nonthreatening fashion, greater diversity in the suburbs than the sturm und drang surrounding recent judicial efforts to insert multifamily housing units into single-family communities.[11]

ACCESSORY USES

Nearly all American zoning ordinances authorize "accessory uses" in residential neighborhoods. These are customarily held to include such amenities as porches and garages; however, courts become more resistant when efforts are made to include self-contained rental apartments in single-family houses, or garage apartments, or separate houses on single-family lots. The "granny house" or "echo house" is said to be a familiar European institution; the two-family home or duplex apartment the rental from one portion of which is used to pay the mortgage is likewise familiar abroad and also has found some recognition in FHA loan legislation if not in common practice[12]: 12 U.S.C. § 1703(b)(1)(B) provides for conversion loans of up to $8,750 per dwelling unit, an amount unchanged since 1981, notwithstanding that loan limits for trailer homes have since been greatly liberalized.[13] "In the Federal Republic of Germany owner-occupants who build two dwelling units, one for owner-occupancy and one for rental, can deduct [against taxes] 5 percent of the cost for 8 years and 2-1/2% thereafter," while Finland allows the first $650 in rent from an accessory apartment to be disregarded for income tax and social security purposes. Local subdivisions have on occasion been permitted to qualify for federal community block grants under 42 U.S.C., § 5301 on the basis of "the development of shared housing opportunities in which elderly families . . . benefit as a result of living in a dwelling.in which the facilities are shared with others."

There has been enhanced interest in this type of housing in recent years. The American Planning Association has published a monograph including model ordinances,[14] and a similar study has been published by the Canadian Mortgage and Housing Corporation. Two books have been published in support of expanded use of such apartments; one by Patrick Hare, a Washington land-planning consultant, and one by Professor Martin Gellen of Berkeley.[15] A number of subdivisions, significantly among them the prosperous and secure suburban areas of Montgomery County, Maryland; Marin County, California; Fairfax County, Virginia; and various towns in Fairfield County; Connecticut have legislated in support of this concept, as have the states of California and Hawaii.[16] It is no accident that the legislation has first appeared in jurisdictions celebrated for high-cost housing.[17] It has been estimated that nearly 40 percent of American suburbs now recognize the concept in some form.[18]

This considerable movement has been in large measure spontaneous. The concept has not generated great support from any organized interest group. "No one [in Mr. Hare's words] is going to make enough off them to afford promotion, or at least no major companies are. The concept has generated little opposition, for it is nonthreatening." The ordinances expand and do not impair the rights of property owners. "Towns seldom resist a change that ought to increase tax revenue by lifting land value assessments and therefore tax receipts."[19] Because the apartments thus created are characteristically small and therefore usually inhabited by single persons or the elderly, the impetus to "fiscal zoning" to exclude families that will burden municipal services is absent. Racial fears are assuaged by the "Mrs. Murphy's boardinghouse" exemption to the Civil Rights Act of 1968,[20] which excludes from coverage buildings with four apartments or less "if the owner actually maintains and occupies one of such living quarters as his residence." The appeal of this concept is enhanced by the opportunity to create an additional housing unit for a construction cost estimated to typically be $16,500.[21]

However, the major impetus for this change is felt need, arising from recent social changes. These include demand for living units by an increasing number of elderly persons priced out of nursing homes,[22] the increased entry of women into the workforce and consequent need of women with children for income obtained from renting extra space, the decline in the marriage rate,[23] and, most dramatically, the decline in household size resulting from these factors and the tendency of families to have fewer children, rendering much housing built in earlier periods needlessly large.[24] The average number of persons per household declined from 3.14 in 1970 to 2.76 in 1980, to 2.69 in 1985, and to 2.67 in 1986, a decline of almost 15 percent in sixteen years. The number of persons over the age of fourteen living alone increased from 7,064,000 in 1960 to 20,602,000 in 1985 and to 23,6000,000 in 1994. The number of households containing six or more persons declined from 6.8 million in 1965 to 3.6 million in 1985. "At a generous maximum space standard threshold of three rooms per person, 7.5 million units or one-seventh of all owner-occupied dwellings in the United States can be classified as containing surplus space." These changes have caused one observer to estimate that 2.5 to 3 million accessory apartments are already in use in the United States, a number equal to six or seven years average rental housing production.[25] It has been observed that "[tlhe herculean job of the planner, aware of the clouded condition of his crystal ball, is . . . to try to figure out how the inevitable shifts in today's demands and the obsolesence of today's techniques can be absorbed at minimum social and economic cost."[26] The recent experience with accessory apartments suggests that, in this sphere, planners need not plan; the crying need is for them to get out of people's way.[27] For even the most widespread use of accessory apartments (particularly if they are restricted to owner-occupied buildings) is unlikely to give rise to use intensities as high as those for which most large homes were built, and provided the usual restrictions against disfiguring exterior changes are present, there will be no effect analogous to nuisance on the neighborhood. In Richard Babcock's words: "The neighbor can insist on protection from the hazards of contagion and fire and from the use of residential streets for four axle trucks . . . if he decides . . . to build a duplex but maintain the single-family density, it is beyond me why I should be able to call down constitutional imperatives to stop him." The benefits of enhanced use of accessory apartments are manifold: Persons of reduced means (the elderly, female heads of broken families) who would otherwise have to sell homes are enabled to retain them.[28] The elderly, who are increasing in number, and for whom inexpensive housing is in limited supply, can obtain housing in good neighborhoods and can frequently both receive services (transportation, home health care) and provide services (child care), the burden of which might otherwise fall on the state.

A revival of the extended family may be fostered, since most people desire propinquity—but not too much propinquity—with their parents, and "granny houses" or apartments with separate entrance and cooking facilities meet this need. The "babushka," though un-American and not a technological innovation, may reduce fashionable demands for expensive and publicly supported day care A more diverse suburban population in terms of both age and income may result, thus also insuring that the entry of women into the workforce does not cause neighborhoods to be populated during the day predominantly by latchkey children, with attendant problems of delinquency. The number of young adults in suburban communities available for the teaching force may be increased. Minority and lower-income persons may benefit directly by being introduced to suburban neighborhoods in small numbers, vouched for by landlord-neighbors, and, indirectly through the phenomenon of "filtering" which follows each creation of a new housing unit. Professor Bernard Siegan has summarized the literature as establishing that: "The construction on the average of 1000 new units, both houses and apartments, makes it possible for a total of about 3,500 moves to occur to different and likely better housing conditions . . . beginning with the third succession of moves poor families were represented in approximately the same proportion which they represent of the population."[29]

A very large number of new housing units will be provided at very limited public or private cost. At a time when each new subsidized unit costs upward of $75,000, accessory apartments may be brought on line at a third or less of this cost. Moreover, the units thus created are in better quality buildings. "Projects provide examples of four or five year old buildings that are in much worse condition than buildings more than ten times their age."[30] Accessory apartments, unlike subsidized housing, also enjoy the benefit of owner-occupied management. Again, to quote Professor Siegan, "Historically, low and moderate housing requires great maintenance and management expertise. It is not unusual for a poorly managed project to fall completely apart after five years." Further "subsidy programs may entail some conventional construction and may not provide housing of the same quality as would have been provided through the normal operation of the filtering process. Because rental and purchase terms are subsidized, these units usually have a great competitive advantage over conventional housing that may be superior in quality." "The apartments promise to provide low income housing in communities in which earlier efforts to do so have been fruitless."

The jurisdictions tha' have opted to liberalize their accessory housing ordinances have had little difficulty in doing so. The usual restrictions imposed are the familiar building-code restrictions relating to required plumbing and privacy arrangements, required parking spaces, minimum window space and ceiling levels, and the like, which operate to circumscribe damp basements and cramped attic apartments.[31] There are commonly restrictions on additional entrances on the front of a building and sometimes on exterior exit stairs (though the fire protection benefits of the latter even as to single-family dwellings should ordinarily outweigh the aesthetic concerns).

Finally, there are restrictions designed to alleviate concerns about neighborhood character, such as the requirement that the converted building have been in existence for five years (thus discouraging developers from selling duplex rental units as such, a doubtful provision since this arrangement is highly popular in Europe) and the more reasonable, indeed indispensable, requirement that an existing building be owner-occupied for at least one year as of the date of creation of a new unit to discourage speculators. Some jurisdictions impose additional restrictions by making permits annually renewable as special exceptions, or, more doubtfully, by restricting to a small percentage the number of homes within a given radius that may have accessory apartments or by imposing consent restrictions.[32]

Many jurisdictions authorizing accessory apartments do not impose such restrictions, and apartments in others may be built without hindrance in rural zones and where sufficient land is owned to support two or more houses. Finally, the decision of the Supreme Court in *Moore v. City of Cleveland*,[33] though a classic no-clear-majority decision, may be read as invalidating restrictions on creation of accessory apartments to be occupied by relatives of the owner.

Although no fortunes may be made from construction of accessory apartments, various interest groups have reason to support the concept: home improvement contractors, lenders, realtors, organizations of the elderly and of divorced parents, hospital discharge planners, and large employers, including school systems.

The fact that there is a perceived problem of homelessness in a nation that prior to the 1970s is said, albeit by supply-side enthusiast George Gilder, to have spent "eight times more of its capital on housing than countries in Western Europe and three times more than Japan"[34] suggests that housing problems involve not physical shortage, but failure of adaptation. If the predicted collapse of housing values materializes, the prevalence of second mortgage and equity loan borrowing and the "equity gains [which] made people feel rich enough to plunge into unprecedented levels of consumer debt" will result in a major social and economic crisis if homeowners are prevented from adapting their principal asset to earn additional income. One may call to mind William H. Whyte's prophecy of thirty years ago:

> Suburbia does not condone shabby gentility. The amenities that a severe cutback in expenditures would put in jeopardy are not marginal; to the family on the edge of the

middle class they are social necessities. The prime fear is the fear of "going back." Psychologically they have more to lose than any other group in our society and a turndown that would be moderate by the standards of two decades ago would place them in a perilous position. They are not going back and if their fears were exploited, their discontent could become ugly indeed. If our economy has an Achilles heel, this might be it.[35]

HOME OCCUPATIONS

The growth of accessory apartments, both those sanctioned by law and those created in defiance of it, at once results in and contemplates the addition to suburban life of groups not previously represented in large numbers—the elderly and single persons of modest means. This in turn creates a need for greater access to retail and service establishments, traditionally excluded from residential neighborhoods except for a limited class of mostly professional "home occupations." Although nearly all residential zoning laws authorize "home occupations," many cases define 'home occupation' restrictively to exclude businesses and limit permitted uses to those previously customary.[36] The logic of this is not clear. In Babcock's words: "In Winnetka the ground rules call for doing money-making in Chicago; local money-making is bad."[37] The exceptions in favor of professional offices are said to rest not on function but social class, and the prohibition of retail establishments on an unwillingness to make the distinctions necessary to appropriate regulation. "Absolute prohibition paradoxically seems to involve less government control than does detailed regulation."[38] "[It] is not harmful to my status to have a professional office in my neighborhood [and] is perfectly genteel for the widow Corruthers to make out with a little homestitching in her parlor but a beauty shop or a mom-and-pop grocery store is unacceptable. If the test were convenience to the neighbors, the beauty shop would be more acceptable than the lawyer's or broker's office, and the mom and dad grocery store with its liberal credit policy and its willingness to cater to special tastes and odd hours would justify first consideration."[39]

It is not easy to justify on any functional ground the prohibition of very-small-one-room retail establishments.[40] The absurdity of the health-and-safety rationale for prohibition has been clear since the dawn of zoning, one of whose fathers, Albert Bettman once confessed, many years before Mrs. Thatcher: "There have been mighty healthy kids raised over grocery stores."[41] Traffic as a ground for exclusion is difficult to justify, at least where acceptance of deliveries from large trucks is prohibited. In any case, notes Babcock, "if our test were based on traffic annoyance, the church would be the first to be excluded from the residential district."[42] The danger of retail uses in residential areas is restricted by the fact that the uses are self-limiting. "[Alny 'home occupation' which depended upon and stimulated vehicular traffic would not remain in the residential area but would locate in areas accessable to large-scale traffic movement."[43] Siegan's study of an unzoned city, Houston, has suggested that "[Al limited number of commercial uses probably no more than 5 percent of structures on local streets, might in time enter the subdivisions . . . most of which would provideservices for local residents and thereby augment the viability of the area"[44] even if there were no restrictions on permitted size of retail uses. As to more affluent subdivisions on large lots, "[t]he high cost of the homes coupled with the fact that they are on low-traffic streets would make it economically unfeasible for purchase by a commercial user."[45]

The interest of existing residents in avoiding depreciation of their homes by the advent of such uses is limited. "Changes will not occur very rapidly. It usually takes a considerable period of time before new uses develop in built-up areas." Moreover, "many property owners tend not to live long periods of time in the same houses for various reasons having nothing to do with changes in the character of property uses. Their discomfort may be short-lived and devoid of financial detriment" even if full-scale retail uses are allowed.

The benefits of small-scale retail uses in residential neighborhoods are several. The first is simple convenience. "The problem in Levittown [according to a study of it by Professor David Popenoe of Rutgers] . . . is the lack of neighborhood shops within walking distance; a loaf of bread entails an automobile trip—often of a sizeable distance. This limits shoppers to drivers, a problem in some families, and restricts the shopping participation of children."[46] It also burdens the scarce time of two-earner families.

The absence of facilities within walking distance likewise renders residential suburban communities inhospitable to the elderly.[47] The segregation of the aged has become an especially vigorous trend in the U.S. What has been said of the poverty of libraries, youth centers and recreational facilities in American suburbs applies also to retail establishments. "This deficit places a special burden on certain types of people, on those persons in fact who are most dependent on the resources of the local environment."[48] As with the aged, so with children who are disadvantaged both as shoppers and as potential employees. In Jane Jacobs' words, "Children are at the mercy of convenience more than anyone else, except the aged,"[49] and in those of David Popenoe, "The most common complaint of teenagers in Levittown is that "there is nothing to do here."[50] Few of the facilities are neighborhood-based; because of this they seem distant to the residents, even though the actual time spent getting to them by car is not great. And the necessity for a car sets up a double dependence situation: Not only must the facility be available, but a car must be available if the facility is to be utilized. This situation holds true especially for retail facilities, the most commonly used ones in any community."[51] "The youth's transportation frustrations and boredom are compounded by the great dependence on parents for something as vital as transportation, which comes at a time when the teenager is striving for greater independence. The situation can lead to deep underlying resentment on both sides and adds to the confusion and sometimes hostility that often seems to mark parent-teenager relationships in the U.S." The same author pertinently observes: "The availability of part-time work, especially in the summer, is one of the best solutions to the problem of teenage idleness."[52]

As with teenagers, so with women: "Many features of Levittown make the life of a working woman there a greater struggle. It is more difficult to find suitable employment within reasonable commuting distance; there is almost total dependence on the automobile (what happens if she can't drive, can't afford a car, or the car breaks down). As the women's movement succeeds . . . boredom may change to active resentment."

To banish commerce is not only to banish employment opportunuties but to create an artificial social situation, or lack thereof, in which "one's quality of life depends heavily on the extent to which the microenvironment is embellished with private possessions."[53] Further, to quote Jane Jacobs, "The opportunity (in modern life, it has become a privilege) of playing and growing up in a daily world composed of both men and women is possible and usual for children who play on lively diversified city sidewalks. I cannot understand why this arrangement should be discouraged by planning and by zoning."[54] It is an uncommon family which can provide all the things which a complete and well-rounded community could offer—facilities, a sense of participation in ongoing community activities, places where teenagersand adults can spontaneously meet, and a chance to observe life as it is lived outside of living room and yard."[55] Small scale retail uses assume particular importance in marginal low-income suburbs in danger of becoming the slums of the future, Jane Jacobs's "gray areas." Professor Siegan has noted, "Separated uses are out of place in new-city locations because of the lack of mobility of low-income residents"[56] "For the family that does not own an automobile, the existence of a nearby grocery store . . . may be a great convenience if not actually a necessity. The same may be true, for the family whose one car is used by the husband during the day."[57] "[Thus] the existence of so-called incompatible uses may increase rather than decrease the viability of a lesser-income area."[58] Further, "[Almong those who will also gain are the relatively few who desire to use homes entirely or partially for business purposes. Areas of diverse use have served well the interest of small and beginning businesses."[59] It is also important to remember that the business use of homes provides a safety net in hard times, "During the twenties and then again under the strain of the depression, small businessmen gave up establishments like beauty parlors, barber shops and real estate offices and conducted their businesses in their homes, which were in zoning districts where such uses were prohibited."[60]

There are also values of competition that are fostered by home occupations. One may recall Jane Jacobs's strictures in the context of city life upon "monopolistic shopping centers [which] cloak under the public relations hoohaw, the subtraction of commerce from the intimate and casual life of cities."[61] Professor Garrett Power, a student of Baltimore City zoning, has noted that "preexisting groceries, filling stations, laundries and confectioneries located in districts now zoned exclusively residential thrived on the absence of competition."[62] Further, "zoning enthusiasts touted the advantages to the suburban retail store which was 'protected from the destructive competition of an unnecessary number of similar stores.'"[63]

The existence of local monopolies resulting from restrictive zoning finds confirmation in a number of respects, both in the "customary judicial view that zoning changes affect only a very small geographic area"[64] and in findings that in the view of middle-to upper-middle-class homeowners "the grocery store or beauty shop or auto repair shop might be an asset if it were a block away, but in any event possibly not harmful at that distance."[65] Professor Popenoe's study of Swedish housing found that "[alt a distance of over five to six hundred yards, the use of many [nonretail community] services drops off precipitously. This is especially true in the age of young people and for working class households. . . . centralization of services is a form of deprivation for some people; it deprives them of the useof the service in a way not dissimilar to the absence of that service entirely."[66]

As suburbs increasingly acquire offices and industry, the concentration of traffic around the few areas zoned for commerce becomes less acceptable. To quote Jane Jacobs: "Whenever people are thinly settled . . . or wherever diverse uses occur infrequently, any specific attraction does cause traffic congestion."[67] Further:, "duplication of car parking is also familiar in suburbs. The schools, the supermarkets, the churches, the shopping centers, the clinics, the movie, all the residences must have their own parking lots and all this duplicate parking lies idle for much of the time. Suburbs, at least while they remain suburbs, can stand this land waste and this high ratio of private automobile travel because of their lack ofconcentration. Here it would seem is that elusive point of equilibrium. Yet the moment work is introduced into the mixture, even in a suburb, the equilibrium is lost."[68] This is so because commuting and industrial traffic is added to the concentrated retail traffic resulting from the principle that "[tlhe more territory, planned or unplanned, which is dull, the greater the pressure of traffic on lively districts."[69] Obviously also "we increase transportation demand by forcing people to leave their residential zone to shop."[70]

Finally, home occupations combat the monotony of Jacobs's "wasted time and dull environments." The coming of age of the electronic office[71] and liberalizedtolerance of home occupations may avoid the stricture that "those thin dispersions 'lack any reasonable degree of innate vitality, staying power or inherent usefulness as settlements. Few of them, and these only the most expensive as a rule, hold their attraction much longer than a generation; then they begin to decay in the pattern of city grey areas."[72]

There are of course desirable restrictions on home occupations. While the restriction against retail sales should be swept aside, Mr. Babcock has suggested "protection from the common law nuisance (whether in the form of a hen house or a noisy window air conditioner) is the minimum [the neighbor] is entitled to expect . . . [he or she] should have the right to insist that there be provided the equivalents of the open space and light that would exist if the single family detached dwelling style had been maintained . . . protection from the hazards of contagion and fire and from the use of residential streets for four axle trucks."[73] Size limitations and requirements that the building's primary use be as a home with a limited number of employees from outside the residence can be justified. Jacobs's point that "grey areas areunequipped to handle strangers"[74] is a valid one, although the absence of heavily trafficked streets itself will operate to restrict the appeal of home-based establishments. Indeed, it has been contended that the need of large businesses for traffic causes substantial businesses to avoid residential locations even when—as it is in Houston—they are permitted to situate themselves there.[75] There may in addition be a case for severely prohibiting or restricting home occupations in a buffer area of a block or so where the residentially zoned area directly infringes on a commercial zone. Not only are the retail uses less needed by residents with a commercial district in the immediate proximity,but also such restrictions protect "those [described by Professor Siegan] who may bemost adversely affected [by allowance of home occupations] . . . the owners of homes backing up onto those on major thorofares . . . if the latter homes are replaced by or used for strip commercial purposes, values may be jeopardized for such adjoining homes." It has been suggested that the governing principle should be, "No regulation may infringe on the right of any resident to use a minor portion of a dwelling for gainful employment that does not change the character of the surrounding residential area."[76] This undoubtedly is an oversimplification: If one valid object of restrictions is to limit use to residents of the neighborhood, size restrictions and restrictions on number of employees (frequently "no more that two persons other than a member of the immediate family occupying said dwelling") have a part to play, as do limitations of signage (commonly to "flat nonilluminated signs not more than one square foot in area") and restrictions on deliveries by large trucks.[77] With these qualifications, however, it is difficult to justify most restrictions on home occupations by reference to objective performance standards since, if these are taken seriously, all window air conditioners and as Babcock wryly observes, "nearly all power mowers and . . . the emission from a number of house chimneys would be illegal."[78]

As with accessory apartments, there are weighty social considerations, not present in like measure at the time of the *Euclid* decision, that weigh in favor of greater generosity toward home occupations. "In the early years of Levittown [Popenoe observed] the teenager, the elderly person, the widowed and divorced female head of household, the working class woman living in tight financial straitsand cut off from relatives were unfamiliar figures."[79] Whether or not "working at home is on the increase and may be a factor which will serve to strengthen family life" or whether as suggested by a legal commentator, Professor Roberts of the Wake Forest Law School, "Economic pressures and high energy costs increase the likelihood that in order to avoid expensive commercial office space and reduce travel more people will "moonlight" at home where part time work is feasible,"[80] it is not unreasonable to suggest that existing prohibitions deserve another look. In an age of diminishing personal savings and reduced agriculture, the home is the principal capital asset of most families. A society that affects respect for private property and individual self-reliance and suspicion of needless government regulation should hesitate before denying individuals and families, in good times or bad, freely available recourse to what is for most the sole cushion against personal, social, and economic dislocations. Any federal administration with a commitment to frugality and market-based approaches would do well to look with favor on the West German tax credit scheme as a device to dramatize and popularize creation of accessory apartments and on liberalization of the FHA lending limits to at least correspond to those provided mobile homes. It should also make the point, forcefully, that talk of housing shortages is premature until existing barriers to use of the housing stock have been relaxed.

NOTES

1. Bernard Siegan, *Land Use without Zoning* (1972), a highly intelligent and provocative work, supplies the best example.

2. "In a society where so high a fraction of behavior and attitude relates to consumption paterns, there must be grave doubt whether income mixing is a plausible social policy. Government efforts to promote income mixing should concentrate not on making higher income neighborhoods available to all lower income people, but on supplementing a greater than usual degree of effort for people who put housing high in their value-preference ranking." M. Mayer, *The Builders* (1978) at 425.

3. E. Freund, *Some Inadequately Discussed Problems of the Law of Zoning*, in *Planning Problems of Town, City and Region* (1929) at 93. By contrast, Freund noted: "People [in Europe] do not mind a little store around the corner a bit. When you go to Vienna you find that the palace of one of the great aristocratic families has a big glass works display room on the lower floor. We wouldn't have that in this country because it is not conformable to our ideas."

4. *Ambler Realty Co. v. Euclid*, 297 Fed. 307, at 316. Judge Westenhaver's opinion was of course reversed on appeal. It is quoted at length in numerous recent works on zoning, including Siegan, op. cit. note 1, supra; and Toll, *Zoned American* (1977).

5. Toll, supra. note 4, at 280.

6. *Lindsey v. Normet*, 405 U.S. 56, 74 (1972). Cf. Simons, *Economic Policy for a Free Society* (1948) at 28-29: "A society based on free responsible individuals or families must involve extensive rights of property. The economic responsibilities of families are an essential part of their freedom, and like the inseparable moral responsibilities are necessary to moral development. Family property in the Occidental sense of the primary family, moreover, is largely the basis of preventive checks on population and of the effort to increase personal capacity from generation to generation, that is, to raise a few children hopefully and well or to sacrifice numbers to quality in family reproduction."

7. "Middle income projects as they age tend to contain a significant (or at least articulate) proportion of people who are fearful of contact outside their class." Jacobs, *The Death and Life of Great American Cities* (1961), at 40.

8. Babcock, *The Zoning Game* (1966), at 51. Other inducements to immobility include moving costs, fixed rate mortgages, the nontaxation of imputed rent, property-tax relief through circuit-breaker credits (see Tomassen, *Circuit Breaking and Life Cycle 'Lock-In'*, 31 National Tax Journal 59 (1978), cited in Gallen, infra note 15 at 100, the income tax deductibility of mortgage interest and property taxes, and capital gains tax deferrals; (see Newman and Reschovsky, *Federal Policy and the Mobility of Older Homeowners* (1985)).

9. "We did not know what general welfare meant, or at least how it could help us in defining the zoning principles. We knew that dark rooms, dark streets, dust, noise, flies, vermin, vibration all those things have some effect on safety or health or morals and our code was built up with great trepidation on these bases. It was a little hard to see why retail business coming into a residence district really affected health and safety." Alfred Bettman, one of the fathers of zoning, in Proceedings of the National Zoning Conference (1938) at 20-21, quoted in Toll, supra, at 281.

10. J. Jacobs, supra, at 446. It has been suggested that the *Euclid* case on its facts does not support the exclusion of two-family homes from residential districts. Gellen, infra note 15 at 118-20; compare *Miller v. Los Angeles*, 195 Cal. 477, 234 P.381 (1927),

with *Brett v. Brookline*, 250 Mass.78, 145 N.E. 271 (1924).

11. See P. Hare, *Accessory Apartments and Echo Units* (National Council of State Housing Agencies, 1987); Hare and Hollis, *Echo Housing: A Review of Zoning Issues and Other Considerations* (Amer. Assn. of Retired Persons, 1983).

12. It is said that FHA appraisal practices developed during the depression discouraged loans for two-family homes. Gellen, infra, citing C. Harriss, *History and Policies of the Home Owners Loan Corporation* (1951).

13. Public Law 98-181, § 105(d), 97 Stat. 1163 (1983). On the foreign schemes, see Howenstine, *Attacking Housing Costs: Foreign Policies and Strategies* (1983) at 104.

14. American Planning Associaion, *Accessory Apartments: Using Surplus Space in Single Family Homes*, Planning Advisory Service Report No. 365 (1981).

15. See Hare and Ostler, *Creating an Accessory Apartment* (1987); Gellen, *Accessory Apartments in Single Family Housing* (1987) (by far the most comprehensive work to date). See also People for Open Space, *Second Units: An Emerging Housing Resource* (1987). On the property tax effects, which are said to be modest, see Calvan, *Local Taxes and Accessory Dwellings* (1983). See also Frazis, *Second Unit Legalization: Issues and Policies* (1985); McGough, *Additions to Housing Supply by Means Other than New Construction* (1982); Sternlieb and Hughes, *The Future of Rental Housing* (1981); Minnesota Housing Finance Authority, *Analysis of the Market and Economic Feasibility of Accessory Apartments in Minnesota* (1982). Popularization of the approach will require consideration of the effect on homestead exemptions. Liberalization is endorsed in the *Report of the President's Commission on Housing* (1982) at 53.

16. Calif. Govt. Code, § 65852.2, enacted by Senate Bill 1534 (1982) (the "Mello Act"), see also Calif. Acts, 1984, ch. 1630.

17. Typical ordinances limit such apartments to one per lot, require that the house be five years old and owner occupied for one year, require that the apartment be internal to the house and have parking and a separate entrance away from the front street. See generally Simons, *Single Family Homes Adding Illegal Apartments to Meet Economic Realities*, *Washington Post*, August 10, 1981; Santry, *Legalizing Single Family Conversions* (Tri-State Regional Planning Coinmission, New York, 1981); Goldberg, *Accessory Apartment Ordinances in the D.C. Region*, *Realtor Magazine*, November 1984, at 15: Brooks, *Wide Appeal for Accessory Apartments*, New York Times, January 3, 1982.

18. Hare and Ostler, supra, at 14.

19. J. Gottmann, *Megalagopolis* (1962) at 253 referring to commercial and industrial uses.

20. 42 U.S.C. § 3603(b)(2), see *Fred v. Kokinokos*, 347 F.Supp. 942 (D.C.N.Y. 1972), but see *Morris v. Cizek*, 501 F.2d 1303 (7th Cir. 1974) (possible private action under 1866 Civil Rights Act).

21. Hare and Ostler, supra. The usual costs are for a kitchen, additional plumbing, thicker walls and separate entrances. Conversions are facilitated by postwar design features such as split-levels and basement rooms with installed plumbing.

22. During the period 1970-78, a short period historically, the life expectancy of a woman of 75 is said to have increased by 57.5 percent. Hare and Ostler, supra. at 60. The aging of the population and resulting pressure on social benefits for the elderly may result in a shift in the trend away from the extended family. "As late as 1950 about 58% of women aged 65 and older who had no spouse present lived with families of their kin, especially children. This percentage had been gradually declining since 1910 and started dropping sharply during the 1940's. By 1970 it had fallen to around 29% and further to

18% by 1980." Gallen, op. cit. supra, citing Sharers, *Older People and Their Families*, 41 Journal of Marriage and the Family 9 (1980).

23. The percentage of men never married increased from 17.3 percent to 25.2 percent from 1960 to 1985; the corresponding figure for women from 11.9 percent to 18.2 percent. The percentage of never-married women between the ages of 25 and 29 increased from 10.5 percent in 1960 to 26.4 percent in 1985. U.S. Bureau of the Census, summarized in 1988 World Almanac and Book of Facts.

24. "[W]ith the exception of elderly widows, divorced and unattached persons prior to 1950 represented a relatively small part of the population. The YMCA and YWCA hotels developed by early twentieth century social reformers were an attempt to provide standard quality housing for this sector of the population which for various reasonswas not being served by the market." Gellen, op. cit. supra, at 66, citing Rose, *Interest in the Living Arrangements of the Urban Unattached*, 51 Am. J. Sociology 483 (1948). Eighteen million units had 2.5 rooms per person or more in 1982. Gellen, op.cit. supra, at 91-93. "Whereas the number of one and two family households grew by 140% between 1960 and 1980, the number of efficiency one and two bedroom units [constructed] increased by only 54%." *Report of the Maryland Housing Policy Commission to the Governor and General Assembly* (1985), at 27.

25. Hare and Ostler, supra. Gellen, op. cit. supra, at 41, estimates the number of conversions of owner-occupied apartments at 50,000 to 65,000 per year, or about one-fourth of the number of unsubsidized rental units completed during the years under study. The proportion is said to have accelerated to about half of new completions since 1980. See Downs, *Rental Housing in the 1980's* (1983) at 126, 147, recommending various incentives including loans, grants, property tax deferrals and selective housing code enforcement to foster accessory housing.

26. Babcock, op. cit. supra. at 136. "The Bureau of the Census estimated in 1979 that there were 12.2 million households of two persons or less in which the head was over 55 and the household occupied 5 rooms or more, not counting basements or garages. Council of State Housing Agencies, Accessory Apartments and Echo Units (1987), at 1.

27. Id. at 142.

28. "Teachers have also been a worry. There is a high turnover of younger teachers in any community, but Park Forest is at an especial disadvantage in this matter. There aren't any bachelors around." Whyte, *The Organization Man* (Anchor ed., 1957), at 424. See Rothblatt, et al., *The Suburban Environment and Women* (1979); Stimpson, *Women and the American City* (1982), at 93, cited in Gallen, op. cit. supra.

29. Siegan, *Land Use without Zoning* (1972), at 92, citing Survey Research Center, University of Michigan, *New Homes and Poor People* (1969); Kristof, *Filtration and Housing Policy Objectives*,A Study for the Committee on Economic Development (1971). "The proportion that Negroes represent of families in the sequence of moves is about 70% of what would be predicted 33 percent of all moves by blacks leave someone still occupying the former home, compared to 17 percent of whites. The filtering effect may convert along the line into a thinning effect," at 94.

30. Siegan, supra, at 189, quoting Biderman, *Shelter for Whom, Barron's*, December 27, 1971, at 5. Rudel, *Household Change, Accessory Apartments and Low Income Housing in Suburbs*, 36 *Professional Geographer* 174 (1984) disclosed average rents in accessory apartments in the community studied of $240 for relatives and $375 for nonrelatives, as against $513 for conventional rental housing, $179 for federally subsidized housing, and $155 for federally owned housing.

31. Montgomery County, Maryland thus requires window areas equal to 8 percent of floor areas, 70 square feet for a single occupant or 50 square feet for each occupant, 7-foot ceilings subject to some variation for attic apartments, and separate kitchen and bath facilities and heat controls.

32. Cf. *Cusack v. Chicago*, 242 U.S. 526 (1917). The Boulder, Colorado, ordinance limits accessory apartments to 10 percent of houses within a 300 foot radius, thus creating a potential closed class as well as, paradoxically, creating an incentive to race to join the magic circle. The validity of age restrictions has been questioned, see *McMinn v. Town of Oyster Bay*, N.Y.S.2d (1985).

33. 431 U.S. 494 (1977). See Comment, *Single-FamilyZoning: RamificationsofState Court Rejection of Belle Terre on Use and Density Control*, 32 Hastings L.J. 1687, 1696-97, 1717 (1981); cf. *Town of Durham v. White*, 115 N.H. 645, 348 A. 2d 706 (1975). *Farr v. Board of Adjustment, N.C.*, 349 S.E. 2d 576 (1986), held occupancy of an apartment by a family member to be a permitted accessory use.

34. Gilder, *Wealth and Poverty* (Bantam ed. 1982), at 211.

35. Whyte, supra, at 34.

36. Compare *Boreth v. Zoning Board*, 396 Pa. 82, 151 A.2d 474 (1959), and *Perron v. Concord*, 102 N.H. 32, 150 A.2d 403 (1959) with City of *Rockford v. Eisenstein*, 63 Ill. App. 2d 128, 211 N.E. 2d 130 (1965); *Dellwood Dairy v. New Rochelle*, 7 N.Y. 2d 374, 165 N.E. 2nd 566 (1960).

37. Babcock, supra, at 25, see Fishman, *Bourgeois Utopias* (1987).

38. See Note, *Zoning, Accessory Uses and the Meaning of the Customary' Requirement*, 56 B.U.L. Rev. 542 (1976); see Pratt, *Legal Barriers to Home Based Work* (1987).

39. Babcock, supra at 143. A publication of the American Society of Planning officials observed: "The situation requires the kind of standards where decisions can be made rapidly without extensive investigation or background reports." Toner, *Planningfor Home Occupations* (A.S.P.O. Report 316, 1976), at 1.

40. Babcock, supra, at 142.

41. Id.

42. Id. at 143.

43. Siegan, supra, at 235.

44. Siegan, supra, at 243-44.

45. Siegan, supra at 237.

46. Popenoe, *The Suburban Environment: Sweden and the U.S.* (1977), at 185.

47. Id. at 229.

48. Id. at 139.

49. Jacobs, op. cit. supra at 84.

50. Popenoe, op. cit. supra, at 139.

51. Id. at 195.

52. Id. at 199.

53. Id. at 177, 179.

54. Jacobs, op. cit. supra, at 84.

55. Popenoe, op. cit. supra, at 164.

56. Siegan, op. cit. supra, at 44.

57. Id. at 43-44.

58. Id. at 25, see also Babcock, op. cit. supra, at 27.

59. Id. at 43.

60. Toll, op. cit. supra, at 281, citing *Proceedings of the Zoning Conference* (1938), at 20-21.

61. Jacobs, op. cit. supra, at 4.

62. Power, *The Unwisdom of Allowing City Growth to Work Out Its Own Destiny*, 47 Md. L. Rev. 626, 659 (1988).

63. Id. at 659, quoting Comey, *The Value of Zoning to Business*, Balto. Mun. Journal, March 9, 1923, at 6.

64. Babcock, op. cit. supra, at 140. It is hard to be moved by one ground for prohibition set out in the leading American Society of Planning officials study of the subject: "By locating in commercial districts many businesses absorb costs they would not otherwise have if they were to operate out of their homes. Consequently the home occupation ordinance can ensure that like uses are treated in the same fashion, thereby eliminating the potential for cost discrimination." Toner, op. cit. supra, at 4. See Hamilton, *Zoning and the Exercise of Monopoly Power*, Journal of Urban Economics, January 1978, at 116.

65. Siegan, op. cit. supra, at 44.

66. Popenoe, op. cit. supra, at 70-71.

67. Jacobs, op. cit. supra, at 229.

68. Id. Another writer, noting the migration of business and industry to the suburbs, describes the new suburb, with its enhanced traffic problems, as a "Technoburb" and proclaims the death of the suburbs. Fishman, *Bourgeois Utopias* (1987), ch. 7. See also Cervero, Suburban Gridlock (1986), on the new suburban traffic problems.

69. Jacobs, op. cit. supra, at 357.

70. Harwood, *Using Land to Save Energy* (Environmental Land Institute, 1977), at 77. See Federal Highway Administration, *Nationwide Personal Transportation Study* (1972); No.7; *Household Travel in the United States*, and No. 10: *Purposes of Auto Trips and Travel.*

71. See Macrae, *The Next Ages of Man*, 309, Economist No. 7582, at 18.

72. Jacobs, op. cit. supra, at 445.

73. Babcock, op. cit. supra, at 141.

74. J. Jacobs, op. cit. supra, at 229.

75. Siegan, op. cit. supra, at 43.

76. Harwood, op. cit. supra, at 77. See the not dissimilar language of Vt. Stat. Ann. Tit. 24, § 4406(3).

77. Barr and Bartley, *The Text of a Model Zoning Ordinance, With Commentary* (Amer. Soc. of Planning Officials, 3d ed., 1966), at 71, proposes a limitation to 25 percent of floor area, sometimes varied to one room, or one room or 25 percent of area, whichever is less. See, e.g., the ordinances quoted in Toner, supra at 18, 19.

78. Babcock, op. cit. supra, at 132.

79. Popenoe, op. cit. supra, at 164.

80. Roberts, *The Regulation of Home Occupations Under Zoning Ordinances: Some Constitutional Considerations*, 56 Temple L.Q. 49, at 92-93 (1983): "Because zoning is the most universal of all the legal tools for shaping the character of the municipality, any unwise use of the process has a far greater impact upon our national character than does the abuse of a less widely employed device for control of land use." Babcock, op. cit. supra, at 124.

11

The Schools: Nostrums and Reforms

THE FINANCIAL FALLACY

For the last thirty years, inordinate amounts of judicial time and energy have been spent on the disposition of a series of constitutional challenges to state school-financing formulas. These claims were rejected by the Supreme Court in 1972 in *San Antonio v. Rodriguez*, a case in which the writer was amicus curiae for approximately thirty state governments and a number of local subdivisions. Undaunted, and supported by books such as Jonathan Kozol's *Savage Inequalities*, an unremitting assault on existing statutes has continued in state courts. Some states, like Maryland, are in their third round of abortive litigation. States whose courts have been unwise enough to allow constitutional claims have generated ten or twelve reported appellate cases, as each successive effort at compliance by their legislatures is challenged or found wanting. The entire subject is unsuitable for judicial manipulation, for a variety of reasons most of them insufficiently appreciated.

One must first take note of the complete failure of either the decided cases or plaintiffs in them to square their results with the traditional constitutional doctrines holding that "in taxation even more than in other fields legislatures possess the greatest freedom in classification"[1]—that "there need be no relation between the class of taxpayers and the purpose of the appropriation," that states "have the attributes of sovereign powers in devising their fiscal systems to insure revenue and foster their local interests," and that "the constitution does not empower this court to second-guess state officials charged with the difficult responsibility of allocating limited public welfare funds among the myriad of potential recipients."[2] It is only by ignoring an enormous quantity of undisputed long established constitutional doctrine relating to the limitations on the roles of courts as to questions of public finance that decisions such as *Serrano v. Priest* may be rendered possible. The problems of enforcement that such decisions these present must necessarily be of concern to the lower courts. The California, New Jersey, and Texas courts boldly responded to these concerns by postponing the effective dates of their decrees and by exempting from their decisions certain categories of educational expenditures, those for debt service, but for some reason not those for expenditures under pending teachers'contracts. Courts applying the California and New Jersey precedents will follow the example of the lower courts which have already acted. They will fearlessly delay, temporize, and bluff. It has been suggested quite unconvincingly that there are other avenues of coercion open to them. It is said that they can close down school systems until states comply, explaining all the while that they are killing the patient so that they may cure him. It is said that they may channel local taxes voted by local voters for local purposes into a statewide fund for state uses while forcibly preventing the local legislative bodies from repealing the exactions thus reappropriated by the courts. It is even said that they may levy and enforce the collection of additional state taxes to upgrade the level of expenditures in poorer districts, the unexpressed hope of all those who bring these education and welfare cases. But as Professor Geoffrey Hazard pointed out in another contemporary context, that of the welfare cases, "taxation without representation is tyranny."[3] No one seriously believes that the Supreme Court or any save the most carefully chosen and eccentric lower courts are going to attempt to impose such remedies. The unexpressed hope is that, as in the reapportionment cases, a declaratory judgment or a decree nominally binding the legislature will be enough and that after an initial show of resistance the legislatures will acquiesce in this new assertion of judicial power. But in fact, as Professor William Fischel of Dartmouth has demonstrated, *Serrano* gave rise to Proposition 13, with its restrictions on all local taxing authority, in rich districts and poor; the California schools, once among the nation's best, are now ranked with the nation's worst.

The reason that the plaintiffs have not really been successful, even in states in which they initially prevailed, is clear. What we are talking about here is not the interests only of incumbent legislators or the highly diluted and attenuated interest of citizens in the political makeup of the legislature, a matter which touches and affects their lives only remotely and over an extended period of time. What we are talking about here is the immediate assertion of a power to raise taxes, to reduce services, to close schools, to foment teachers' strikes, all relating to the subject of the education of children, which, as the busing controversy should have taught us, is uniquely freighted with emotion and with the capability of inciting both disinterested benevolence and disinterested malice. The courts at this extremity take note of Professor Crane Brinton's observation that virtually all the great national revolutions and social upheavals have involved either centrally or importantly issues of the legitimacy of taxation. Even the California court could not defy Proposition 13.

Let us turn from the law to questions of educational and economic policy. First, one must begin with the realization that it is as certain as such things can be that the immediate short-run result of compliance with a *Serrano* or similar decision would be massive increases in state school costs. During the Nixon administration, backup papers were prepared by the President's Commission on Educational Finance relating to the costs of equalizing state school expenditures at the ninetieth percentile, the ninety-fifth percentile, and so on. Those costs were enormous. More than six billion 1970 dollars (today probably more than twenty billion) would be required to equalize to the level of the ninetieth percentile, and more than nine billion 1970 dollars to equalize to the ninety-fifth percentile. No one can seriously believe that the sums required may be easily found by the state governments, or for that matter by the federal government. A few examples will serve to illustrate this. For the Commonwealth of Massachusetts, a state that does not have especially notable inequalities in its educational spending, to raise average expenditures in all its districts to the ninetieth percentile in all districts would have cost according to the president's commission, 236 million 1970 dollars annually. Massachusetts has a sales tax. Increases in that sales tax are rarely popular, but sometimes by dint of much travail the legislature can be persuaded to approve one. A 1 percent increase in the Massachusetts sales tax on its 1970 base, which is a fairly typical base, would have produced annual revenues of 53 million dollars, a bit less than one-fourth of the amount required to raise average expenditures in that state to the ninetieth percentile. To raise expenditures to the ninetieth percentile in Maryland would have required an additional 3 percent on the state sales tax, to do so in Illinois, approximately an additional 2 percent; to do so in California, approximately 1.75 percent; to do so in New York, 1.5 percent; in Ohio, 3 percent; in Pennsylvania, 3 percent; and so on. If the States avail themselves of income taxes rather than sales taxes for this purpose, the exhaustion of their income tax bases is just about as dramatic. The proponents of the changes involved here like to assume that states will immediately rush from the supposedly benighted property tax to a progressive state income tax, but it is quite clear that those such as New York, Oregon, and Maryland that already have high state income taxes will not be free to do so and that in some states there are constitutional and other limitations upon state income taxes. Moreover, it is difficult indeed as a matter of practical politics to enact a highly progressive tax in association with a supposedly progressive benefits program, if one is interested in developing the coalition of interests necessary to produce political majorities.

Second, not only do these decisions impose great costs upon the state governments, but it is highly likely that these costs will be allocated among state taxpayers on an essentially regressive basis. This is so for the political reasons I have indicated; it is also so because the most progressive tax, the income tax, has largely been preempted by the federal government. State and local taxation generally is probably no longer regressive in its impact, but there are few who would contend that it is highly progressive. Put differently, any benefits which the poor among our citizens may derive from the expenditures side from changes followingthese decisions will in all probability be more than offset by the adverse effects upon them from the revenue side. If the federal government comes to the aid of the state governments by a large-scale assumption of education costs, it is even more certain this result will follow. No one really believes there is a great appetite in the modern democracies for additional direct taxation. The recent experience of virtually all the European countries is against it. If these decisions are imposed and taken seriously, they will almost certainly guarantee the enactment of a value- added tax.

Third, the emotional fuel behind this litigation comes from a desire to elevate the educational standards of the poor generally and minority groups in large cities in particular. Published statistics on these questions almost totally contradict plaintiffs' postulates. There are at least six recent studies relating to the impact of a full state-funding or equal- spending rule upon the interests of large cities and the interests of areas with below- average income. The United States Office of Education in a monograph published in 1972 entitled *Finances of Large-City School Systems: A Comparative Analysis*[4] found that, contrary to popular myth, most large cities have by reason of the concentration of commercial and industrial property in them above average per capita assessed valuations. Sixteen out of twenty-five representative large-city school systems were found to have such above-average assessed valuations. Moreover, the tax effort for education of most large cities, contrary to popular myth, is below average. Indeed, sixteen out of twenty-five also had average or below-average tax rates for education. This is so because the fiscal problems of large cities come not from their rather ordinary educational expenditures but from police and fire protection, health services, and in some states welfare. The study further found that if all the states collected all presently collected local funds for education and redistributed them on an equal-funds-per-pupil basis, only twenty-nine of the eighty-four urban school systems studied would receive more funds. Similar conclusions were reached in a study published under the auspices of the Mondale Committee by Professor Joel Berke of Syracuse. Professor Berke found that if present local school property taxes were replaced by a state school property tax whose proceeds were distributed to localities on an equal per-pupil basis, most of the large cities including the cities of Boston, Buffalo, New York, Rochester, Philadelphia, Pittsburgh, Providence, Chicago, Indianapolis, Detroit, Minneapolis, St. Paul, Kansas City, St. Louis, Columbus, Milwaukee, Atlanta, Louisville, New Orleans, Los Angeles, San Francisco, Oakland, Denver, Portland, and Seattle would have suffered. Indeed, the only cities that would benefit, the only cities in which the mythological syndrome of high tax rates for education and low per pupil assessed valuation exists, are a few eastern cities where boundaries encompassing small land areas were frozen at an early date, chiefly some of the New Jersey and Ohio cities. There are at least four studies in specific states that have reached similar conclusions. Although the Fleischmann commission in New York recommended full state funding, the important thing to note about its report is that the effect of its recommendations at least in the short run would entail sharp tax increases for the "big six" New York cities as well as a reduction in their available funds. There were in addition three studies of the effect of a

Rodriguez-Serrano rule on particular states, one by Professor Ridenour in the *Kansas Law Review*, one by Professor Davies in the *National Education Association Proceedings* for 1967, and one in a 1972 issue of the *Yale Law Journal* dealing with the effects of full state funding and equal distribution. With respect to all these[5] jurisdictions, it was found that application of such a rule would, in Professor Ridenour's words, result "in effective discrimination against taxpayers with little income." Professor Davies observed, "California's present criterion of wealth imputes to the high wealth counties ability that on the basis of income they do not possess." Professor Ridenour further observes, "The practical result of the *Serrano* rationale in California and Kansas is to strike down de jure discrimination between pupils on the basis of assessed value per pupil in favor of a scheme of de facto discrimination on the basis of income per pupil. It can be argued that there exists in Kansas almost an inverse correlation, districts with highest income per pupil have low assessed value per pupil and districts with high assessed value per pupil have low income per pupil." The *Yale Law Journal* study of Connecticut reached similar conclusions and added the conclusion that the most ruinous change in school finance that could possibly take place, viewed from the perspective of the interests of large cities, persons with low income and minority groups, would be the removal from local tax rolls of commercial and industrial property and state assessment and collection of taxes on such property. That was one of the magic panaceas advanced by Professor Coons and his colleagues.

None of these conclusions is surprising once one thinks about them. Notwithstanding the movement in recent years, most commerce and industry is concentrated in large cities. Those whose boundaries have been permitted to expand and those whose boundaries were generously defined possess substantial commercial and industrial tax bases, denied suburban and rural areas. It is not astonishing that large cities taken as a whole have higher than average commercial and industrial tax bases nor should it be surprising that low income persons reside in disproportionate measure in areas of high per capita property wealth. Such persons do not, at least in metropolitan areas, characteristically reside in areas that are zoned exclusively for residential use, nor do they commute by car and dwell at a great distance from commercial and industrial establishments. It is true there are a very few suburbs, Scarsdale, Bronxville, and the like which one hears so much about, that have significantly higher per- capita income and per-capita school expenditures than the cities they adjoin. The important thing to note is that these entities are not characteristic of the suburbs even in their own metropolitan areas, let alone in the nation as a whole. To the findings that I have already summarized one more may be added. It has been found that in both California and Connecticut the majority of minority-group citizens and particularly of black citizens reside in the districts of above-average assessed valuation. This is not true in Texas. It is true in virtually all the northern states in which the migration of blacks from the South has tended to be migration to large cities. So one must conclude that even when one thinks in terms of relative advantage, a *Serrano-Rodriguez* rule will not operate to the benefit of minority groups, poor people, or cities generally, even if one excludes the effects upon the tax system from one's consideration and even when.one looks solely at relative advantage. The chief effect of the *Serrano-Rodriguez* rule is to pour vast sums of money into rural areas with low costs and few pressing social and educational problems, most of which never knew they needed such resources.

In Maryland, for example, if the trial court decision in *Rodriguez* became the law and all districts were raised to the level of the highest county, approximately three-fourths of the resulting expenditures would be distributed to suburban and rural areas of the state and approximately one-fourth to Baltimore City. Baltimore City's share of the new money would be less than its share of the population of the state as a whole. A shower of blessings would descend upon various small eastern shore and western Maryland counties, four of which were once alone in declining to impose local income taxes at the maximum allowable rate and nearly all of that have property tax rates for education and total property tax rates which are far below the state average and, indeed, far below those prevailing in Montgomery County, the richest suburban county. To put the matter bluntly, this country has higher priorities today then the use of twenty or thity billion dollars or a large portion of it in raising teachers' salaries in rural areas.

Of course, it is sometimes said that under a Serrano-Rodriguez regime, states would have to rethink their education formulas and undoubtedly would skew them to the benefit of urban districts; but they are perfectly free to do that now. Many of them, including Maryland, provide special assistance for urban districts; and as the *Washington Post* pointed out some years ago, it is hardly likely that the representatives of suburban areas would be more disposed to vote such special funds for city problems in a period when their own expenditures were being forcibly held down.

We have come by imperceptible degrees to another major effect of the California and New Jersey decisions, the extent to which they will usher in statewide teachers'unions. As Senator Moynihan has pointed out, the real beneficiaries are not the school children but the teachers, not the poor but a portion of the middle class. One need not labor the Coleman Report issue that is present in all these cases, the question whether there is in fact a relation between educational spending and educational accomplishment. There are studies indicating that there is no correlation or that, if there is such a correlation, it is neglible; and there are even studies, some say a majority of the pertinent studies, that indicate that there is a negative correlation between class size and educational. achievement at least in some age groups. It is clear that spending differences, even viewed a priori have little to do with education. They result from differences in class size, from differences in teachers' salaries and in some degree from the presence in schools or their curriculum of things like swimming pools, driver-education programs and so on. The lion's share of added spending will go to reduce class sizes marginally and to provide higher salaries to people who are presently teaching. It is hard to think of any area of public policy where large infusions of public funds can be expected to produce fewer proportionate benefits, since it cannot be assured and there is no way to assure that increments in spending resulting from these decisions will be utilized for the introduction of new programs or new methods. If improvement in education is required, it is more appropriately achieved either by a reallocation of existing funds to other uses or by particularized new appropriations, state or federal. It is precisely such narrowly focused efforts which will be discouraged by implementation of *Serrano-Rodriguez* decisions. Certainly if the federal government is to find massive sums to assist the states in pursuing statewide equalization, it can scarcely be believed that further expansion of the Title I program will be forthcoming. As for actions on the state level, one of the first casualties of the new cases was the Bateman Act in New Jersey—an act thatrestructured that state's equalization formula to focus funds on districts with high percentages of AFDC recipients.

Maryland has a program of density aid of which Baltimore City is the sole beneficiary, a program enacted and several times increased by its legislature with substantial suburban support. Since the filing of the latest wave of cases there has been no discussion whatever of the possibility of further increases in this program. I add in passing that these cases seem little more than an effort to undo some of the political results of the reapportionment decisions. Those decisions, so enthusiasticallysupported by urban interests, had the effect of transferring political representation from rural areas to suburbs. The principal effect of the present cases is to transfer economic resources from suburbs and cities to rural areas. Some may say that if the rule does not comfort the afflicted it at least afflicts the comfortable. But the suburbs have their own problems, unfashionable though they may be—high costs, high social mobility, high teacher turnover, and a paucity of community institutions and cultural and recreational facilities. Notwithstanding all this, we find the Urban Coalition and like groups in the forefront of both reapportionment and equalization movements. One need not share all or indeed any of the views of the late Arthur Krock to appreciate his reference some years ago to "a society sickened by quack cure-alls."

It is hard to believe seriously that the problems of assimilation that exist in our large cities are going to be effectively resolved or even significantly mitigated by five or ten years of storm and fury about educational aid formulas, tax increases, and conflicts between judges and legislators. What has gotten lost in the course of this entire controversy and what will continue to be lost if additional available funds are directed solely at general-purpose equalization is the exploration and application of new educational methods and the alleviation of the social conditions which breed educational failure. One of the leading proponents of the new decisions, Professor Charles Benson has observed, "There is strong reason to believe that performance of schools with respect to disadvantaged youth is itself extremely sensitive to these very kinds of expenditures that might suffer if states move toward compliance with *Serrano*. This would subvert whatever equalitarian purpose exists in *Serrano*."[6] Indeed, after reading portions of the vast quantities of somewhat turgid literature that have been generated on these problems, I am led, as an amateur, to two apparently unorthodox conclusions. The first is that the use for educational equalization of funds that might better be directed toward the relief of urban unemployment is, in light of the Coleman Report and like studies, a grotesque misallocation of resources. The second is that attention might also more usefully be directed at the findings and recommendations of the leading British report on these questions, the so-called Plowden Report,[7] published in 1967, with its conclusion that "the variation in parental attitudes can account for more of the variation in children's school achievement then either the variation in home circumstances or the variation in schools" and its allied conclusion that "our evidence suggests that parents' occupation, material circumstances and education explain only about a quarter of the variation in attitudes leaving three quarters or more not accounted for. This implies that attitudes, could be affected in other ways and altered by persuasion."[8] The report goes on to suggest, "Our findings can give hope to the schools, to interested parents and to those responsible for educational policy. Parental attitudes appear as a separate influence because they are not monopolized by any one class. Schools can exercise their influence not only directly upon children but also indirectly through their relationships with parents." The recommendations of the Plowden Report, though there are financial recommendations, focused primarily upon such things as programs for contact with children's homes through such devices as school care committees, arrangements for private talks with parents, special efforts to make contact with parents who do not visit the schools, the fullest possible use of primary schools outside of school hours, the provision of various forms of literature[9] to parents, the evening use of school buildings, and the like.

While costs are undoubtedly associated with measures such as these, these costs are as nothing to the costs associated with reduction in pupil ratios and increases in teachers' salaries that will be the primary result of *Serrano-Rodriguez* decisions. In all of the literature on this subject.in this country I have seen no suggestion, aside from some rather ill-defined talk about community schools, that measures of this sort would be useful or that they ought to be promoted by federal and state authority through focused and separately funded programs. Such measures, of course, will not be pursued or funded if we are compelled for the next ten or twenty years to embark upon a carnival of waste.

We may conclude with two further sets of observations, the first relating to fiscal policy and the second relating to the implications of the doctrines of these decisions for the political structure of this country. The proponents of these decisions in an effort to minimize their scope have frequently suggested that these decisions have nothing whatever to do with the desirability or undesirability of the property tax and that jurisdictions remain as free under a *Serrano-Rodriguez* rule to utilize property taxes for the support of education as they are free now to do so. The proponents of these decisions repeatedly claim that full state funding is not a necessary result of these decisions and that there remains available and is intended to remain available the option of power equalizing. This is almost certainly an illusion. The salient fact to note about district power equalizing, the elaborate scheme, never adopted anywhere, that is said to be a viable alternative, is that it presupposes an accurate and uniform measure of district taxing power. One cannot ensure that the tax resources available to any school district have been equalized without a uniform measure of taxing power, that is to say, without state rather than local assessment of real property. Only three or four states presently have such state as distinct from local assessment of real property. Only a handful of states have state property taxes, and "the decision does not invalidate the property tax but itrequires that if that tax is to be retained the distribution of the income generated by it must be reformed. This probably cannot be done unless the manner in which the tax is collected is also reformed." But I would not describe as reform a shift from local to state assessment; rather, it is likely to be reform's opposite. The property tax is a good local tax, it is a worse state tax, and it would be an atrocious national tax. It is not for nothing that unapportioned federal direct taxes are prohibited by the Constitution. This is so because property assessment is not an exact science and because it is impossible to equalize over a broad geographic area the principles of assessment. At present, individual homeowners sometimes have reason to complain of unequal assessments, but even they must acknowledge that the inequalities are visible and subject to ready ascertainment by comparison with properties in an immediate vicinity usually assessed by the same assessors. Under a regime of state or national assessment, there would be no such assurance of visibility or uniformity; and instead of aggrieved individual homeowners, we would have aggrieved localities, aggrieved regions, and aggrieved industries. The notion that the integrity of the tax system is enhanced by aggrandizing and projecting onto a broader scale the inevitable inequalities inherent in property taxation is one which seems strange indeed. It is clear, therefore, that implementation of these decisions would in fact result in a shift away from property taxation. It is suggested that this shift would be beneficial. I doubt it. Apart from the fact that the property tax is an efficient way of raising large amounts of revenue, it is not notably unjust either in its application to businesses or in its application to individuals. Most of the objections to property taxes arise from the fact that they are highly visible. Perhaps taxes should be highly visible. To the extent that the tax is a tax on businesses, it frequently has the effect, as has often been pointed out, of reaching industries, particularly the mineral extracting industries, that otherwise are practically exempt from corporate taxation. The effect of restriction of property taxes would be to confer a windfall on many industries. It is certainly true that the local character of this taxation means that many industries and industrial plants are unequally treated. It does not follow unless one is prepared to contemplate with equanimity massive effects upon industrial location and massive disturbances of vested interests, that state assessment of commercial and industrial property would be an improvement over the present local assessment. This is particularly so since one effect of state assessment would be the virtual destruction of the remaining tax base of large cities.

This discussion brings us to the much maligned residential property tax. It is said that this tax is regressive and that it is terribly unjust. Perhaps as some of the "circuit breaker" laws suggest, accommodations of the local property tax are in order with respect to its bearing upon elderly persons or those of exceptionally low income. It is hardly rational, however, to go further than that. As that great student of taxation Professor Henry Simons pointed out many years ago, any sweeping reduction of residential property taxes has the effect of conferring a windfall on the present landowners and real estate speculators.[10]

As Professor Lowell Harriss of Columbia has pointed out, there is no reason to believe that the distribution of even residential property is regressive in relation to income classes.[11] It is not astonishing that the wealthy own more residential property than the less wealthy and that the very poor own little residential property at all. There is one further point about the residential property tax that is very often overlooked. Like the commercial property tax in its bearing on extractive industries, it also plugs an income tax loophole. Virtually every student of income taxation who has attempted to define the appropriate scope of a comprehensive income tax base has recognized that the imputed rental value of owner-occupied land is conceptually income. The tax systems of Great Britain and of virtually every advanced industrial nation, other than our own, have at one time or another taxed the imputed rental value of owner occupied land as income. Yet those who would restrict or abolish the residential property tax are rarely heard to suggest that this change in the income tax base be initiated in the United States. I add that I do not suggest this change as a matter of policy. This country has not been served badly by the preferences that its income tax laws give to owner- occupied housing. I merely suggest that recognition that the present income tax structure provides it with great benefits supplies a nearly full answer to the loose rhetoric that we frequently hear about the inequities and evils of the residential property tax.

The ideological presuppositions underlying the rules in these cases deserve some final comment. The first of these is that education should not be a function of parental wealth. It is clear that position threatens private education and all parental supplements to education. It is also clear as a practical matter that one effect of compulsorily restricting expenditures in suburban schools will be to increase the attractiveness of private education and decrease political support for public education. If this movement is not to render the result of these cases meaningless, in terms of the ideals of their proponents, there will inevitably follow efforts to constrict parental rights in education. It is not merely local governments but families, and if we are to believe Professor Coons, eventually state governments whose rights with respect to educational matters are under attack. As Professor Kurland observed some years ago, in one sense equality of rules is always inconsistent with a multiplicity of rulemakers. Professor James

Coleman has put the matter differently:

There are two very different conceptions of the relationship of schools to the social order. One conception is that of schools as agents for the transmission of knowledge, culture and social norms, thus as agents for the maintenance of the social order. The other conception is that of schools as crucial institutions of social change. On the issue of social change, national governments are more often on one side, the side of change, and the local authorities are more often on the other, the side of stability—modern totalitarian regimes following a coup or revolution move quickly to take control of the schools in order to indoctrinate the new generation with the ideology of the regime. Such attempts at change meet with increasing resistance at lower levels of social organization, all the way down to the family. What is true in totalitarian regimes is true to a lesser degree in democratic ones. The national government is more likely to see the schools as instruments of social change than is the local government. What is evident in this type of conflict is in a sense the self- preservation interests of two social units, the nation and the community.[12]

It should be clear to everybody, despite Professor Coons' wistful essays about voucher systems, that one effect of these cases is to give a powerful push toward greater state and national influence over schools and diminished local and family influence over them, with the political implications to which Professor Coleman has adverted.

The second major premise of these decisions, made particularly explicit in the *Serrano* opinion, may be summed up in the phrase, "in the beginning was the state." These opinions hold that states may not by delegating taxing and other powers to local governments produce inequalities among residents of local districts of the sort that would not be suitable if there were full state funding of schools. A false analogy has been drawn to the desegregation cases which hold that the state may not conduct segregation nor may it do so indirectly by authorizing its local subdivisions to segregate. But it is one thing to say that the state may not empower local units to treat their own citizens unequally; it is another thing to say that permissible inequalities may not result from differences between the local units to which the state delegates its authority. The power of states to define units of local government has usually been thought to be almost plenary, with a minor qualification as to racial gerrymandering. To hold that local governments may not freely tax their citizens for education if they happen to be wealthier than the average is to fly in the face of most of our established doctrine about delegation of authority and has implications for all diferences resulting from local home rule.

Hitherto, it has been thought to be an advantage of our system of government that states and localities are not precluded by the absence of a national majority or by the lack of means to carry out reforms on a national scale from addressing needs that command majority support in their own jurisdictions. It has similarly been thought to be an advantage of our system that local governments may address needs not recognized by a statewide majority and that private individuals can spend funds for social purposes not recognized by a majority at even the local level. Yet these cases effectively hold that there must be full state funding, or at the least, a system of excises on wealthy districts that will effectively discourage local supplementation in them and that, in consequence, locally recognized needs must go unalleviated until the means and the statewide majority can be found to generalize them on a statewide scale. One may recall here Professor Simons' observation that the way to create large problems is to neglect little ones. One may add to this the observation in the last volume of General de Gaulle's memoirs that one of the great advantages of the American system of government as distinct from the centralized system of France is that local grievances about education and the like do not automatically become grievances against the national government of the nature that he experienced in 1968.[13] These cases are recipes for a society in which political controversies are fought out at ever higher levels for ever higher stakes by ever more violent means and in which the safety valves traditionally inherent in federal pluralistic and limited government will have become constricted to the point of extinction.

These decisions of are concern for yet another reason of interest not alone to lawyers. They are founded not at all upon the case law, they find their acknowledged source and origin entirely in academic writings. An academic commentator has recently alluded to the developing shift in the law of this, country from a reliance on case authorities and the essentially empirical method of the common law toward the civil law or code system characteristic of the continental nations, in which legal doctrine is developed by embroidering upon relatively general statutory or constitutional provisions. These cases are the most dramatic possible illustration of that tendency. It would be wrong to regard this development as simply a deriviation or deduction from the reform movements in American jurisprudence earlier in this century: the sociological jurisprudence of Roscoe Pound and the legal realism of Karl Llewellyn and his associates. For those efforts at legal reform were essentially fact oriented. These recent cases are, however, a horse of a different color. The late Justice Walter Schaefer of the Illinois Supreme Court has observed, "It is true I think that the style of legal argument and perhaps even the technique of legal research have shifted in recent years. It seems to me that much more than in the past the lawyer's quest has become a search for quotable words which regardless of.their initial context can be read in the abstract to bear upon the situation at hand. The pressure is thus toward a jurisprudence of words or phrases divorced from facts and capable of generating new words and phrases with independent lives."[14] That, of course, is a repudiation of the essence of legal realism. It is only necessary to compare the method of these cases with the four standards of adjudication outlined by Justice Cardozo in his liberating lectures of forty years ago, where he described the method of logic, the method of sociology, the method of custom and the method of history. These decisions find sanction not in the logic of prior cases nor in the established custom of the American states and nation, nor in historical materials, nor in the needs of the time. They represent instead deduction from a preconceived ideology—an effort to apply ideological presuppositions to rather intractable bodies of fact. That method of proceeding is inconsistent with the genius of our institutions, political and judicial, and where it has been tried on a large scale it has left the nations that have tried it either the captives of tyranny or saturated in blood. It has been said that these cases and the reaction to them, whatever one thinks of the details of their results, have something important to say about contemporary American education. They do, but not for the reasons usually given.

SCHOOL GOVERNANCE

The problems of our schools and particularly of our urban schools arise less from inadequacies of finance than from flaws in their governance.

American schools are both overly large and overly centralized. While the conventional wisdom for most of this century has favored the consolidation of small districts and small schools in the interest of offering students a wider range of subject matter, a heavy price has been paid for this development. Many schools are large, impersonal, and impossible to effectively regulate and discipline. Many school district offices have become remote and bureaucratized.

These tendencies have been enhanced by increased regulation at the state level. Since in the Kennedy administration, there has been a federally supported explosion in the size of state departments of education. These agencies do not deliver services; they proliferate rules. These rules generally deny local principals and local school boards the power to hire staff not graduates of schools of education. Competence in subject matter is almost a disqualification for a teaching position in many states. The homogeneity of background of most teachers, usually the products of the weakest department at the weakest colleges, in turn leads to unionization and the introduction of additional rigidities. Elaborate grievance procedures render inadequate teachers virtually irremovable. Even more seriously, union contracts fasten on schools rigid seniority systems that require each school principal to fill vacancies from seniority lists, that preclude transfer of teachers, and that prevent any principal from assembling a harmonious team.

In addition to these impiositions from the state level, federal interference further undermines the governance and autonomy of schools. Judicial excess and Congressional excess have combined to undermine discipline. In 1975, the Supreme Court held, over the vehement dissent of four justices, that a notice and a due-process hearing were necessary for a student to be suspended from a public school, even for a single day. The decision held "for the first time" in the dissenting words of Justice Powell, a former school board president, "that the federal courts, rather than educational officials and state legislatures, have the authority to determine the rules applicable to routine classroom discipline of children and teenagers in the public schools."[15] In the same year, Congress passed a carelessly drawn statute, the Education of the Handicapped Act, requiring the "mainstreaming" of mentally handicapped students, including within the definition of "handicapped" students with serious emotional disturbances. In 1987, the Supreme Court held that this law prohibited schools from changing the placement of students without their parents' consent until long and tedious review proceedings were concluded and further held thsat there was no "emergency exception for dangerous students" other than that provided by a federal regulation allowing suspensions for not more than ten days.[16] Since school boards can be amerced in damages for violations of these principles, a collapse in disciplinary practice ensued.

Other cases limit drug testing, school uniforms, the separation of the sexes in secondary schools, and even requirements that students take showers after gym class. Sweeping school busing orders destroy parental confidence and neighborhood involvement in public schools; bilingual education has been inflicted on schools that have trouble providing even a basic program in one language. Presidents, congressmen, and federal judges possess no special competence in balancing the relevant interests. They can only demoralize and drive from the system able people who might improve local schools.

The path of reform is that marked out in Britain, Australia, and New Zealand and by the Catholic schools in the United States. Each school should be largely self-governing. Each school should have its own board, which should be partly chosen by government, parents, and teachers but which should for the most part fill its own vacancies, like the board of a private school. At the high school level at least, schools should compete for students. Public schools must be rendered drug-free; their faculties must be drawn from all who are competent to teach; they must possess the power to discipline their students; their teachers must be persons selected for their value to a particular school and must be subject to removal and transfer; they must have self-governing boards, rooted in their communities; and they must be free of arbitrary and sudden pupil-assignment schemes imposed by the courts. When these conditions are met, it will be appropriate to consider increases in the financial rewards of those teachers who perform well and are adequately trained, to render teaching a true profession, as it is on the European continent.

SCHOOL DRUG TESTING

Beginning in 1985, nearly five million members of the military underwent routine drug testing, a program that continues to this day and that is credited with having virtually eliminated from the military the serious problems of drug abuse that afflicted it following the Vietnam War. That program is generally adjudged a successful one, though it has inspired remarkably little interest on the part of the mass media. In 1986, as a result of the new program of the military, sixteen American high schools had instituted random testing, and 27 percent of principals favored it.[17] Yet, despite the fact that drug-associated homicides are now a leading, and in some places the leading, cause of death among young black males, the movement for drug screening in the schools has gone no further.

This discussion suggests that the time has come for another look at this subject and attempts to address serially a number of relevant questions.

Q. Why did the movement toward school drug testing stop?

A. Almost entirely because of litigation and the fear of litigation. In 1986, the Carlstadt school district in New Jersey instituted a program of drug screening for all entering students. This program was instituted in a year in which a national survey of high school students revealed that 25 percent had consumed marijuana and 10 percent cocaine within the preceding month. Within one week of the inception of the program, without any adverse action having been taken against any student, suit was brought against it by the American Civil Liberties Union. The ensuing adverse trial court decision, *Odenlein v. Carlstadt School District*, was extensively publicized in two front-page articles in the *New York Times*, and was not further appealed. In addition, the trial court ordered the school district to pay the ACLU $23,000 in counsel fees. This decision was referred to in the widely disseminated *Bulletin of the National Association of Secondary School Principals* in March 1987. A subsequent similar lower-court decision in Arkansas was also extensively publicized. The only other relevant litigation on this issue has involved drug testing of student athletes, as to which the majority of decided cases support testing, including a decision of the Seventh Circuit Court of Appeals which expressly rejects the premise of the *Carlstadt* case and which has now been upheld by the Supreme Court in 1995.

Q. What has the Supreme Court said about this subject?

A. By a six-to-three majority, it has upheld drug testing of student athletes, using broad language which also supports general drug testing of students. One of the six majority justices, Justice Ginsburg, wrote a separate concurrence disassociating herself from this broad language. Significantly, none of the other five majority justices joined her opinion. Several earlier decisions suggested that appropriate systems of screening or testing might be upheld.

In *New Jersey v. TLO*, Justice Powell, for the court, applied a relaxed "reasonable suspicion" standard to school locker searches for drugs and weapons and significantly noted: "We do not decide whether individualized suspicion is an essential element of the reasonableness standard . . . the Fourth Amendment imposes no irreducible requirement of such suspicion [where] other safeguards are available to assure that the individual's reasonable expectation of privacy is not subject to the discretion of the official in the field . . . [there are] commonality of interests between teachers and their pupils . . . without first establishing discipline and maintaining order, teachers cannot begin to educate their students. And apart from education, the school has the obligation to protect pupils from mistreatment by other children and also to protect teachers themselves from violence."

In *Michigan Department of State Police v. Sitz*, breath testing of adult drivers at sobriety checkpoints was upheld, notwithstanding that fewer than 1 percent of those examined tested ositively. In the Von Raab and Skinner cases, the Supreme Court upheld drug testing of certain classes of federal employees and of railroad workers, noting that the program provided for "no direct observation of the act of urination" and that "the combination of EMIT and GC/MS tests is highly accurate."

Q. We have just had two conservative national administrations. Why didn't they do anything in this field?

A. They preferred to begin with workforce testing, where there was no adverse lower-court case law. Education Secretary William Bennett's *What Works: Schools without Drugs* noted that "the few courts that have considered this issue so far have not upheld urinalysis to screen public school students for drugs." However, the final report of the earlier White House Conference for a Drug-Free America noted that drug testing, as a deterrent, must be recognized as an effective mechanism for prevention. Drug testing also helps identify drug use much earlier than it can be identified through other means, and early identification means a greater likelihood of derailing drug use . . . social and peer disapproval must be brought to bear against the drug user."

Q. Doesn't the military have sanctions to apply that schools do not?

A. Of course. As General Colin Powell has noted, military personnel are voluntary enlistees, who do not want to lose their careers. By contrast, suspension or expulsion holds no terrors for manv high school students. However, school programs are not without some teeth. These include: (a) peer pressure, which will increase as programs become established; (b) the threat of reporting to parents, some at least of whom will be ignorant of or disapproving of drug use; (c) the usual array of sanctions for noncooperation in school, which have an impact on many though certainly not all students; and (d) the possible transfer of students not correcting their drug problem to schools for the disruptive or, in extreme cases, civil commitment to in-patient treatment programs.

Q. Isn't it wrong to require testing where treatment may be unavailable?

A. Not necessarily, since the peer and parental pressure resulting from testing may have deterrent effects. The provision of adequate drug treatment to the young ought in any case to be regarded as a first call on local, state and national revenues. Some forms of treatment, such as participation in Narcotics Anonymous, involve little or no costs and may be valuable in dealing with less firmly established addictions.

Q. Isn't urine testing worthless if not done on a surprise basis, and aren't there dangers of false positive results, dilution and substitution of samples, and gross intrusions on privacy?

A. All of these problems have been addressed in what are now the well-established testing programs of the military, the federal employee workforce, and corporations, and recognized protocols exist. The most serious problem, that presented by the inability of urine testing to detect substances ingested more than a few days previously, may be obviated through increased use of hair testing.

Q. Isn't hair testing uncertain and expensive?

A. "Sample collection is easier than that for blood or urine, and is also less prone to substitution or alteration than urine . . . a 1 1/4 inch sample of hair will permit the detection of drugs used anytime in the previous 3 months."[18] Its cost in 1990 was said to be $28 to $65 per sample, and it was used in some company and parole system programs. Hair testing obviates the concern expressed by justices Marshall and Brennan, dissenting in *Doe v. Renfrew*, that since urination is "among the most private of activities," testing involves "mass governmental intrusions upon the integrity of the human body." Its advent makes feasible many testing programs heretofore renounced, as the former drug czar in the Nixon administration, Robert Du Pont, recently pointed out.[19] Discussions of the ethical problems associated with it makes clear that they are only variants of those surrounding urine testing; the main such argument, that its greater backward reach covers meriods unrelated to work performance, is irrelevant in the school setting.

Q. Aren't there valid civil liberties concerns?

A. Certainly. As pointed out in the White House conference report "when drug testing is conducted as part of a regular physical exam, for specific cause or as a random procedure, it should be done in a way that guarantees reliability, accuracy, and confidentiality and with a system to handle results properly." There are three further concerns: (1) that results be confined to the educational system and not shared with law enforcement (2) that they be used to refer students to treatment programs in the first instance, and to the disciplinary system or schools for the disruptive in the event of nonparticipation in treatment, and not used simply to detect occasions for punishment; and (3) that they not become part of a permanent record that will pursue the student later.

Q. Won't students suffer prejudice from being identified to parents or fellow students as drug users?

A. Undoubtedly, though reasonable efforts should be made to preserve confidentiality so as not to use publicity as a form of punishment. Prejudice of this sort is the inevitable result of any sort of school discipline and may be a benefit to the student's further development.

Q. Isn't it overkill to inflict this on all schools and all students?

A. No one suggests that this be attempted where a system does not want it, and a case can be made for reposing discretion at the level of the school principal. As a practical matter, a period of experimentation would in any case be required; there should be no sudden leap into full system adoption.

Q. Doesn't this overdramatize the whole subject of drugs?

A. In many schools, the subject cannot be overdramatized. Any dangers of this sort can be minimized by assimilating drug tests to the normal school medical procedures, such as hearing and vision testing and lead screening. This is particularly feasible if the need for surprise is eliminated by using hair testing.

Q. Isn't this likely to be prohibitively expensive?

A. The more routine hair testing becomes, the lower its costs will be. Costs can be further reduced and deterrent values maintained by selecting students to be tested, either at random, by certain classes, on the basis of documented academic, truancy, or disciplinary probiems, or on the basis of documented observed symptoms of drug abuse. It should be possible to draw protocols that avoid charges of discrimination.

Q. Isn't the true answer that suggested bv the ACLU, decriminalization of drugs?

A. This is so only if one considers the problem as one of drug-related crime and homicide rather than drug addiction. Even if conflicts among drug sellers were eliminated and addicts were relieved of the need to commit crimes to raise money to purchase drugs, the physical and psychological effects of addiction remain and should be of great concern in any rationally conceived school health program. The repeal of Prohibition did not abolish alcoholism.

Q. Why hasn't there been more public discussion of school drug testing?

A. David F. Musto, a historian of the narcotics problem, has observed: "The practical value of urine testing led observers to speculate that the drug tests would become a part of routine physical examinations—but that was in the 1970's, an era of drug tolerance and assumption of a right to bodily privacy with regard to drugs. In such an atmosphere, the tests did not become common." More recently, however, two criminologists, professors Frank Zimring and Gordon Hawkins, whose devotion to civil liberties is unquestioned, have observed, in their *The Search for Rational Drug Control* (1992): "Consider a program of universal compulsory urine testing for drugs in secondary schools patterned after the program currently in use in the U.S. military. A credible claim for public health justification based on finding out whether students are using any of a wide spectrum of legal and illegal substances and referring them to treatment and support programs that are avowedly nonpunitive might pass constitutional muster, while a drug testing program aimed at suspending or expelling those with positive urine tests for illegal drugs could be viewed as overreaching either Fourth Amendment standards or the government's obligation to protect the young."

Q. What should the response to this issue be in a city like Baltimore?

A. In the first instance, a resolution of the School Board reading approximately as follows: Drug screening of students in particular schools is hereby authorized, subject to the following conditions: Screening must be requested by the principal of the school and thirty days' notice of the request given to all students and parents. Schools will be screened in the order that requests are received, subject to limits of available funds, which may include private contributions. The superintendent shall appoint a screening coordinator qualified in the fields of medicine or public health, who need not be a municipal employee. The principal in agreement with the coordinator shall designate the persons to be screened, who may be chosen by classes, according to objective academic, attendance, or disciplinary standards or on the basis of observed and documented symptoms of drug abuse. The coordinator shall determine the method of testing. Retesting of contested results shall be provided. No testing shall be conducted at a school until the principal and coordinator have identified treatment facilities including, at a minimum, Narcotics Anonymous chapters, in reasonable proximity thereto. Positive tests suggesting current drug consumption shall be reported to students and parents and counseling and references to treatment facilities given, and such students shall be subject to retesting as determined by the coordinator. Students may not be subjected to discipline for positive tests but may be disciplined or transferred from the school for failing to provide evidence of participation in drug treatment if a positive result is repeated on retesting. The coordinator, if qualified to do so under state law may seek civil commitment of such students to treatment facilities subject to the limitations of state law. Results shall not be disclosed to law enforcement authorities or made part of a student's permanent record. The resolution shall expire in eighteen months unless renewed.

NOTES

1. *Board of Education v. Oklahoma*, 409 F. 2d. 665 (10th Cir. 1969).

2. The quotations are from *Madden v. Kentucky*, 309 U.S. 83 (1940); *New York Rapid Transit Co. v. New York*, 303 U.S.573 (1938); *Allied Stores of Ohio v. Bowers*, 358 U.S. 522 (1959); and *Dandridge v. Williams*, 397 U.S. 471 (1970).

3. *Hazard, Social Justice through Civil Justice*, 36 U. Chi. L. Rev. 699 (1969).

4. Select Committee on Equal Educational Opportunity, United States Senate, *The Financial Aspects of Equality of Educational Opportunity and Inequities in School Finance* (1972), at p. 67.

5. The documents in question will be found at *Report of the New York State Commission on the Quality Cost and Financing of Elementary and Secondary Education*, p. 2.33; 20 Kansas Law Review 213 (1972); National Education Association, *10th Annual Conference on School Finance* 199 (1967); 81 Yale L. J. 1303 (1972).

6. Mondale Committee Hearings, supra, note 4 at 7669.

7. Central Advisory Council for Education (England), *Children and Their Primary Schools* (2 Vols. 1968) (H.M.S.O.).

8. The quotations are from id., vol. 2, page 181; id. ol. 1, pg. 36; id. vol. 1, pp. 40-49.

9. *Economic Policy for a Free Society* (1946), at 67.

10. Issues and Interpretations, 155 The Bankers Magazine no. 2 (1972).

11. The Struggle for Control of Education, in Bowers (ed.), *Education and Social Policy: Local Control of Education* (1970).

12. de Gaulle, *Memoirs of Hope: Renewal and Endeavor* (1971), at 323.

13. *Book review, [of Jaffe, English and American Judges as Lawmakers (1969)] 84 Harv. L. Rev. 1558 (1971).*

14. *Goss v. Lopez*, 419 U.S. 1565 (1975).

15. *Honig v. Doe*, 484 U.S. 305 (1988).

16. *Education Week*, September 10, 1986.

17. G. Andtadt, *Hair Analysis in Drug Screening*, 32 J. Occ. Med. 666 (1990).

18. *Operation Tripwire Revisited*, 521 Annals 91 (May 1992).

19. *Hair Analysis for Drugs: Technical Breakthrough or Ethical Quagmire*, 88 Addiction 163-65 (1993); 89 Id. 295-300 (1994).

12

New Forms of Neighborhood Organization: Land Readjustment Associations, Street Associations, Old Age Clubs, Playgroups, Advice Bureaux, and Volunteer Probation Officers

Ralph Kramer, in his *Voluntary Agencies in the Welfare State* (1981), in comparing the social welfare systems of four countries, observes:

> Most significant [American] social service legislation originates on the federal level, and it typically provides for both state and local participation in financing and administration. Therefore, voluntary organizations must be represented in Washington and in the state capital, as well as in their local communities. This helps explain why national voluntary agencies in the United States stress advocacy, standard setting and research and do not operate service programs, as is the case in England where pressure groups and public opinion are less important in the policy making process.

It is doubtful that Tocqueville, were he to return today, would again laud Americans' gifts for voluntary organization. The price that we pay for our highly legalistic approach to social welfare, with its destruction of individual casework, is suggested by an examination of British voluntary institutions that have no counterparts in the United States, as well as examination of the old age clubs of Japan, street associations in Germany and the Netherlands, and land readjustment associations in the Far East and Western Europe.

In an age conditioned to large-scale government and corporate action, little attention has been paid to small-scale private and governmental bodies and the contribution they can make to addressing our most pressing social problems. General talk about the revival of civil society is usually unaccompanied by illustrations, particularly institutions that have stood the test of time in major nations. Accordingly, it seems useful to describe a number of foreign institutions and practices that might be adapted to American conditions:

LAND READJUSTMENT ASSOCIATIONS IN EUROPE AND ASIA

Americans assume that only two methods exist for the assembly of land for purposes of urban renewal. The first is eminent domain, the condemnation of land, which is sold off to developers. Since the postwar decision in *Berman v. Parker*, there are few restrictions on this technique, though it has disadvantages. Since each property owner has a right to jury trial, there are delays and unpredictable costs, "planning blight" descends, and constructive endeavor ceases. Few condemnees are enthusiastic about their fate, since juries are drawn from taxpayers and are frequently parsimonious. The public authority must pay as values are determined and hold land through the construction process, incurring capital and carrying costs.

A second method is private acquisition, such as that practiced by the Rouse Company preparatory to the creation of Columbia, Maryland. This requires great stealth and the use of dummies, and the last landowners to sell must be paid exorbitant prices.

The combination of cost, coercion, and planning blight have discredited American urban renewal; and private assembly is rarely attempted in cities, where news of buyer interest travels fast. It is less costly for private developers to acquire exurban land.

There is, however, a third method, popularly referred to as "land readjustment," that has been in use in major countries other than the United States and England for a century and has proven especially useful in reclaiming decayed slums and repairing war damage. At a time when many American inner cities resemble war zones, with vacant lots and vandalized buildings, use of this technique deserves exploration.

Under land readjustment, a specified supermajority of owners is permitted to establish a redevelopment area by petition approved by public authority. When its boundaries are established, dissenting owner-occupiers have the right to be excluded. Other dissenters can insist that the petitioners immediately buy them out at an impartially appraised value, a remedy like that given dissenting shareholders in corporate reorganizations. The remaining petitioners then receive proportionate shares in the common enterprise. A committee is elected to manage, which either funds construction by borrowing against land values or enters into joint ventures with builders. When work is complete, each petitioner receives either a building representing his pro rata share of the new development, together with fractional cash payments, or a pro rata share as owner in common.

The petitioners thus have a profit incentive to cooperate rather than holding out. The scheme makes possible redevelopment without the necessity of raising funds for land acquisition and carrying costs. As long as the scheme is approved by public authority and provides adequate compensation for dissenters, it presents no constitutional difficulties. Similar mechanisms have been used in America to reconsolidate lots in failed recreational developments.

This system originated in Germany. Because of the lack of primogeniture and resultant splintering of agricultural land, mechanisms were provided to consolidate holdings. The burgomeister of Frankfurt, Franz Adickes, agitated for ten years for similar measures for urban land. Under the Lex Adickes (1902), prior owners received shares in the newly plotted land proportionate to their original shares. Unavoidable differences in value were settled in money. An English writer[1] observed that "the mere possession of the power to compel unwilling owners to come into the pool made its application unnecessary. During the first ten years 14 areas with a total extent of 375 acres were pooled and redistributed, with the assent of the owners. Originally consisting of 643 lots belonging to 149 different owners, the land was reparcelled into 198 after a deduction ranging from 25 to 40 per cent for street purposes." The Adickes plan was extensively utilized in the reconstruction of postwar continental cities, including Kiel and Rotterdam; and variants of it accounted for more than half of reconstructed Japanese housing, in addition to much housing in Korea and Taiwan. Its possible application in America has been discussed in W. Doebele (ed.), *Land Readjustment: A Different Approach to Financing Urbanization* (1982), and in M. Shultz and F. Schmidman, "The Potential Application of Land Readjustment in the United States," 22 Urban Lawyer 197 (1990). A summary of the principal foreign enactments follows:

Germany. The Lex Adickes was for Frankfurt only. By 1902 similar legislation had been enacted in Hamburg (1892), Baden (1896), and Saxony (1900). In 1950, the principles of the law were extended to land containing structures; in 1960 a system of valuation boards was introduced, regulated by the Ordinance on Principles for Assessing the Market Value of Real Estate of 1972. The 1976 Federal Building Act reaffirmed the principles of the 1902 law. In 1987, this legislation was made the fourth part of Baugesetzbuch of that year. A collection of local variations was published in 1984.

Japan. The first land readjustment enactment in Japan was the City Planning Act of 1919, though this was preceded by the Agricultural Land Consolidation Law of 1899. The 1919 act extended the ALCL system to urban areas and was extended by the Special City Planning Law of 1923 following the great earthquake of that year. A special Town Planning Act, focusing on war reconstruction, was enacted in 1946 and was in turn supplanted by a comprehensive land readjustment law in 1954. In 1975, a special law allowed towns to designate readjustment areas of at least five hectares in their town plans and to intervene if private land adjustment does not get underway within two years.

Korea. Land readjustment was introduced in Korea during the Japanese occupation of 1905-45, the critical enactment being the Korean Land Readjustment Act of 1934. In 1966, a Land Readjustment Project Act was enacted that, while permitting readjustment by private initiative, placed greater emphasis on readjustment initiated by local authorities. Korea is unique in its effort to use land adjustment for the purpose of creating low-income housing by provisions in the 1980 Korean Master Plan for Public Housing Construction and National Urban Land Development.

Taiwan. Article 143 of the 1949 constitution expressly refers to land readjustment, which was regulated by Articles 136 and 139 of the Land Law of April 1946, as supplemented by Articles 13 and 14 of the regulations issued by the National Executive Council in October 1946. By a protocol dated 9 July 1959, the National Executive Council approved readjustment regulations for the City of Kaohsiung. Land readjustment on the national level is also regulated by articles 56, 76, and 161 of a by-law to the Equalization of Urban Land Rights law of 1957.

Australia. Land readjustment began with enactment of the Town Planning and Development Act of Western Australia in 1928, the First Schedule of which authorized land pooling. It is now codified as Sections 6, 7 and 13, of the Town Planning and Development Act of 1928-1979. In practice, its application has been confined to the Perth region.

France. Legislation in 1865 and a decree of 1927 authorized formation of land development syndicates. This permitted involuntary inclusion of landowners by prefectoral resolution. In 1967, initiation of schemes by landowners was authorized. The method was outlined in detail in two publications of the Ministere de L'Equipement in 1975 and 1977. A law of 18 July 1985 codified the rules.

India. Land readjustment was introduced in the 1915 Bombay Town Planning Act and continues in the successor states of Maharastra and Gujarat.

Sweden. A Joint Development Act of 1 July 1987 authorized land readjustment, though only after prior municipal authorization and without coercion of dissenters. Its operation has been confined to recreational developments.

WOONERVEN IN THE NETHERLANDS, GERMANY AND DENMARK

The woonerf, or residential street-government regime, is a Dutch innovation of the 1970s, although precursors can be found in laws in England and New York allowing the closing of playstreets. These earlier mechanisms involved transfer of street uses from traffic to people. The Dutch innovation rested instead on what Rodney Tolley has called the "startling and revolutionary notion that in residential areas traffic and people should not be segregated but instead should be integrated . . . admitted on the residents' terms . . . slowly and without superior rights."

Woonerven in the Netherlands began in 1976, when a law authorized elimination of curbs and the integration into one surface of sidewalk and road areas, giving the visual impression of a residential yard. "Pedestrians may use the full width of the road within an area defined as a woonerf; playing on the roadway is also permitted. Drivers within a woonerf may not drive faster than [about 8 to 12 mph]. They must make allowance for the possible presence of pedestrians, children at play, unmarked objects . . . traffic approaching from the right at whatever speed always has priority. Drivers may not impede pedestrians. Pedestrians may not unreasonably hinder the progress of drivers."

This innovation offers important benefits to the upbringing of children, to safety, and to the creation of a sense of community in both suburban and city areas.

Traffic in woonerven is controlled by ramps, speed bumps, narrowings, changes in axis, street furniture, planters, and trees. Parking is permitted only in specially designated spaces. Woonerven in the Netherlands may be petitioned for by a 60 percent vote at a meeting attended by a majority of neighborhood citizens. Because they result from local initiative, woonerven have proven highly popular. By 1983, 2,700 woonerven had been created, leading to a 50 percent reduction in injuries within them. In Germany, there was a 20 percent reduction in accidents and a 50 percent reduction in severe accidents.

Advocates maintain that children and the elderly "should not have their links to the outside world severed by traffic flows past their doors." The creation of these zones has become a major environmental cause in Germany.

An OECD study in 1986 stated as requisites to success the prevention of residential areas being used by through traffic, regulations and signage influencing driver behavior to follow planned routes at moderate speeds, and the use of physical measures in support of regulations. In Britain, where only physical measures in new developments have been used, the concept has been slow to take hold, because of the absence of legal provisions for its creation on neighborhood initiative.

The mechanism has been highly popular in Denmark. This may be due to the fact that many Danish streets in new developments are in private ownership. "Residents, if they wish [calming], must pay for it themselves," the cost approximating that of a new refrigerator. Similar private street regimes exist in parts of St. Louis and in many of the newer American residential community associations.

The popularity of woonerven on particular streets has led to broader efforts to calm traffic in residential areas generally, through the use of 30 kph speed limits, numerous four-way stop signs, and street narrowings, speed bumps, and other speed reducers, popularized in the United States by Oscar Newman and others promoting concepts of "defensible space" to protect neighborhoods; HUD has issued a pamphlet written by Secretary Cisneros sounding similar themes.

If woonerven are to be used and accepted here, they must be perceived as being an expansion of the legal rights of property owners. This result can be achieved through use of the Dutch mechanism for creation on neighborhood application or by including their creation within the arsenal of powers of residential community associations as defined by their deed covenants, or by street privatization on the St. Louis model. In the short run, the Dutch mechanism is simplest and has been found to result in "stronger social cohesiveness, much brought about by the involvement of the residents themselves in a sophisticated process of planning their own surroundings."

The developers of Seaside, Florida, found that in order to avoid street width and curb regulations, it was necessary to characterize woonerven as parking areas. In Germany, civil engineers resisted the encroachment of landscape architects into their field; it is now established that the former design the subsurface and the latter the surface. Traffic-calming, however, has some natural allies other than residents. According to Rodney Tolley's *Calming Traffic in Residential Areas*,[2] the most recent survey of the field, "The employment effects of traffic calming are labor intensive, with few machines being used and much planning and discussion required...employment effects are reported to be 4 or 5 times higher than the employment effects of conventional large scale road construction."

There is a large literature on traffic-calming, beginning with the pioneer work of the late Donald Appleyard, an American, *On Streets* (1970), and including several books by Carmen Hass-Klau, Annette Moudon, and Rodney Tolley.[3]

The paradox is that a form of privatization is needed for streets to fulfill the function of public property identified by Carol Rose: "In the absence of the socializing activities that take place on inherently public property, the public is a shapeless mob, whose members neither trade nor converse nor play, but only fight, in a setting where life is, in Hobbes' all too famous phrase, solitary, poor, nasty, brutish, and short."

THE OLD AGE CLUBS OF JAPAN

Japanese strategy for the delivery of services to the aging heavily emphasizes the use of volunteer workers organized on a neighborhood basis and the organization of old age clubs for mutual assistance. While the success of this system rests in part on traditional respect for family solidarity and the interests of the elderly, it is in some ways a recent social construct that has lessons for the United States.

The system was formalized by a law governing volunteer workers in welfare services in the early 1970s and by related policy changes throughout the 1980s. These changes were a response to felt need: an unusual graying of the population resulting from Japan's low wartime and postwar birth rate. At its peak (in 2020) the old age population of Japan was estimated in 1980 to reach 18.8 percent. The peak old age population then projected in western countries was much lower: 14.1 percent in Britain (in 1980), 16.1 percent in Sweden (in 1990), and 13.7 percent in France (in 2000). Subsequent improvements in life expectancy have caused some to estimate that the proportion of the aged may go as high as 24 percent by 2025. The population over 65 is estimated to increase from 10 million in 1979 to 26 million in 2020. The ratio of productive-age population (15 to 64) to the elderly is projected to decline from 7.5:1 in 1980 to 6.2:1 in 1990, to 4.5:1 in 2000, and 3.3:1 in 2020. At the same time, Japan has been beset by many of the same disintegrating influences on family structure as the West, including greater mobility, a rising divorce rate, and the large-scale entry of women into the labor force.

Government response to this projected problem has included curtailments in health care expenditures designed to increase the already high savings rate and efforts to affirmatively promote the extended family and neighborhood institutions. The elderly must now bear a portion of the cost of hospitalization, a measure taken to limit government spending and provide incentives to save. Tax credits are allowed to caretakers of the elderly. The government actively promotes "a land policy aimed at pressing for three family generations to live in the same place or for family members to live within easy reach" and provides government loans for home remodelling in order that an elderly person may join the household.

As late as 1988, a five-country study revealed that while only 3 percent of Americans over the age of 60 wanted to live with their children, 58 percent of the Japanese expected to do so. For this reason, nursing home care, except for very short stays in acute cases for people without relatives, is little developed in Japan, and recent government spending has focused on day-care centers and home health services. As of 1980, 70 percent of persons over the age of 60 lived with children, as against 28 percent in the United States and 42 percent in Britain.

The basic premise of Japanese policy toward the elderly is that they "are expected to provide for themselves," with the aid of family members. One major notion is that, while the elderly are ill more than the general population, most of the elderly are not ill most of the time and are in a position to render mutual assistance. In addition, for practical purposes, social work as a profession is virtually unknown in Japan. Instead, government administrators have built upon two preexisting institutions: the voluntary welfare worker, or minsei-iin, who numbered about 15,000 by 1930, and old age clubs, a development of the 1950s. The resulting system is described in a number of works in English, for example, Eyal Ben Ari's *Changing Japanese Suburbia* (1991).

Under the law concerning volunteer workers, minsei-iin are appointed for three-year terms, and are assigned to separate districts, where their task is to identify those in need of welfare services and to promote and foster community organizations. In a representative Japanese city of 244,000 there are said to be 344 minsei-iin, collectively carrying out work that would require 140 paid officials. Each was recruited by recommendations from neighborhood associations, though formally appointed by the prefectural governor. They typically call on elderly people and inquire of neighborhood organizations and storekeepers to identify those who have problems and remind the elderly of the availability of free annual medical examinations and x-rays. They arrange for attendance at day centers and for home health care and other benefits. Unlike the situation during and prior to World War II, these neighborhood leaders do not supply the sole route to local services and do not function as political bosses.

Old age clubs are organized by the minsei-iin to create networks of friends who can visit each other when someone is sick, call a doctor in time of need, and run errands. The involvement of the elderly in club activities also provides respites for younger caretakers. The minsei-iin attend meetings once a month called by the District Council to explain regulations and programs and receive suggestions and complaints, including complaints about particular cases. Minsei-iin receive no compensation other than reimbursement of expenses, but they are regarded as civic dignitaries and treated as such at graduations, sports days, and other public functions and are accorded meetings with high officials of city government. Typically they are women in their fifties.

The old age clubs, or roojinkai, have been fostered as a matter of government policy. The percentage of persons over the age of 60 participating in them is said to have increased from 12.8 percent in 1962 to 47.2 percent in 1973. Among their functions are the organization of trips, social events, and hobby clubs, the maintenance of community rooms, lobbying for local improvements such as changes in bus routes, and organizing the receipt of certain city health services such as free medical massages, quarterly health classes at which the elderly are instructed in diet and exercise and taught to measure blood pressure, and above all mutual aid, particularly to those who are ill. The overriding object is providing information, referring to municipal services, and building networks of mutual aid.

Because the minsei-iin are volunteers and there are few professional social workers and because the old age clubs are not precluded from engaging in neighborhood advocacy, the system does not involve rigid top-down government control. Old age clubs receive approximately 60 percent of their financial support from membership dues and contributions, roughly 20 percent from neighborhood associations, and roughly 20 percent from the city, administering funds provided by the Ministry of Health and Welfare. Since annual dues approximate 2,500 yen per year ($25), the amounts provided by government are exceedingly modest, perhaps $10 per member. Yet the availability of this modest subsidy was a large inducement to the expansion of old age clubs in the 1960s and 1970s. The quid pro quo for the subsidies was the conversion of the clubs from purely recreational entities to organizations providing health and education classes. In any view of the matter, a great deal of social capital was created at very little cost.

What are the lessons of this development for the United States? Obviously, our more mobile, less family-centered society will require more government services than that of Japan. It would also be difficult, given our present rates of female labor-force participation, to recruit a comparable cadre of volunteers or to give them meaningful authority and honorific positions where they are being supervised by our large social work profession. There would also be greater fear of political abuse or government control. However, it could and should be government policy to foster the self-organization of old age clubs. This might be fostered in two ways: (1) by widespread distribution, to millions of elderly, of guides to organization of such organizations, including samples of by-laws, lists of possible activities, and listings of government and private organizations in a position to provide further resources to interested clubs, particularly those relating to health maintenance and home care, and (2) by providing a very small tax deduction or credit for the first $50 or $100 in dues paid to such organizations. The cost of this would be extremely modest. Assuming 30 million elderly, 12 million of whom participated in clubs, a $50 deduction would cost about $240 million but would do much to foster organizations of great social value.

BRITAIN'S PRESCHOOL PLAYGROUPS

With the widespread entry of American women into the labor force, demands have risen for better day care. In 1990 Congress provided parents with tax credits so that they may find their own day care or not be disadvantaged if they choose to stay home. Demands for government-supported full-time nurseries continue to be asserted by the Clinton administration and by feminist organizations dominated by professional women of better than average education and income. The interests of many other less prosperous women who would rather be at home, working part-time, when their children are young tend to be neglected in the national debate. Even for welfare recipients, the administration has sought full-time, government-supported day-care places. While this discussion continues, much day care for the less prosperous is provided by untrained babysitters.

In 1961, a mother in London, Belle Tutaev wrote a letter to the *Manchester Guardian* about her predicament as an employed mother of limited means who wanted to have greater contact with her three to five-year-old children and to assure that they received education as well as custodial care when she was at work. She received an overwhelming response; after borrowing a typewriter and setting up a duplicator in her garage, she created an educational charity that today organizes care for 800,000 British children. These groups function with supervisors, usually themselves mothers, three fourths of whom (45,000) are paid, and with unpaid volunteer helpers, most of them parents serving in rotation for half a day a week. It has been discovered that "Children learn better when their parents are involved. Seeing their own families validated and powerful gives them a secure base from which to progress, and parents are in a better position to reinforce at home the learning which has occurred in the group . . . becom[ing] confident partners in the world of education rather than mere consumers." The playgroups conduct their own fundraising, liaison with local authorities, parents' meetings, and training courses. They characteristically meet in church halls or other rented premises. Most children attend playgroups for two or thee half-day sessions a week, though there are now many playgroups offering extended hours for working mothers.

The Plowden Report[4] in 1968 recommended replacement of the policy discouraging nursery education that had prevailed since 1933, except in wartime, with a policy favoring the establishment of half-day public nursery schools: "Our evidence is that it is generally undesirable to separate mother and child for a whole day in the nursery." A lone dissent by Mrs. M. Bannister recommended the policy that was ultimately adopted by reasons of cost. She criticized nursery education as "disrupt[ing] the mother, child and sibling relationship" and urged that playgroups rather than nurseries be encouraged except in "educational priority areas." The provision of large numbers of nursery teachers, she said, would divert talent from the nursing and teaching professions at a time when the pool of available single women was declining. Concluding, she declared that nursery education "does little to enable mothers to participate in the early school experiences of their children. The mothers' loneliness and boredom are also major social problems which play centers and groups might help to solve."

The Plowden objectives for nursery education were formally abandoned in an education White Paper in 1985, and Lady Plowden herself in 1972 became chairman of the Pre-school Playgroups Association PPA. The government became instead "committed to the continuation of a range of provision that will meet a variety of needs, in both the public and private sectors." In 1990 only about one-third of playgroups[5] received external funding, this funding amounting to about 10 percent of the budgets of the groups receiving it. Overall, parents paid about L250 million in playgroup fees, as against L10 million in public aid. Any view of playgroups as elite institutions is dispelled by the fact that 23 percent of children of skilled non-manual workers and 20 percent of those of skilled manual workers attend them, as well as 10 percent of children of manual workers and many children of mothers on state benefit. In 1994 26 percent of British three to four year-olds were in nurseries, 21 percent in school reception classes, and 42.7 percent in playgroups.

The PPA offered a foundation course of 120 hours with approximately 8,200 students annually for playleaders stressing child development, educational play, and group organization. Shorter programs of from 10 to 25 hours were given to 40,000 parents annually. More elaborate courses of from 40 to 240 hours, followed by some local civil service examinations, were provided to about 1,200 group organizers. The annual cost of ten sessions per week in a playgroup was estimated at L420 per year in 1987,or less than $1.50 per session, as against L1039 in a nursery class and L1505 in nursery school. The activities of the national association now include a magazine, *Contact*, with a circulation of 15,000 playgroup leaders, a quarterly, *Under-5*, with a circulation of 100,000, and three television series dealing with the organization and operation of playgroups. Its catalogue of publications includes workbooks on good practice, session outlines, rota notices, constitutions and rules, course materials, and workbooks for such activities as sand and water, glueing, woodplay, wordplay and fingerplay, maths, language, science and music. Pending British government proposals would "voucherize" nursery education, allowing mothers to utilize L1100 vouchers to choose between nursery schools and playgroups as their needs require rather than concentrating government nursery expenditures on the state sector. The movement has spread to several other countries, including the Netherlands, where playgroups in 1986 enrolled 38 percent of the relevant population, and Ireland, where they enroll about 15 percent.

Expensive schemes for government nurseries are not in order unless and until the private sector is fully mobilized, through widespread dissemination of information about the British experience, including its training manuals, courses, and videotapes.[6] As of now, the promotion of voluntary playgroups has scarcely begun in the United States, although three associations of cooperative preschools have recently been established in the Washington, D.C., area.[7]

CITIZENS' ADVICE BUREAUX IN COMMONWEALTH NATIONS

Citizens' Advice Bureaux, another distinctive British social institution, were established at the outset of World War II by the National Council of Social Service, having been planned beforehand. Two Hundred of these bodies began operations on the day war was declared; 1,000 existed by the end of the war. Their initial function was assisting the public in dealing with wartime call-up, evacuation, and rationing regulations. Although called into existence by the exigencies of total war, their close fit with the individualist casework philosophy of the Charity Organization Society COS was attested by the fact that the COS itself operated eighty of the new offices when the war began. The successor to the COS, the Family Welfare Agency, an organization of much-reduced size and prominence, continued to operate fourteen Citizens' Advice Bureaux and two Legal Advice Centers as late as 1958.

At the end of the war, a National Standing Conference of Citizens' Advice Bureaus was established, and the functions of the bureaux redirected to assisting individuals with the regulations of the welfare state, including housing, hire purchase, and consumer protection legislation. By 1969, according to Mary Morris,[8] the agencies had between 5,000 and 8,000 volunteers, 75 percent of them women, chiefly housewives and retired teachers, nurses, social workers, or professional men. Three-fourths of participants in bureaus were volunteers; the remainder were part-time employees. Some 500 bureaus existed, a modest increase over the 416 that survived in 1960, and a number close to the objective of 900-one for each population center of 30,000 or more persons. Each bureau has an average of ten workers, each serving for at least one session (an average of 1.5 sessions) per week, mostly during working hours on weekdays. Only five had full-time solicitors.

By 1977, according to another study, there were 700 bureaus, in addition to twenty-three law centers, one hundred consumer advice centers, and two hundred housing aid centers, processing 2.75 million inquiries at an average cost of 60p. This number further increased to 936 by 1982-83. By 1993-94, there were 724 bureaus and 803 associated outlets. A study by the National Consumer Council revealed that 80 percent of the population had heard of CABs. Staff numbered 9,000. By 1982, there were 4.8 million inquiries; by 1986 the number had reached 6 million, and by 1993-94, 7.6 million, of which about 24 percent each related to social security and debt and consumer matters, and about 10 percent each related to family, housing, and employment matters. The last comprehensive government study of the system in 1984 disclosed 13,500 workers, only 1,000 of whom were paid; by 1993-94, there were 27,000 workers, 90 percent of them unpaid.. Two-thirds of the bureaus functioned without paid help, and only nine had solicitors. However, in 160 offices, volunteer solicitors provided advice on a part-time basis.

In their emphasis on casework and in their rendering of advice divorced from material aid, as well as in their rendition of services without a means test, the bureaus represent a survival of the Charity Organization Society philosophy. Far from being adjuncts of the state, the bureaus have been described by Geoffrey Finlayson as "a watch-dog in keeping the statutory services up to the mark." A board member, Sir Wyndham Deedes, observed in 1978, "If all the knowledge which resides in a movement of this kind were made available for the use of men who make legislation, we should have a force for the welfare and well-being of mankind second to none."

In recent years, the national CAB has increasingly spoken out on defects of administration. In January 1984, it criticized the administration of housing benefit schemes; in June 1987, it threatened to sue the Department of Social Services over delayed processing of supplemental benefit claims; in April 1991, it noted the dire effects on some persons of increases in water charges; in June 1992, it issued a report on worthless loan protection insurance offered consumers.

The financing of the CAB has always been precarious. Grants from central government ended in 1950 and were not renewed for ten years. In 1963, pursuant to recommendations of the Molony Committee, the CAB received a grant from the Board of Trade to assist in consumer education and advice and relatively nominal annual grants from a number of central government agencies. Later, in 1973-74, the CAB received a development grant of L2 million over five years. From 1974 to 1977, a total of L4.4 million in grants to local authorities to create Consumer Advice Centers CAC were made available, 120 such centers being created by 1979. In that year, grants to CACs were merged with the grant to NACAB, which was increased from L1.85 million in 1879 to L4 million in the following year, gradually increasing to L6.04 million in 1983-84 and to L12.2 million in 1993-94; local authority grants to centers approximated L10 million in 1983-84 and to L37 million in 1993-94. In that year, about one-fourth of the national grant was passed through to local bureaus.

In March 1983, after the advent of the Thatcher government, a major crisis arose when the responsible minister, Gerald Vaughans, shortened to six months the annual central government allocation to the CAB based on displeasure with the activities of some prominent members, including one who was active in the Campaign for Nuclear Disarmament. A backbench revolt led to the restoration of the cuts, the replacement of the minister in the cabinet reshuffle following the June elections and his permanent departure to the backbenches, and the appointment of an investigatory panel, universally regarded as a face-saving measure for the government. The CABs received vehement support from prominent conservative M.P.s, Mark Carlisle declaring, "I have never heard of any suggestion of political bias," Brian Mawhinney describing their performance as "excellent," and Peter Bottomley declaring that "there is unanimous support in this House" for the CABs. Another Conservative member declared, "among those who are at the forefront of the CABs in my constituency, there are relatively few . . . who are either members of the Labour party or supporters of CND." The value of the services rendered by volunteers was estimated at L64 million, which on an American scale would translate to $500 million in that year, the number of volunteers having since doubled.

The ensuing Lovelock Review of the National Association of Citizens' Advice Bureaus found that the CAB "provides exceptionally good value for money" and recommended an additional central government allocation of L400,000, together with a further L500,000 subject to local matching. The report felt that CAB activities involving debt counseling and representation before tribunals should be given second place and defined its publicity function as alerting authorities to facts, as distinct from arousing public opinion, a distinction not always easy to observe. It defined the principles of the CAB as impartiality, confidentiality, independence, freedom from charges, and provision of a generalist service and noted that its reference and training materials-800 items in a four-drawer filing cabinet, supplemented monthly, received universal praise. As of the date of the report, there were 83 persons in the central office and 127 in twenty-one area offices, the area offices supervising training and assessment. Each CAB had a management committee, chosen by members, employees, and representatives of local organizations. The chairman of each management committee together with the area representative chose the local organizer, one fourth of whom were paid by local authorities, one fourth of whom served without compensation, and the balance of whom received nominal honoraria averaging L1000 per year. A national council included twenty-one area representatives, twenty-two committee officers and representatives of various voluntary organizations, and a nonvoting observer from central government. Its composition is being changed to ensure that less than half its members are CAB employees, in order to comply with the 1992 Charities Act.

Later, financial concerns arose as a result of the abolition of metropolitan government in London and other cities, which raised fear that the CAB would lose L1 million in local aid. In 1989, there were again threatened decreases in funding by central government, and in 1991 similar concerns were expressed about local funding. A short-lived flap in 1988 centered on a central office circular relating to discrimination against homosexuals, leading to allegations that the group had been hijacked by activists; this was dispelled by the resistance of the local affiliates. The greater conservatism of the local affiliates was also attested by their resistance to proposals for the addition of a legal advice function. This proposal was rejected in 1986, before finally being accepted in 1993. In 1994, the CAB began to recruit debt advisers.

The extensive training programs for volunteers is described in the 1969 Aves report on Volunteer Workers in the Social Services. Active and successful efforts have been made to recruit volunteers from racial minorities. Sixty percent of persons seeking advice are not working, 11 percent are single parents, 27 percent are black, and 90 percent have below-average income; 3.4 percent of volunteers are from ethnic minorities, which make up 5.1 percent of the population, 2.7 percent are disabled persons, and 54 percent are over the age of 55.

Margaret Wynn, in her 1964 study, *Fatherless Families,* noted another aspect of the advice bureaus that resembles the original COS design: "We have to act as a family service. Of course we give factual information as well but that's only half the job. Sometimes we are in close touch with mothers-and fathers-for years on end and we fight like tigers to keep children from going into care." Unlike bureaucratic agencies, the advice bureaus are said to offer their clients "the luxury of time to talk," and volunteers are expected to present all options and abstain from revealing their political complexion.

Margaret Brasnett has noted that the advice bureaus have been successfully imitated in many countries. A significant number of bureaus have been established in Ghana and Israel, and the concept has found more limited use in South Africa, Zimbabwe, India, and Guyana. Councils of Social Service in a number of Australian states have also imitated the service. However, the proposals in Alfred J. Kahn's 1966 study of neighborhood information centers sponsored by the Columbia School of Social Work were stillborn. The American "War on Poverty" was explicit in its favoring of class advocacy over individual casework; and its neighborhood offices were manned by professionals, not volunteers,and devoted themselves to efforts to overthrow, rather than to produce conformity with, existing social institutions. The prevailing ideology in American programs has stressed legal services rather than social work and has fostered a culture of complaint rather than constructive endeavor.

The comment of Charles Loch Mowat on the advice bureaus is a just one: "As long as social work is done in the manner of the COS, by casework, and in the spirit of the COS,concern for the individual and the family, the Welfare State will be drawing on the legacy of the Victorians who made the C.O.S. and devoted themselves to its work nearly a century ago."

VOLUNTEERS AND PROBATION

Probation, it has long been said, is a wonderful idea that has never been tried. Contemporary Americans are apt to think of the typical probation officer as an overworked and harassed bureaucrat, who is frequently the last to know of adverse developments affecting the lives of his charges, and who possesses little in the way of resources allowing him to assist them with employment, housing or family problems. At best, probation is thought of as a low-cost way of penalizing nonviolent offenders, by subjecting them to a certain amount of systematized aggravation; belief in its efficacy as a means of reintegrating offenders into the community has largely disappeared, at least in the United States.

Yet there is an earlier tradition in which participation in the rendition of probation services was regarded as a form of civic service. The early British probation officers were civic volunteers, frequently ministers of religion. Though driven from the field in the 1920s by the creation of professional probation bureaucracies in England, volunteer probation officers continue to play an important role in other countries, notably Japan, Austria, Denmark and Sweden.

Probation in the Anglo-american tradition was originally provided for by the British Probation of First Offenders Act, 1887, enacted at the instance of police court missionaries. The first full-time workers were employed in 1907 but in 1922, when the Report of the Departmental Committee on Training Appointment and Payment of Probation Officers[9] recommended a professional service, probation in England was carried on by 784 volunteer workers. In 1957, one of the early volunteers recalled that "The volunteer probation officer of the old days was a private citizen who interviewed his cases in a private house or a church vestry. The delinquent did not feel on such premises the restraint that inhabits him when he makes his fortnightly visit to a room in the court-building or to an office that looks like a department of a public organization." The Criminal Justice Act of 1925 established an almost purely professional organization, and a substantial role for volunteers in the British probation service was not restored until the aftermath of the Reading report, *The Place of Voluntary Service in After Care*, in 1967. By 1980, there were approximately 5,000 volunteers; by 1985 there were roughly equal numbers of professionals and volunteers in the British service, though professionals handled much the larger number of cases. The recent approach of the Conservative government has expanded the use of volunteers by Home Office circulars in 1984[10] and 1991[11] and has also proposed the "contracting out" of probation services to private sector managers.

Other nations in the Western tradition make much more extended use of volunteers.[12] In Austria, 579 volunteers supervise 25 percent of the caseload,[13] there being only 189 full time officers; in Denmark 1,000 volunteers[14] supervise 45 percent of the caseload, there being 194 full-time officers; in Sweden 9,000 volunteers, 48 of each professional officer, handle 75 percent of the caseload. In Japan, professional officers each supervise 65 volunteers, each of whom works with about 4 clients, there being in all more than 56,000 volunteers.

A different approach, the use of collective entities to supervise probationers, has been pursued in both Russia and France. In Russia, parol of offenders to the custody of neighborhood or workplace organizations has long been prevalent;[15] in France, supervisory functions are frequently reposed in private organizations such as the Emmaus Community, the Croix Bleue (anti-alcohol league), the Red Cross, and the Secours Catholique. Proposals of the similar use of church and community organizations have been made in the United States by Robert Woodson.[16] Parole to a neighborhood collective certainly represents a greater intrusion on liberty and privacy than the relatively secret and anonymous supervision by a probation professional, but probation by definition is intended to be a punishment and an intrusion on civil rights, and community organizations are far better placed than government officials to inculcate values and give tangible assistance. This seems particularly true in respect to juveniles and less dangerous adult offenders. Rediscovery of the usefulness of community and voluntary institutions is a major effect of the new welfare reform bill. Extension of this approach to the criminal justice area also seems called for. So long as revocation decisions are finally reposed in courts, no intrusion on ideas of impartial justice results from allowing private individuals or church or community organizations to supplement or even supplant the public probation services.

CONCLUSION

From the experience of these organizations, it is clear that there are functions that can be discharged by organized volunteers at which the state dismally fails or which it can perform, if at all, only at far greater cost. Much of social casework may be part of those functions. Even staunch defenders of the welfare state have noted the distinctive role that can be played by volunteer organizations. Attlee, in the third year of his premiership, on becoming president of a settlement house declared, "Alongside everything done by the local authority and by the state there are people who want to do a bit more . . . I believe that we shall always have alongside the great range of public services, the voluntary services which humanize our national life and bring it down from the general to the particular."

The institutions we have considered well illustrate this proposition, yet they have no counterparts in the United States. In the provision of that administration, the organized volunteer has a much larger role than he has been accorded in the recent history of the United States. If Americans are to be summoned to national service, that service is appropriately rendered by true volunteers, not disguised conscripts; in local communities, rather than in ideologized national institutions; by adults, not adolescents; and with something approaching what Adlai Stevenson called "the serene commitment of a lifetime," not merely for a season or a year.

NOTES

1. W. Dawson, *Municipal Life and Government in Germany* (1916).

2. Beffi Press, 1995.

3. Useful surveys appear in volume 12 (1986) of the magazine *Built Environment* and in Eran Ben-Joseph's *Changing the Residential Street Scene* in the Autumn 1995 issue of the *Journal of the American Planning Association.*

4. *Children and their Primary Schools.*

5. but three-fourths of those in London.

6. The workbooks and curricula of the British organization can be obtained from the Pre-School Learning Alliance, at 45-49 Union Road, Croydon CR0 2XU, England, fax 0181-684-0485.

7. *Washington Post*, November 10, 1995.

8. *Voluntary Work in the Welfare State* (1969).

9. Cmd. 1601.

10. Home Office; *Probation Service: Statement of Natural Objectives and Priorities.*

11. Home Office, *Community Work and the Probation Service.*

12. C. Curtledge, *Probation in Europe* (1981).

13. H. Becker, *Justice in Modern Sweden* (1976).

14. W. Ames, *Police and Community in Japan* (1981); W. Clifford, Crime Control in Japan (1976).

15. D. Treadgold, *Soviet and Chinese Communism* (1967); T. Friedgut, *Political Participation in the USSR* (1979).

16. R. Woodson, *A Summons to Life* (1981).

Conclusion

Americans have become accustomed to thinking of the present American system of conditional federal grants-in-aid as a natural or inevitable system of government. Yet in fact this uniquely cumbersome system is the product of a historical accident: the fact that the Supreme Court, in the years 1935-38, denied the permissibility of direct federal action under the Commerce clause while upholding indirect federal suasion through conditional grants from the federal fisc. "The spending power, my dear, the spending power is all you need," Justice Stone is supposed to have told Secretary of Labor Frances Perkins after the decisions checking the New Deal in 1935. The result has been sixty years in which the federal government has expanded its role, not through direct action but through coercion of the states. This regime, as demonstrated in the second chapter, is the direct opposite of the federal role contemplated by the framers, who gave the federal government taxing powers precisely in order to avoid the need for coercion of the states. Conditional grants-in-aid are not merely ineffective as a method of carrying out federal purposes; they have the added vice of demoralizing and trivializing state governments. In other federal systems, notably Canada, Germany, Switzerland and recently even in France and Italy, a different method has been practiced: revenue sharing, accompanied by the drawing of relatively clear lines allocating responsibility among levels of government. "Responsibility," Justice Brandeis was wont to observe, "is the great developer of persons." The centralization of recent years in the United States has gained respectability from the civil rights movement. But measures necessary to advancement of minorities when they were disenfranchised in large areas of the country become counterproductive once enfranchisement has occurred. Blacks in the United States are now far better represented in the local and state legislatures than in federal organs. The centralized institutions legitimated by the civil rights movement have now been captured by other economically well situated interests, and are now employed to impose the agenda of an urban professional middle class whose claims are frequently antithetical to and destructive of the local and religious institutions that have aided immigrant groups in their rise in society.

The involvement of the national courts and national government in all controverted questions has rendered every political grievance a grievance against the central government. It was in an explicit effort to end this phenomenon in France that General de Gaulle proposed the decentralization reforms that led to his fall from power but were later implemented by his successors.

Celebration of the achievements of the American civil rights movement should not blind us to two malign legacies resulting from the judicial extravagances committed in its name. One of these is the vastly extended reach of federal criminal jurisdiction blessed by cases like *Katzenbach v. McClung* and *Katzenbach v. Morgan* and only recently checked in *United States v. Lopez.* A second is the enhanced power of a concentrated mass media resulting from the immunities conferred by *New York Times v. Sullivan* and its progeny, the restraints placed on antitrust enforcement, and the judicial curtailment of the autonomy and power of competing institutions such as the universities, the professions, the churches, and state and local governments. A polity in which free and diverse political expression ceases to be a reality and one in which the freedom from fear of political actors is subject to the influence of an ever-growing national police bureaucracy is not the polity contemplated by the framers of the Constitution. The first two parts of this work discuss the changes in constitutional doctrine necessary to relieve these perils. The last portion discusses some of the local and sublocal institutions that will become relevant when we are enabled to practice a politics not so fully dominated by what passes for constitutional discourse. The examples of other countries illustrate that such sublocal entities, far from being weak, outmoded, or ineffectual, play a vital role in some of the most effective systems of care for the young and old, education, law enforcement, and urban renewal. When our judges relearn the importance of judicial restraint to liberal democracy, a culture of civic participation can begin to supplant our present culture of complaint.

Select Bibliography

PRE-SCHOOL PLAYGROUPS ASSOCIATION

Brophy, J., *Playgroups in Practice: Self-Help and Public Policy* (London: HMSO, 1992) Central Education Advisory Committee for England and Wales.

Children and Their Primary Schools (Plowden Report), London: HMSO, 1968. Committee of Inquiry into the Quality of the Educational Experience Offered to 3 and 4 Year-Olds (Rumbold Committee), *Report* London: HMSO, 1990.

Crowe, B. The Playgroup Movement 3d ed., London: PSPA, 1977.

House of Commons, Education, Science and Arts Committee, *Education Provision for the Under Fives*, (London: HMSO, 1989.

Mastel, S. et al., "The Role of the PSPA after 25 Years in England and Wales," 27 *Early Child Development and Care* 393-417 (1987).

Scottish Education Department, *Provision for Pre-School Children*, Edinburgh: HMSO, 1990.

Statham, J. et al., *Playgroups in a Changing World* London, HMSO, 1989.

Statham, J. et al., *Playgroups in Three Countries*, London: Thomas Coram Research Unit, U.of London, 1989.

CITIZENS' ADVICE BUREAUX

Aves, G. *Voluntary Workers in the Social Services*, (London: Allen and Unwin, 1969)

Borrie, B. *Advice Agencies*, (London: HMSO, 1989)

Brasnett, M. *Story of Citizens' Advice Bureaux*, (London: Natl. Council for Social Service, 1964)

Finlayson, G. *Citizen, State and Social Welfare in Britain*, (Oxford: Oxford U.P., 1994)

Morris, M. *Voluntary Work in the Welfare State*, (London: Routledge, 1969)

Review of the National Association of Citizens' Advice Bureaux (Lovelock Report), (London: HMSO, 1988)

Richards, J. *Inform, Advise and Support*, London: Lutterworth Press, 1989.

WOONERVEN

Anderson, S. *On Streets*, Cambridge, Mass., MIT Press, 1978.

Appleyard, D. *Liveable Urban Streets*, Washington, D.C.: GPO, 1970.

Ben-Joseph, E. *Changing the Residential Street Scene*, Journal of the American Planning Association (Autumn 1995).

Kray, J. *Woonerven and Other Experiments in the Netherlands*, 12 Built Environment 20 (1986).

Moudon, A. *Public Streets for Private Use*, New York: Van Nostrand, 1987.

Tolley, R. *Calming Traffic in Residential Areas*, London: Beffi Press, 1995.

OLD AGE CLUBS

Ben-Ari, E. *Changing Japanese Suburbia*, London: Kegan Paul, 1991.

Campbell, J. *How Policies Change*, 1993.

Campbell, T. *The Old People Boom and Japanese Policymaking*, 5 J. Japanese Studies 321 (1974).

Kinoshita, Y. *The Political Economy Perspective of Health and Medical Care Policies for the Aged in Japan*, in S. Ingman, *Elder Care*, Albany, N.Y. SUNY Press, 1995.

Lock, J. *Ideology and Female Midlife*, 25 J. Japanese Studies 46-51 (1994)

Maeda, D. *Decline of Family Love and the Development of Public Services*, J. Eeekelaar, *An Aging World* 1989.

LAND AND READJUSTMENT ASSOCIATIONS

Doebele, W. (ed.), *Land Readjustment*, A *Different Approach to Financing Ur banization*, 1982.

Minerbi, L. *Land Readjustment: The Japanese System*, Cambridge, Mass, Lincoln Institute, 1986.

Shultz, M. and F. Schmidman, *The Potential Application of Land Readjustment in the United States*, 22 Urban Lawyer 197 (1970).

GENERAL

Abrams, N., *Federal Criminal Law and Its Enforcement Minneapolis*: West Publishing Co., 1986. Allen, F., *Ernest Freund and the New Age of legislation*, 13 U. hi. L.S. Rccord 1 (1965).

Bork, R., *The Tempting of America*, New York: Free Press, 1990.

Bryce, J., *American Commonwealth*, New York: Macmillan, 1985.

Burke, E., *Reflections on the Revolution in France*, New York: Anchor, 1973.

Calvocoressi, P., *The British Experience* 1945-1975, New York: Pantheon, 1978.

Chafee, Z., *Free Speech in the United States*, Cambridge: Harvard, 1941.

Cisneros, H., *Defensible Space*, Washington, D.C.: Dept. of Housing and Urban Development, 1995.

Davis, K., *Administrative Law Treatise*, Minneapolis: West Publishing Co., 1958.

de Tocqueville, A., *Democracy in America*, New York: Knopf, 1945.

Devlin, P., *The Enforcement of Morals*, London: Oxford, 1965.

Friendly, H., *Some Sort of Hearing*, 123 U.Pa. L. Rev., 1267 (1975).
Glendon, M., *A Nation under Lawyers*, New York: Farrar, Straus and Giroux, 1994.
Glendon, M., *Rights Talk*, New York: Free Press, 1991.
Hamilton, Al, et al., *The Federalist*, New York: Modern Library, 1937.
Hand, L., *The Spirit of Liberty*, 3rd ed., New York: Knopf, 1960.
Hayek, F., *Law, Legislation and Liberty*, Chicago: University of Chicago Press, 1973.
Hazard, G., *The Ombudsman: Quasi-Legal and Legal Representation*, Chicago: American Bar Foundation, 1969.
Kalven, H., *A Worthy Tradition, New York*: Harper and Row, 1988.
Katz, M., *In the Shadow of the Poorhouse*, New York: Basic Books, 1986.
Kennan, G., *At a Century's Ending*, New York: Norton, 1996.
Mannheim, K., *Criminal Justice and Social Reconstruction*, New York: Norton, 1946.
Meiklejohn, A., *The First Amendment is an Absolute*, 1961 Supreme Court Review, 245 (1961).
Mill, J., *Utilitarianism, Liberty and Representative Government*, New York: Everyman's Library, 1950.
Olasky, M., *The Tragedy of American Compassion*, Chicago: Regnery, 1992.
Reardon, J., *Standards Relating to Fair Trial and Free Press*, Chicago: American Bar Association, 1966.
Richmond, M., *The Long View*, New York: Russell Sage Foundation, 1930.
Richmond, M., *What Is Social Case Work?* New York: Arno Press, 1922.
Simon, W., *The Invention and Reinvention of Welfare Rights*, 44 Md. L. Rev.1 (1985).
Weil, S., T*he Need for Roots*, New York: Putnam, 1952.

Author's Bibliography

LAND USE

A Proposed Revised State Zoning Enabling Act, American Society of Civil Engineers, Housing America in the Twenty-First Century Conference Proceedings, 91 (1992).

Maryland Zoning: The Court and Its Critics, 27 Md L. Rev., 39 (1967).

Suburban Zoning:Two Modest Proposals (Accessory Uses and Home ccupations), 25 A.B.A. Real Property, Probate and Trust Law Journal 1 (1990), reprinted in 32 Municipal Attorney 32 (1991) in 1991 Zoning and Planning Law Yearbook, 81 (Clark, Boardman and Co.), and in 15 Cato Policy Report No.6, 1(1993).

The Chesapeake Bay Critical Area Law: The Evolution of A Statute, Baltimore Daily Record, April 20, 1985, reprinted in expanded form in 19 Coastal Management 451 (1991).

The Modernization of Zoning; Enabling Act Revision as a Means to Reform, 23 Urban Lawyer 1 (1991), partially reprinted in Zoning and Planning Law Report, Summer 1996, and in 19 Regulation No. 2, 71 (1996).

Three Good Ideas from Abroad: Woonerven, Land Readjustment Associations, Accessory Apartments, 7 The American Enterprise 72 (1996).

Unfashionable Solutions to Fashionable Problems: Hopelessness and Day Care, Urban Land, January 1991, 36.

WELFARE AND RELATED SUBJECTS

Addressing Illegitimacy: The Root of Real Welfare Reform, Heritage Foundation (1995)

"Article on Welfare Shows Gullibility" (letter),Baltimore Sun,December4,1994.

Bad Incentives, The Family in America, July 1993,6.

"Don't Invite Problems to the Suburbs" (letter), Baltimore Sun, December, 1995, 2E.

Rebirth of the Maternity Home, 6 The American Enterprise 49 (1995).

The AFDC Conundrum: A New Look at an Old Institution, 38 Social Work 36 (1993).

"Welfare: Got a New Plan?" (letter), Washington Post, December 11, 1993.

CONSTITUTIONAL LAW, JUDICIAL PROCEDURE, AND FEDERAL JURISDICTION

A Dangerous Explosion: The Proposed Federal Criminal Code, 9 Trial No.5, 21 (1973)

Antitrust and the Proposed Revision of Federal Criminal Laws: Penalties, 43 Antitrust Law Journal 409 (1974).

Courtroom TV and the Destruction of Justice, Baltimore Sun, April 8, 1994, 15A.

Delegation to Private Parties in American Constitutional Law, 50 Indiana L.J. 650 (1965).

Economic Crimes: The Proposed New Federal Criminal Code, 27 Business Lawyer 177 (1971).

The Federal Courts and the Federal System, 1973, 62 Kentucky Law Journal 998 (1974).

Fourteen Points for the Forum Chooser, Maryland Bar Journal, January, 1981, 13.

"Justice A La Mode," Baltimore Sun, September 25, 1996, 17A.

Local Discretion and Common Sense Affirmed, 2 J. Law and Education 463 (1973).

Maryland Civil Procedure Forms (2 Vols. 1984) (West Publishing Co.).

Maryland District Court Law and Practice (2 Vols. 1976) (West Publishing Co.).

The Proposed Federal Criminal Code, 56 American Bar Association Journal, 1070, 1176 (1970).

The Proposed Federal Criminal Code: What Does It Mean For Business, Corporation Law Review, 3 (1979).

The Restrictive Practices Court and the Net Book Agreement, 28 Modern Law Review 551 (1965).

COMMUNITY ORGANIZATION

"Business Districts Keep Our Cities Alive" (letter), *New York Times*, December 4, 1995.

Devolution of Power to Community and Block Associations, 25 Urban Lawyer 335 (1993) and 1992 Proceedings of the International Association for Housing Science 668.

The Little Platoons: Sub-Local Governments in Modern History, Praeger Publishers, 1995).

Mum's The Word in British Day Care, Policy Review, May-June 1996, 11.

Testing for Drugs in Schools, Calvert News, Spring 1997, 4.

Voluntary Pre-School Playgroups, Alternatives in Philanthropy, April 1995, 7.

Name Index

Subject Index

About the Author

GEORGE W. LIEBMANN is a practicing lawyer in Baltimore and the author of *The Little Platoons: Sub-Local Governments in Modern History* (Praeger, 1995) and numerous articles on constitutional and administrative law. He has been lecturer at Johns Hopkins University, the University of Maryland Law School, and the University of Salford, and a Simon Industrial and Professional Fellow at the University of Manchester. In 1996, he was a visiting Fellow at Wolfson College, Cambridge.

ISBN 0-275-95886-8

90000>

EAN

9 780275 958862

HARDCOVER BAR CODE